S0-BFA-236

A HISTORICAL
SKETCH OF THE
BRETHREN
MOVEMENT

A HISTORICAL SKETCH OF THE BRETHREN MOVEMENT

H. A. IRONSIDE

LOIZEAUX BROTHERS
Neptune, New Jersey

REVISED EDITION, JANUARY 1985

Earlier edition © Zondervan 1942

Copyright © 1985 by LOIZEAUX BROTHERS, Inc.
*A Nonprofit Organization Devoted to the Lord's Work
and to the Spread of His Truth*

Library of Congress Cataloging in Publication Data

Ironside, H. A. (Henry Allen), 1876-1951.
  A historical sketch of the Brethren movement.

  Reprint. Originally published: Grand Rapids, Mich. :
Zondervan Pub. House, 1942.
  1. Plymouth Brethren—History.   I. Title.
BX8800.17   1985   289.9   84-23414
ISBN 0-87213-344-3 (pbk.)

PRINTED IN THE UNITED STATES OF AMERICA

PUBLISHER'S NOTE

"Among the various manifestations of the work of the Holy Spirit in the last century," Dr. Ironside begins this *Historical Sketch of the Brethren Movement*, "there was one sphere of Christian fellowship and activity, which had its inception in the early part of the nineteenth century, that has had a far wider influence upon Christians generally than many realize…. Though Brethren assemblies have never been large in numbers as compared with the great denominations of Protestantism, their influence has been world-wide, and thousands have accepted their views on many lines who are not openly identified with them."

Included in this "influence" he cites "the present (i.e., 1940's) revolt against modernism," but also of note would be the widespread pioneering activity in missions, and ministry—spoken and especially written ministry—much of which is still available today.

In the many years that *A Historical Sketch of the Brethren Movement* has been out of print there have been numerous requests for it. Suggestions have also been made that it be brought up to date with later developments. This would be no small or easy task, and would certainly merit a book in itself.

There are undoubtedly some errors of fact or explanation in these pages, but Dr. Ironside himself waived any claim to infallibility, pointing out that "many of the booklets contradicted one another and it has been difficult to ferret out the exact facts." However, he added, "I believe I have been enabled to give a fair and straightforward account of what is here recorded." Therefore we are happy to make available once again Dr. Ironside's insights into this complex subject.

LOIZEAUX BROTHERS

October 1984

PREFACE

THE PREPARATION of these papers, both in their original form as a series of articles in a periodical no longer published, *Serving and Waiting*, and in re-editing and adding more and later material for book publication, has been to me a definite labor of love. That the movement some of whose history I have endeavored to trace out has been, and still is, a very definite work of the Spirit of God, though like all other testimonies committed to man, seriously marred by the failing human element, is my sincere conviction.

I have been importuned by many persons to put these papers in permanent form, but for a number of years have refrained from doing this for I was not clear as to whether the doing so would be for the glory of God and the blessing of souls or not. But after much exercise of heart, considerable prayer for guidance, and consultation with leading men among the assemblies of brethren who have encouraged me to accede to this request, I have gone over the original papers, endeavored to correct any inaccuracies, and added much additional material.

The question has been raised as to whether the story of the divisions among the brethren is profitable, and some have suggested it would be kinder to eliminate this part of the story and tell only the other side. This does not seem to me to be right. Common honesty I feel would compel one to set forth the whole truth, so far as possible, in connection with the movement, hoping that the portion relating to strife and dissension might prove to be salutary reading for the brethren themselves, and give warning and instruction to other Christian groups that they may avoid the rocks which proved so disastrous to what was evidently a marked work of God.

I do not pretend to infallibility in discussing the many questions involved. I have had to depend on much ephemeral pamphlet literature. Many of the booklets contradicted one another and it has been difficult to ferret out the exact facts. But after conferring with many older brethren, numbers of whom are now with Christ, I believe I have been enabled to give a fair and straightforward account of what is here recorded.

During the past twelve years I have been pastor of the Moody Memorial Church of Chicago, an independent church standing very largely for the very truths which the brethren love and from which Dwight L. Moody profited so definitely. This has, in measure, cut me off from that full communion with assemblies of brethren which I enjoyed for years, but has in no sense lessened my love and respect for them.

H. A. IRONSIDE

Chicago
August 1941

CONTENTS

CHAPTER ONE

THE BEGINNING OF THE MOVEMENT

AMONG THE various manifestations of the work of the Spirit of God in the last century, reviving and enlightening His people, there was one sphere of Christian fellowship and activity, which had its inception in the early part of the nineteenth century, that has had a far wider influence upon Christians generally than many realize. I refer to what is commonly known as the Brethren movement, or by others denominated Plymouth Brethrenism. Because of the far-reaching influence of this distinctive school of Christian thought it may not be unprofitable to inquire into the causes of the movement, to seek to delineate some of its outstanding features; discover, if possible, the reasons for the antagonisms it has provoked in many quarters, and endeavor to make plain its essential contribution to the fundamentalism of the present day. For that there is a connection between this movement and the present revolt against modernism should be plain to any instructed student of conditions. The Brethren as a whole are fundamentalists. Their fellowship is of such a character that modernism could not be tolerated among them without destroying their assemblies. By far the great majority of outstanding fundamentalist leaders readily acknowledge their indebtedness, in measure at least, to the oral or written ministry of the Brethren, and only the facts that division and dissension have wrought such havoc in their ranks (causing them to seem so hopelessly divided), and that there has appeared among them the manifestation in some quarters of such unexpected sectarian bias, has kept numbers of these from open identification with the assemblies professedly gathered only in or to the name of the Lord Jesus Christ.

That there was a very definite action of the Holy Spirit in exercising many widely separated believers simultaneously along similar lines, eventually bringing them into one outward fellowship, a careful study of the origin of the movement makes plain. As early as between 1812 and 1820, it is proven that letters passed between a group of Christians in New York City, seeking after a simpler and more Scriptural fellowship than they were enjoying, and another group of believers in Great Britain who were also dissatisfied with existing conditions. Some from among these companies were eventually identified with the Brethren, but the true beginning of the movement seems to have been in Ireland in the year 1825.

On missionary fields in South America, notably British Guiana, and in far-away Rangoon, India, similar movements began either at or a little later than this time, and eventually letters were exchanged which showed a remarkable unanimity of views among very widely-separated groups. This does not alter the fact that we must go to southern Ireland for the first public testimony to the conviction which many had timidly expressed.

Though the name Plymouth early became prominent, it was not in Plymouth, England, but in Dublin, Ireland, that the first meeting of the kind was formed. Similar assemblies were shortly afterward found in Plymouth, Bristol, London, and other places; though some of the members composing these groups knew nothing of others similarly gathered together until after the lapse of months or even years.

The first three decades of the nineteenth century were times of much unrest in the Church of England and in the various nonconformist bodies of Great Britain and Ireland. The Wesleyan revival and similar movements had brought new life into communities that had been cold and formal for years. A spirit of inquiry and yearning after better things was abroad. Christians were eagerly searching their Bibles for fuller light as to their responsibilities, both individual and collective. The Napoleonic wars had directed attention to the prophetic Scriptures as never before, and the truth of the Lord's imminent return was rediscovered after it had been seemingly lost for centuries. That much fanaticism was linked with this there can be no question; nevertheless there was a modicum of truth which, followed out, led to a fuller understanding of the prophetic Word. What was afterward misnamed Higher Criticism (since utterly discredited by archeological findings) was just beginning to attract attention, and real Christians were horrified to find unconverted state-paid clergymen readily taking up the new views, and some, like Bishop Colenso, a little later, even deliberately attacking the authenticity of the Holy Scriptures from within the church itself. This led many to despair of the organized church as the "pillar and ground of the truth."

The Tractarian movement with its trend toward Rome, the Irvingite heresy attempting to revive the gifts and the apostolate, the many smaller bodies formed by frequent dissensions among the followers of Wesley and Whitefield, the troubles of the churches of Scotland, and the threatening disestablishment of the Church of Ireland, all tended to cast true believers more upon God and the Word of His grace and to lead them "to seek of him a right way for themselves and their children." And so it came to pass that out of the unsettled state of the professing body, there grew up several very marked movements within the next half century tending to magnify the name of the Lord Jesus, to exalt and honor the Holy Spirit, to reassert the authority of the Bible as the all-sufficient rule of Christian faith and practice, and to carry the gospel energetically to a lost world, independent of clerical pretension. The great world-wide missionary movement is one of these. The Bible societies may be looked at collectively as another. And what is sometimes called "Brethrenism" is a third, and I am persuaded not the least in point of interest. For though the Brethren assemblies have never been large in numbers as compared with the great denominations of Protestantism, their propaganda has been world-wide, and thousands have accepted their views on many lines who are not openly identified with them.

The names of seven men have come down to us as in some sense the founders under God of this movement or as some would call them the first of the Brethren.

In using the term in this sense, I only do so in order to avoid continual circumlocution and lengthy explanations; for those who hold the principles of gathering which I purpose examining in these papers, have from the first refused any names that would be distinctive or that could not be applied rightfully to all of God's people. Therefore, they speak of themselves as brethren, believers, Christians, saints, or use any other term common to all members of the body of Christ. With this explanation, I trust I shall give offense to none in speaking of them hereafter as the Brethren, and using the capital in order to make clear who are intended, though its use is utterly condemned by these Christians themselves.*

The seven above referred to are Edward Cronin, Edward Wilson, H. Hutchinson, William Stokes, J. Parnell afterwards Lord Congleton, J. G. Bellett and John N. Darby. Of these it would seem that Edward Cronin was the chosen instrument to first affect the others, or at least to first act on his convictions, though the last two had been thinking and studying along the same lines independently of the rest for several years.

Mr. Cronin was a young dental student who had been brought up as a Roman Catholic, but had been graciously enlightened by the Spirit of God, and led to personal faith in Christ and into the knowledge of peace with God through resting upon the atoning work of the Lord Jesus. Sometime after his conversion, on account of ill health he was sent to Dublin. This was in the early twenties. After taking his degree as a doctor, he remained in Dublin until about the year 1836, and devoted the major part of his life afterwards to the ministry of the Word. It was during these years from 1825 onward that the movement of which I write really had its inception.

Like many another divinely-quickened soul who for conscience sake had turned his back upon the seeming unity of the papal system, Edward Cronin was greatly disturbed and perplexed by the many divisions of Protestantism. It grieved him much to find Christians of like precious faith divided into ofttimes warring camps, (for sectarian feeling was running high in the early part of the nineteenth century), and so powerless in the face of such desperate need. The argument that they were but like various regiments or battalions in one great army seemed valueless to him when he found them turning their guns, so to speak, upon each other instead of unitedly facing the common foe.

Yet all alike welcomed him when he went among them at first, and rejoiced at his deliverance from Rome. He was allowed to communicate with them at the table of the Lord as a visitor, but when his stay in Dublin became prolonged, he was urged to choose a definite church and settle down there, as church tramps were looked upon with great disfavor and special membership was insisted upon.

---

* I have often said myself and repeat here, that I am only one of "the brethren" as long as no capital B is used.

Which church to choose troubled him exceedingly, but eventually he became a member of the Independents at a meeting on York Street, and sat under the ministry of the Reverend W. Cooper. His mind, however, was not at rest, and he was unable to understand why the one church founded by the risen Lord should be so broken and divided outwardly. At last he decided carefully to read the New Testament in looking for light on this particular subject. As he weighed the utterances of the apostolic writers and studied the history of the early church, he saw no place for denominationalism, as such, in the Word of God. It became plainer and plainer to him that the one church builded on Christ Himself, of which He was the Corner Stone and in which every believer is a living stone placed there by the Holy Spirit, was the only church contemplated in the Bible. He saw that this church was also spoken of as the body of Christ of which the risen Lord is the glorified head, and that believers ever since Pentecost have been baptized by the Spirit into this body, thus becoming members of Christ and members one of another. "The Lord added to the church daily such as should be saved." Membership of denominations, as such, he could not find in Scripture, though he did see that there were local churches, made up of the members of the one body of Christ gathered together for fellowship, for instruction, for the breaking of bread and for prayer in local companies, but apparently one on the ground of the body, receiving one another as such and not as subscribing to special tests or forming minor organizations within the one great organism. How much of this was clear to him at once it would be hard to say, but he soon began to speak of what he was learning to others. He also found growing up within himself a feeling of repugnance to a one-man ministry, for it seemed to him that there was no place for this in the New Testament church, but that gifted men exercised their ministry as led by the Spirit in dependence on the Lord, and that the idea of one minister set over a church was foreign to Scripture. He did not mean by this to deny that in many places the responsibility for preaching or teaching the Word might be largely restricted to some one gifted individual, but he thought he saw a different order for worship meetings, where the Spirit of God might use whom He would to the edification of all, if believers were subject to His guidance.

Writing of his early experiences years afterwards, he says: "This

liberty was continued till it was found that I became resident in
Dublin. I was informed that I could no longer be allowed to break
bread with any of them without special membership. This left me
in separation from them for several months, and then feeling unable
to attend their meetings from the growing feeling of opposition to
one-man ministry, I was left exposed to the charges of irreligion
and antinomianism. This affected me to such an extent that it was
a season of deep exercise of heart, and separation from many that
I loved in the Lord; and to avoid the appearance of evil, I spent
many a Lord's day morning under a tree or a hay-stack during
the time of their services. My name having been publicly denounced
from one of their pulpits (Rev. W. Cooper's), one of their deacons,
Edward Wilson (assistant secretary to the Bible Society), was con-
strained to protest against this step, which led ultimately to his
leaving also. Thus separated, we two met for breaking of bread
and prayer in one of his rooms, until his departure for England."
This was in the year 1825 and, therefore, may be said to be the
first meeting on the ground afterward taken by the Brethren. After
Mr. Wilson left; two of Cronin's cousins, the Misses Drury, also
separated from the chapel at York Street because of sympathy with
their relative's views, and they were joined by a Mr. Tims who
was a bookseller in Grafton Street. These four met together for
the breaking of bread regularly in the back parlor of Edward Cronin's
house in Lower Pembroke Street. Others began to hear of the strange
little meeting with what many considered, the narrow and bigoted
views, and various persons became affected by the same teaching in
regard to the unity of the body and the presence of the Holy Spirit
on earth to direct and guide in ministry. It was in 1827 that H.
Hutchinson found them out, and as the meeting had now increased
somewhat in members, he offered the use of a larger room in Fitzwilliam Square. Very little now is known of Mr. Hutchison, but
he was evidently a gracious holy man, for J. G. Bellett wrote of him
in after years: "His memory is very dear to me and much honored
by me."

It was in 1827 that Mr. Bellett and J. N. Darby became definitely
identified with the little meeting started by Edward Cronin. The
first of these became in after years a well-known writer on Scriptural themes, but not of the kind that appeals to the mass. His books
are deeply spiritual, meditative in character, rich in their ministry

of Christ, and manifesting an insight into the mysteries of God but rarely found in this workaday world. Bellett had literally steeped himself in the truths of Scripture, and his wrapt soul delighted in the Saviour therein revealed. No one can read his "Evangelists," "Patriarchs," or other "Meditations," particularly the "Son of God" and the "Moral Glory of the Lord Jesus Christ," without a spiritual quickening, if at all a lover of Him who is the central theme of the Book of God. Mr. Bellett has left on record a letter giving an account of the movement from the time of his connection with it, though not going back to the actual beginning in 1825. We shall quote from this letter later.

John Nelson Darby was at this time a young curate of the Church of Ireland. Born in 1800 he was, at twenty-seven, a devoted laborer in work and doctrine, whose yearning soul made him count no effort too great if he might be a blessing to others. He had passed through deep waters ere he found his feet firmly planted on the Rock of Ages, and he realized how much people needed establishment in the Word of grace. He says himself that "There were three years in my life when the only Scripture that gave me any comfort was the 88th Psalm, and that was because there was not a ray of comfort in it; yet I was persuaded a saint had written it, or it would not be in the Bible." For a time he had hopefully followed the will-o'-the-wisp of Tractarianism, and as a high churchman, he looked with a bigoted youth's disdain upon all other professing Christians, "hoping they might find grace through the uncovenanted mercies of God," but fearful that they were living and dying "without the benefit of clergy." One who knew him well in his early days, and of whom Mr. Darby had high hopes at that time, but who became one of the first of the modernists, Francis William Newman, brother of Cardinal Newman, has written of him under the title of the "Irish Clergyman":

> "This (John Nelson Darby) was a young relative of his, a most remarkable man, who rapidly gained an immense sway over me. I shall henceforth call him the 'Irish Clergyman.' His 'bodily presence' was indeed 'weak.' A fallen cheek, a blood-shot eye, crippled limbs resting on crutches, a seldom-shaven beard, a shabby suit of clothes, and a generally-neglected person, drew at first pity, with wonder to see such a figure in a drawing-room. It has been reported that a person in Limerick offered

him a halfpenny, mistaking him for a beggar; and if not true, the story was yet well invented. This young man had taken high honors at Dublin University, and had studied for the bar, where, under the auspices of his eminent kinsman, he had excellent prospects; but his conscience would not allow him to take a brief, lest he should be selling his talents to defeat justice. With keen logical powers, he had warm sympathy, solid judgment of character, thoughtful tenderness and total self-abandonment. He before long took holy orders, and became an indefatigable curate in the mountains of Wicklow (Ireland). Every evening he sallied forth to teach in the cabins, and roving far and wide over mountains, and amid bogs, was seldom home before midnight. By such exertions his strength was undermined, and he so suffered in his limbs that not lameness only, but yet more serious results were feared. He did not fast on purpose, but his long walks through wild country and amongst indigent people, inflicted on him much severe deprivations; moreover, as he ate whatever food offered itself (food unpalatable and often indigestible to him), his whole frame might have vied in emaciation with a monk of La Trappe . . .

"I was at first offended by his apparent affectation of a careless exterior, but I soon understood that in no other way could he gain equal access to the lowest orders, and that he was moved, not by asceticism, nor by ostentation, but by a self-abandonment fruitful of consequences. He had practically given up all reading but the Bible; and no small part of his movement soon took the form of dissuasion from all other voluntary study. In fact, I had myself more and more concentrated my religious reading on this one book; still I could not help feeling the value of a cultivated mind. Against this my new eccentric friend (having himself enjoyed no mean advantages of cultivation) directed his keenest attacks. I remember once saying to him: 'To desire to be rich is absurd; but if I were a father of children, I should wish to be rich enough to secure them a good education.' He replied: 'If I had children, I would as soon see them break stones on the road as do anything else, if only I could secure to them the gospel and the grace of God.' I was unable to say Amen; but I admired his unflinching consistency, for now, as always, all he said was based on texts aptly quoted and logically enforced. He made me more and more ashamed of political economy, and moral philosophy, and all science, all of which ought to be 'counted dross for the excellency of the knowledge of Christ

Jesus our Lord.' For the first time in my life, I saw a man earnestly turning into reality the principles which others professed with their lips only . . .

"Never before had I seen a man so resolved that no word of the New Testament should be a dead letter to him. I once said: 'But do you really think that no part of the New Testament may have been temporary in its object? For instance— What should we have lost if St. Paul had never written, 'The cloke that I left at Troas bring with thee, and the books, but especially the parchments?' He answered with the greatest promptitude, 'I should have lost something, for it was exactly that verse which alone saved me from selling my little library. No! every word, depend upon it, is from the Spirit, and is for eternal service.' . . .

"In spite of the strong revulsion which I felt against some of the peculiarities of this remarkable man, I for the first time in my life found myself under the dominion of a superior. When I remember how even those bowed down before him who had been in the place of parents — accomplished and experienced minds — I cease to wonder in the retrospect that he riveted me in such a bondage."

This young man was the youngest son of John Darby of Leap Castle, King's County, Ireland. He was educated with a view to the Irish bar at Westminster and Trinity College, Dublin, but deciding not to practice law, he took orders in the Church, much to his father's disgust. Mr. Bellett writes as follows:

"It was in the year 1827 that the late Archbishop of Dublin, in a charge delivered to the clergy of his diocese, recommended that a petition should go up to the legislature seeking increased protection from them in the discharge of their ministerial duties, as the teachers of religion in these lands. John Darby was then a curate in the County of Wicklow, and often did I visit him in his mountain parish. This charge of his diocesan greatly moved him; he could not understand the common Christianity of such a principle, as it assumed that ministers of Christ in doing their business as witnesses against the world for a rejected Jesus, should, on meeting the resistance of the enemy, turn round and seek security from the world. This greatly offended him. He printed his objections to such a principle in a pretty large pamphlet, and without publishing it or putting it on sale, sent copies of it to all the clergy of the diocese. All this had a very decided influence on his mind, for I remember him at one time a very exact Churchman (as I may speak), but it was evident his mind had now received a shock, and it was never again what it had been. However, he continued in his mountain curacy, at times, as a clergyman, visiting different parts of the country, either to preach sermons or to speak at some meeting of the religious societies."

He was thus just in the state of mind that would make Mr. Cronin's views agreeable to him, and he and Bellett together with others met frequently with Cronin to study the Word of God. On a number of occasions, while still a clergyman in the church, Mr. Darby joined the little company for the breaking of bread, but as the months went on, he felt the incongruity of going on as a clergyman, and he withdrew from the Church of Ireland and identified himself wholly with the Brethren.*

It was a little later that another earnest man threw in his lot with them—Mr. J. Parnell, afterwards Lord Congleton. He was an enthusiastic adherent from the first and soon became a leader among the Brethren. A man of singular devotion to Christ, and yet judged by some to be of extreme and erratic tendencies, his influence was largely felt in the movement. It is painful to have to record that in after years he and his early associates felt they could no longer work together.

Of W. Stokes I have not been able to learn anything more than that he was prominently linked with the company from about the beginning of 1827.

It is a mistake to suppose, as some have thought, that the Brethren movement was founded upon particular views of prophecy. It was not until about 1830 that the truth of the coming of the Lord began to grip these earnest men as they searched the Word of God. What particularly marked them from the beginning was their belief that there is no Biblical warrant for the idea that the Lord's Supper was ever intended to be the badge or exclusive possession of a sect or party; that no ordained clergyman needed to preside in order to render the remembrance of Christ in this way valid, but that any two or three gathered together in the name of Jesus, whether for prayer, worship, or to take the feast of love, were guaranteed His presence in the midst. They did not see in Scripture any evidence of a clerical

---

* For Mr. Darby's own account of his early experiences, see Appendix A.

system in the early church at all, but recognized that the Word taught the priesthood of all true believers having access into the holiest by the blood of Christ. Acting upon this, after much exercise and in fear and trembling at first, they began the breaking of bread on the ground of membership in the body of Christ alone.

Neither were they actuated by what has come to be known in after years as "separation truth." Their concern at first was not so much with separating from the evil that was coming into the denominations, but rather that they desired to find a simple and Scriptural basis upon which all Christians could meet in happy fellowship. Nor did they intend to judge or condemn others, because meeting apart. This is made very manifest by Mr. Darby's earliest tract on the subject, "The Nature and Unity of the Church of Christ." This was published in 1827 and aroused a spirit of inquiry in many places as to the possibility of carrying out the simple principles it enunciated. There is no doubt that Mr. Darby himself saw much more clearly than others of the little company the rising tide of apostasy, and already the loyal Christian's responsibility to separate from evil when fully manifested, was becoming clear to his mind; but it was not until after the Brethren movement was thoroughly under way that he himself set forth his views in a paper entitled "Separation from Evil God's Principle of Unity." In fact, at the very beginning, he himself dreaded anything that looked like schism from the established order. Edward Cronin makes this clear in the following paragraphs which I have taken from a letter he wrote years afterwards, giving his recollections of the origin of the movement:

> "At this time J. G. B. and J. N. D. were more or less affected by the general state of things in the religious world, but were unprepared to come out in entire separation, and looked suspiciously at our movement, still able to attend and minister in the Church of England, as well as to come occasionally to our little assembly.
>
> "We soon began to feel, as humbler brethren were added to us, that the house in Fitzwilliam Square was unsuited, which led me to take a large auction room in Angier Street for our use on Sundays, and, oh! the blessed seasons to my soul, with J. Parnell, William Stokes and others, while moving the furniture aside and laying the simple table with the bread and wine on Saturday evening — seasons of joy never to be forgotten, for

surely we had the Master's smile and sanction in the testimony of such a movement as this was.

"About this time G. V. W. [that is, George V. Wigram] paid us a visit from England, having some intention of joining the Mission party to Bagdad. From that time to my leaving Dublin (1836) there were continual additions of evangelical Christians, all of us with very little intelligence as to the real character of God's movement among us.

"Special membership, as it is called among dissenters, was the primary and most offensive condition of things to our minds, so that our first assembling was really marked as a small company of evangelical malcontents. We all felt free up to this time, and long afterwards, to make arrangements among ourselves as to who should distribute the bread and wine, and take other ministries in the assembly. We were also, from ignorance or indifference, careless as to conscience and godly care one of another. I am led the more to make this observation owing to the frequent way in which some of the early brethren who are now in separation from us accuse us of departure from first principles in our present actings. Nevertheless, I am convinced that even at that time we would no more have tolerated false doctrine than now. The comfort of many who loved us, but never met with us, was our staunch orthodoxy as regards the mystery of the Godhead and the doctrine of grace and godliness.

"I would remark here a feature in the ways of God in the beginning of this movement, how in and through obscure individuals, and in distant places and diverse positions, the substance of His grace and truth dwelt in us; and though, as I have said before, with little intelligence, led us in paths more or less agreeable to the mind of God. It is striking that those able and honored brethren, J. N. D., J. G. B. and G. V. W.,* did not constitute the embryo of it, while God has used, and continued to use them, in divine intelligence and development of principles as to His church, etc.

"I have repeated somewhat on this point, owing to the charge alluded to above; whereas God's ways with us were, and are still, a gradual unfolding of His truth, discovered to us in various

---

* The Brethren have from the beginning been in the habit of designating their leading teachers by the initials of their names with the perhaps mistaken idea that they were hiding the identity of the human instruments in order that God Himself might get the greater glory.

practical details. So that what in the beginning was no bigger, as it were, than a man's hand (when we were few in number, and weak and defective in understanding), has expanded itself to meet the necessities of thousands, gathered on the same principles and to the praise and glory of his grace.''

The references in this letter to Mr. Wigram and to the Bagdad Mission will be more fully explained in the next chapter.

CHAPTER TWO

WIDENING BORDERS

AFTER THE publication of Mr. Darby's pamphlet on the Nature and Unity of the Church of God, to which reference was made in the preceding chapter, inquiries began to reach him from Christians in many parts regarding the practical outworking of what he there set forth. The result was the establishment within the next few years of a number of similar gatherings to the one already under way in Dublin. There was no attempt at first to enforce uniformity of procedure in these meetings, and if I may be allowed to record here my profound conviction as to the chief cause of the apparent failure of the testimony of the Brethren and their eventual breakup into many different groups, I should say that it was through their failing to maintain the principle that unity is not necessarily uniformity. If the Brethren had been content to allow the Spirit of God to have His own way in each place, and had not made the attempt to enforce common methods of procedure and church order upon the assemblies as they did some years afterwards, they might have still presented a marvelous testimony to the unity of the Spirit. That this was Mr. Darby's original thought, the following quotations from the pamphlet in question will make plain:

In the first place, it is not a formal union of the outward professing bodies that is desirable; indeed it is surprising that reflecting Protestants should desire it: far from doing good, I conceive it would be impossible that such a body could be at all recognized as the church of God. It would be a counterpart to Romish unity; we should have the life of the church and the power of the Word lost, and the unity of spiritual life utterly excluded. Whatever plans may be in the order of Providence, we can only act upon the principles of grace; and true unity is the unity of the Spirit, and it must be wrought by the operation of the Spirit . . . If the view that we have taken of the state of the church be correct, we may adjudge that he is an enemy to the work of the Spirit of God who seeks the interests of any particular denomination; and that those who believe in "the power and coming of the Lord Jesus Christ" ought carefully to keep from such a spirit; for it is drawing back the church to a state occasioned by ignorance and non-subjection to the Word, and making a duty of its worst and most anti-Christian results. This is a most subtle and prevailing mental disease, "he followeth not us"; even when men are really Christians . . .

Accordingly, the outward symbol and instrument of unity is the partaking of the Lord's Supper, "for we being many are one body, for we are all partakers of that one bread." And what does St. Paul declare to be the true intent and testimony of that rite? That whensoever we eat of that bread and drink of that cup, we "do show the Lord's death till he come." Here then are found the character and life of the church—that into which it is called—that in which the truth of its existence subsists, and in which alone is true unity . . .

Am I desiring believers to correct the churches? I am beseeching them to correct themselves by living up, in some measure, to the hope of their calling. I beseech them to show their faith in the death of the Lord Jesus, and their boast in the glorious assurance which they have obtained by it, by conformity to it—to shew their faith in his coming, and practically to look for it, by a life suitable to desires fixed upon it. Let them testify against the secularity and blindness of the church; but let them be consistent in their own conduct. "Let their moderation be known unto all men." While the spirit of the world prevails, spiritual union cannot subsist. Few believers are at all aware how the spirit which gradually opened the door to the dominion of apostasy, still sheds its wasting and baneful influence in the professing church . . .

But there is a practical part for believers to act. They can lay their hands upon many things in themselves practically inconsistent with the power of that day—things which show that their hope is not in it—conformity to the world, which shows that the cross has not its proper glory in their eyes . . . Further, unity is the glory of the church; but unity to secure and promote our own interests is not the unity of the church, but confederacy and denial of the nature and hope of the church. Unity, that

is of the church, is the unity of the Spirit, and can only be in
the things of the Spirit, and therefore can only be perfected in
spiritual persons . . . But what are the people of the Lord to
do? Let them wait upon the Lord, and wait according to the
teaching of His Spirit, and in conformity to the image, by the
life of the Spirit, of His Son . . .

But if any will say, If you see these things, what are you doing
yourself? I can only deeply acknowledge the strange and infinite
shortcomings, and sorrow and mourn over them; I acknowledge
the weakness of my faith, but I earnestly seek for direction.
And, let me add, when so many who ought to guide go their
own way, those who would have gladly followed are made slow
and feeble, lest they should in any wise err from the straight
path, and hinder their service, though their souls may be safe.
But I would earnestly repeat what I said before: the unity of
the church cannot possibly be found till the common object
of those who are members of it is the glory of the Lord, who
is the Author and Finisher of its faith—a glory which is to be
made known in its brightness at his appearing, when the fashion
of this world shall pass away . . . The Lord Himself says, "That
they all may be one, as thou, Father, art in me and I in thee,
that they also may be one in us; that the world may believe
that thou hast sent me. And the glory which thou gavest me
I have given them, that they may be one, even as we are one;
I in them, and thou in me, that they may be made perfect in
one; and that the world may know that thou hast sent me, and
hast loved them, as thou hast loved me" (John 17).

From these extracts it must be plain to any unprejudiced reader
that Mr. Darby at this time had no thought of forming a confederacy
of societies, organized or unorganized, all of which were to be more
or less dominated by some one particular rule. It was rather that
he and his associates in those early days realized that the presence
of the Holy Spirit on earth to direct and guide in the church of
God was in great measure ignored in the existing organizations. He
would call Christians back to dependence on the Word and the
Spirit, and each group gathering together to the name of Jesus alone
would be dependent on their glorified Head and His Vicar on earth
to guide them through the Word on all matters of procedure.

By 1830 there were some five or six little meetings in Ireland,
and Mr. Darby had been invited to go over to England to meet some

Christians there who were similarly exercised. It was not, however, until 1832 that he began a work in Plymouth, having gone there at the earnest request of Mr. Benjamin Wills Newton, a fellow of Exeter College, Oxford, whom Mr. Darby recognized as a man largely taught of God and in many respects a kindred spirit. The two were for some years most devoted friends and fellow-laborers, and it is one of the tragedies of the Brethren movement that they were at last utterly estranged from one another. Of Mr. Newton there will be much more to tell when we consider the first great division among the Brethren.

A meeting began in London in the same year through a brother that Mr. Darby met while in Oxford. Some little time before this, a group of earnest Christians had been meeting in the castle of Lady Powerscourt for the study of prophecy. To these meetings Mr. Darby and Mr. Bellett were invited. Here also they met George V. Wigram, who was to become one of Mr. Darby's most earnest collaborators in after years. At these meetings a chairman was chosen, and he indicated who should speak on the subject under discussion. It became soon evident that Mr. Darby's enlightenment on prophetic themes was considerably in advance of most of the others, but the meetings were real conferences, the forerunners of the Bible readings so common in Brethren's meetings, except that in such meetings a chairman is dispensed with. Many clergymen attended, and quite a few who were linked with the Irvingites, thus giving rise to the erroneous impression that the Brethren movement was more or less linked with the "Catholic Apostolic Church." These Irvingites, however, soon dropped out, because the teaching was so contrary to what they held.

It was in these meetings that the precious truth of the rapture of the Church was brought to light; that is, the coming of the Lord in the air to take away His church before the great tribulation should begin on earth. The views brought out at Powerscourt castle not only largely formed the views of Brethren elsewhere, but as years went on obtained wide publication in denominational circles, chiefly through the writings of such men as Darby, Bellett, Newton, S. P. Tregelles, Andrew Jukes, Wigram, and after 1845 William Kelly, whose name was then linked with the movement, C. H. Mackintosh, Charles Stanley, J. B. Stoney and others.

It was but natural that from the first the question of the Christian's responsibility to carry the gospel to "the regions beyond" pressed upon the hearts of these energetic believers. Messrs. J. Parnell and E. Cronin were ardent believers in missions, and shortly after the start of the movement they made the acquaintance of Anthony Norris Groves, in whom they found a kindred spirit. He was a man of singular piety, most catholic in his attitude towards other Christians, and deeply impressed with the solemn responsibility resting upon the church to carry the gospel to "the uttermost parts of the earth" before the return of the Lord, which to him seemed most imminent. He went out himself to Bagdad in Mesopotamia to investigate conditions, accompanied by John Kitto, and here he was shortly afterwards joined by E. Cronin and his sister, J. Parnell and others. They left in September, 1830, sailing for France, intending to cross the Syrian desert for Bagdad. Opposition developed of a serious character and this, with the ill-health of various members of the party, soon led to a disbanding of the mission and the return of most of its members to Great Britain and Ireland. Groves, Cronin and Parnell came back to Dublin, and all were prominently identified with the movement in various ways in after years. Kitto returned to the Church of England, and is well-known as the author of a helpful series of notes illustrating the Scriptures. Though the Brethren's first mission seemed to end in failure, they have ever been a missionary people, yet this work has been greatly hindered by the divisions that have come in among them.

In the early thirties an apparently independent work of the Spirit of God broke out in the southern part of India, where a number of British army officers began to meet together for prayer and the study of the Word. They came to similar conclusions as to the present state of the church and their responsibility to meet in a simpler manner, taking the New Testament alone as their guide. Many of these gentlemen began preaching in the various districts where they were located, and the work spread until there was quite a stir in British army circles. A number of retired officers in Plymouth took up the testimony and were early identified with it in a public way.

Mr. Darby's gifts and knowledge caused him to be greatly in demand, and he went from place to place strengthening the little assemblies, and proclaiming the Word of God to saint and sinner. In 1837 he felt the Lord was leading him to Switzerland where, he learned, a remarkable work of God was going on in connection with the free churches. At first he was cordially received everywhere, but gradually a line of demarcation was drawn between the free churches as such and Brethren meetings. The work has never ceased in that little republic. It spread from there into France, Germany and Holland. In all of these countries Mr. Darby labored earnestly. His knowledge of French and German enabled him to preach in these languages, and he published many of his works in them also. Translations were made into Dutch and Scandinavian when the work opened up in the northern countries.

George Muller and Henry Craik were co-pastors of an independent church in Bristol, England, but in the early thirties both became much exercised as to the New Testament order of ministry and worship. They were used of God to spread the teaching in their own communion, and practically the entire church took the form of a Brethren's meeting. Mr. Muller's great work of faith in connection with the Ashley Downs Orphan Houses has made his name well-known throughout Christendom. It is pathetic to have to record that he and Mr. Darby were perhaps the most prominent parties on the two sides in the first great division among the Brethren. Some one has well said, "If the two could have gone on together, the one would have balanced the other, for Mr. Darby will ever be remembered as the man of truth and Mr. Muller as the man of faith." This, of course, is not to imply that the truth had not likewise gripped Mr. Muller's heart, nor that Mr. Darby was not a man of faith, but it is simply placing the emphasis where it clearly belongs.

From 1832 until 1845 Plymouth was one of the chief centers of the movement. There were at one time over 800 Brethren in fellowship there, and many devoted men of God were linked with them. Their first meeting place was known as Providence chapel, and the persons gathering there were known to the townsfolk generally as Providence people, because they refused all sectarian names; but as evangelists and teachers went out from the chapel into the surrounding parts ministering the Word, they gradually began to be spoken of as "some of those Brethren from Plymouth," and this naturally led to the nickname "the Plymouth Brethren." This name, of course, was never accepted by them, nor by Brethren elsewhere, but it is the cognomen by which they are generally designated today in English-speaking countries. On the continent of Europe they are

generally called Darbyists. Writing of the early days in Plymouth
Mr. Andrew Miller says:

> There was great freshness, simplicity, devotedness, and separa-
> tion from the world. Such features of spirituality have always
> a great attraction for certain minds; and many no doubt, who
> left their respective denominations and united with the Brethren
> had very undefined thoughts as to the nature of the step they
> were taking. But all was new: they flocked together, and gave
> themselves to the study of the Word of God, and soon expe-
> rienced the sweetness of Christian communion, and found the
> Bible—as they said—to be a new book. It was, no doubt, in
> those days of virgin freshness a most distinct and blessed work
> of God's Spirit, the influence of which was felt not only through-
> out this country, but on the continent, and in distant lands.
>
> It was no uncommon thing at this time to find valuable jewelry
> in the collection boxes, which was soon turned into money, and
> given to the deacons for the poor.

This last item is interesting because it emphasizes one side of
things that the Brethren stressed from the beginning; namely, that
God's work should be supported by God's people. Their preachers
and assemblies have almost invariably sought to act on the principle
enunciated in 3rd John where, speaking of traveling servants of
Christ, the apostle says:

> We therefore ought to receive such, that we might be fellow-
> helpers to the truth. Because that for his name's sake they went
> forth, taking nothing of the Gentiles.

In order to carry this out, public collections were taboo, but when
the Brethren gathered together for the observance of the Lord's
Supper they sought to carry out the letter and the spirit of I Corinthians 16:2:

> Upon the first day of the week let every one of you lay by him
> in store, as God hath prospered him.

I do not mean that all the money thus laid by went into the offering boxes, but these sums were disbursed privately by the individual
as he felt led of the Lord, or put together in a common collection
for the spread of the gospel and for ministry to those in need.

What was true of Plymouth was equally true of many other places where, in their first love and their new-found liberty, companies of warm-hearted believers came together to remember the Lord on the first day of the week according to what seemed to them to be the apostolic pattern; and to search the Scriptures daily and seek to make known to others the precious things they were discovering in them. From the first the evangelistic note was very prominent. It was a new thing in many parts of Great Britain to have these so-called "lay preachers" and in many instances ex-clergymen who had renounced all their stipends, emoluments and ecclesiastical titles, preaching in barns, public halls, theaters, on village greens, the street corners, by the seaside, at race-tracks and in all other places where the public could be gathered together. It was with amazement that people listened to uneducated men from the humblest walks of life, and cultured gentlemen from the highest society, even titled personages at times, all preaching with fervor and holy enthusiasm the same wondrous truths. It was no uncommon thing to hear Brethren spoken of as "walking Bibles"; for, having turned away from traditional views, the Scriptures were their one source of instruction and their one court of appeal. "They found it written" settled everything for them. "Thus saith the Lord" was absolutely authoritative. Troubled with no questions as to degrees of inspiration, they accepted the entire Bible as the very Word of the living God, and the Old Testament was as precious to them as the New, for they realized as Augustine of Hippo wrote so long ago that—

> *The New is in the Old concealed;*
> *The Old is by the New revealed.*

Great emphasis was placed upon the utter depravity and ruined condition of the human race, man's inability to save himself or in any way acquire merit; the great fundamental truths of the Holy Trinity; the incarnation, sinless humanity and true deity of the Lord Jesus Christ; the personality and indwelling of the Holy Spirit who had come to earth to baptize believers into one body and to take care of the church in the absence of its glorified head; the substitutionary character of the atoning work of the Son of God, who not only bore our sins in His own body on the tree but in matchless grace was made sin for us that we might become the righteousness of God in Him; new birth through the Word, thus giving eternal life by faith in Christ; the believer's eternal security as "accepted in the Beloved," whose intercession in heaven prevails against all the opposition of the enemy; the second coming of the Saviour to call His own to Himself in the air, where in glorified bodies they will be manifested before His judgment seat to be rewarded according to the measure of their service for Him on earth, thus distinguishing between the judgment of a believer's works at the Lord's return and the judgment of the wicked at the Great White Throne; the great tribulation following the rapture of the church; the awakening of Israel; the visible return of the Lord to establish His kingdom on earth and His glorious millennial reign to be followed by the eternal day of God, when God shall be All in All in the new heavens and new earth. This is but a bare outline of the precious truths preached and taught by the Brethren. It is not to be supposed that all of these lines of teaching were made clear at once, but as time went on these were the predominant views promulgated by these enthusiastic Christians.

In numbers of instances, as the teaching became known, clergymen and their entire congregations accepted them with deep exercise, and bodily separated themselves from existing systems where these truths were denied. In many cases the breaking of bread was carried on in the simple way with which the Brethren began and with no human leader, but under the direct guidance of the Holy Spirit, at an early hour, after which some gifted brother took the platform and ministered the Word to edification. If again the writer may be permitted to express his sincere conviction, he would say that had this practice been more universal, the tragic failure of the movement might not have been so marked. This, however, is merely the writer's judgment, and many will think it open to serious question.

Some of the assemblies were, if one may so say, much more organized than others. Many of them repudiated all thought of leadership, nor would they recognize any systematic arrangements of any kind. Others believed they saw in Scripture that godly elder brethren, answering to the description of bishops given in Titus and Timothy, should be accorded a special place in the local assemblies, and that the direction of things should be largely in their hands. All alike, however, repudiated the idea of a one-man ministry; though it is to be admitted that this often gave occasion to another abuse equally as dangerous perhaps as that which was rejected; namely, an any-man ministry. Mr. Darby and others sought to correct this by insisting on the responsibility of the local assembly to refuse ministry that was not for edification, even going so far as to counsel the saints to rise and leave the room, if an unfit man persisted in attempting to preach or teach after he had been informed that his ministry was not to edification. Perhaps, if the Brethren everywhere had been more particular about this, it would have been better for all concerned.

It will readily be understood that Satan would labor with unwearied energy to destroy so gracious a work of the Spirit of God as that which we have been considering. As long as the opposition to the truth came only from without, the Brethren prospered, and multitudes received the Word with gladness, and many through deep exercise of soul were added to them, but, as in the early church and in practically every movement of the Spirit of God since, Satan set himself to stir up dissension within. It could hardly be expected that it would be otherwise. Jealousies among ministering Brethren, differences of views as to age-old questions like the subjects and mode of baptism, details as to prophetic events; even serious doctrinal divergences, soon came in to mar the peace and happiness of the little assemblies. There were, too, some grievous cases of backsliding, thus bringing the truth into great dishonor. A new line of tradition grew up to supersede the old views left behind, and at last divisions came in among Brethren which have never been healed to this day. These we must sorrowfully consider in our next chapter, hoping thereby to glean some lessons that will be for the blessing of God's people today who sincerely desire to do His will.

To those looking on from the outside it has often seemed that one great weakness of the movement has been the failure to recognize the true pastoral office. They have felt that in seeking to avoid the Scylla of Diotrephian clericalism, the Brethren were shattered on the Charybdis of extreme individualism.

CHAPTER THREE

GATHERING CLOUDS

IT HAS BEEN a comparatively simple thing thus far to trace out the beginnings and early progress of the Brethren's meetings. A far more difficult task is now before me; namely, to tell the story of the first great schism that divided them into the two camps of "exclusive" and "open" meetings. To do this in an impartial way, keeping severely to the historical and non-partisan method, requires, it seems to me, an almost superhuman wisdom, something to which the present writer can make no claim. While endeavoring to be strictly impartial, one's prejudices and predilections are bound to be manifested. It may as well be acknowledged at once that the "exclusive" principle, if not pushed to an extreme, seemed to me for many years to be most nearly Scriptural; but I hold no brief for that wing of the movement, and I have come to the conclusion that it may require greater spirituality to act upon it than most of us possess. I have the warmest admiration for many of those who conscientiously differ from me as to this. I only give this explanation here to make my own position clear, for I fear I shall please neither conservative "exclusives" nor radical "opens" in telling the story as I understand it.

I have already pointed out that all was not harmonious in the Brethren's ranks during the years that have occupied us. As they increased in numbers and meetings were multiplied, difficulties arose that they had not foreseen in the first happy days.

At this time, while J. N. Darby was undoubtedly the leading figure among the Brethren in Ireland, B. W. Newton was perhaps the man whose learning, ability and piety outshone all others in England, though many remarkable men had become identified with the movement. It was he who was used of God to begin the work at

Plymouth, where for fifteen years he was the accredited leader, and from which center his influence, through his printed ministry and frequent visits to other parts of the country, extended far and wide. By 1840 there were over 800 gathered together at the Ebrington Street meeting, where he exercised the teaching and pastoral gifts. By 1845 the number had increased to 1,200. It is questionable if any other assembly of Brethren has ever grown as rapidly. This in itself is proof of the esteem in which he was held.

Mr. Darby did not come to Plymouth until the meeting there was well under way. He was at first warmly received by Mr. Newton, who had met him previously at Oxford, and the saints meeting with him; and he visited them frequently; though for the first few years he preached generally in Anglican pulpits, as he had not yet completely separated from the Church of England. Mr. Newton attended a number of the Prophetic conferences, in Ireland, until it became evident that he and Mr. Darby were hopelessly at variance, both on prophetic teaching and in regard to the nature, calling and order of the church. Mr. Newton was warmly supported in his views by the learned Dr. Tregelles, the textual critic who was in the Plymouth meeting. Mr. Newton was a voluminous writer, as was Mr. Darby; but the works of the former are of a much more finished character than those of the latter, though there is a depth of spirituality about the writings of Mr. Darby that few have attained to. His friends have described Mr. Newton as a polished, scholarly speaker, gentlemanly in his bearing, and most gracious in his demeanor. On the other hand, his opponents dwell on his irritation if crossed, and his unyielding and relentless pressing of his own views in opposition to those of other gifted brethren. He lived to be ninety-three years of age, and after his separation from the Brethren became the pastor of an independent congregation characterized by his particular teaching, in the city of London.

The late venerable man of God, Mr. Henry Varley, well known as an evangelist and Bible teacher in Europe, America and Australia, said to me on one occasion: "If I were asked to name the godliest man I have ever known, I should unhesitatingly say, Benjamin Wills Newton." He described him as tall and of patriarchal bearing, with the calm of heaven on his brow, and the law of kindness on his lips. His intimate associates loved him devotedly and listened with rapt attention to his expositions.

This was the man who was destined to be the means of rending the Brethren asunder, or at least he was the figure over whom the storm broke. In the minds of many he is to this day the very incarnation of iniquitous teaching.

He viewed with extreme disfavor any departure from Puritan theology, except on eschatological lines. For him, the church included all the faithful from Abraham down. He considered Mr. Darby's dispensational teaching as the height of speculative nonsense. He was vehemently opposed to the idea of the church being a special company of whose calling and destiny the Old Testament knows nothing, a line of things emphasized by Mr. Darby, Mr. Bellett and their intimates. When at the Powerscourt meetings the idea of the cancelled seventieth week of Daniel, beginning after the rapture of the church, was suggested by Sir Edward Denny and Mr. Darby, it was readily accepted as the key to the prophecies by G. V. Wigram and J. G. Bellett. It was, however, utterly rejected by Mr. Newton, who maintained that the church must go through the final tribulation and that the "rapture" would be coincident with the "appearing." Other differences gradually led to Mr. Newton's absenting himself from these gatherings in after years. He remained at Plymouth with the avowed intention of making that place a center and a model for other assemblies, and by printing press and in public meetings he sought to oppose what many believed to be the special work of the Holy Spirit in recovering precious truth long lost through the church's declension and partial apostasy.

In April, 1845, he issued a statement showing wherein he differed from the rest, and setting forth what he felt called upon to maintain. I give it in full, though the reader will probably find it ambiguous in some particulars:

"It is my desire to maintain,—

"I. That the twelve apostles of our Lord and Saviour do represent *believers* standing in acknowledged acceptance before God, through the name of Jesus, and that they represent such only.

"II. That the Gospels of Matthew, Mark and Luke are Christian Scripture, in the same sense in which the Gospel of John is Christian Scripture.

"III. That the Pentecostal church was not in a semi-Jewish or semi-Christian condition, or in any sense 'earthly,' or 'formed for citizenship in the earth;' but in a true church position, as 'partakers of the heavenly calling.'

"IV. That the Epistles of Peter, and the Epistle to the Hebrews or Galatians, are not to be regarded as having a lower character than the Epistles to the Ephesians or Colossians.

"V. That the introduction or presence of Jewish circumstances or characteristics into any particular passage, does not necessarily make the subject-matter Jewish.

"VI. That Peter and the Pentecostal church testified to the ascension and heavenly glory of Jesus, equally with St. Paul.

"VII. That there is no salvation and no life apart from union with the person of the Son of God, and that all who so rise in Him are sons of God.

"VIII. That the church is under covenant promise and dispensation, as much as Israel will be; and is in no sense above dispensation, except in the sense in which all the redeemed receive their calling to blessing in Christ Jesus before the foundation of the world, and therefore independent of circumstances here.

"IX. That the resurrection of Christ, and resurrection in Christ, is never regarded in the Scripture, save as abolishing all personal distinctions such as that of Jew and Gentile, among the partakers thereof.

"X. That heavenly blessings, as well as earthly, were included in the promise to Abraham, and that God never purposed or proposed to accomplish one branch of these promises, without also adding the other.

"XI. That 'the household of faith' is an equivalent expression to 'church.'

"XII. That the various expressions, etc., applied in Scripture to the church, afford various aspects or positions of the same body, but do not imply that the church is correspondingly divided into distinct and separating compartments.

"XIII. That Abraham and the Old Testament saints are equally with ourselves included under such passages as the following:

" 'The dead in Christ shall rise first.' 'As in Adam all have died, even so in Christ shall all be quickened.'

" 'All onewise.' "

During the years that these views were being developed at Plymouth, Mr. Darby was busy preaching and teaching in Great

Britain and Ireland, and on the continent of Europe, particularly in Switzerland where many gatherings had been formed. As assemblies were multiplied difficulties increased, and questions of reception, discipline, and internal arrangement became prominent. The early meetings, as we have seen, were of the simplest character. Persons wishing to commune were not examined as to where they had come from, but were received freely if they gave evidence that they belonged to Christ. As time went on, however, there was a tendency to restrict communion in a way that caused some to fear the Brethren would soon become a sect like those about them.

Mr. A. N. Groves wrote in 1828:

> "My full persuasion is, that inasmuch as any one glories either in being of the Church of England, Scotland, Baptist, Wesleyan, Independent, etc., his glory is in his shame, and that it is anti-Christian; for as the apostle said, 'Were any of them crucified for you?' The only legitimate ground of glorying is, that we are among the ransomed of the Lord by His grace. As *bodies* I know none of the sects and parties that wound and disfigure the body of Christ; as individuals I desire to love all who love Him. Oh, when will the day come when the love of Christ will have more power to unite than our foolish regulations have to divide the family of God! As for order, if it be God's order, let it stand, but if it be man's order, I must examine whether or not it excludes the essence of Christ's kingdom; for if it does, I remember the word, 'Call no man your master upon earth; for one is your Master, even Christ, and all ye are brethren.'"

That this was the mind of practically all these early Brethren I think has already been made clear, but this word from Mr. Darby written in 1839, in a letter to Rev. J. Kelly, will serve to clinch the subject:

> "Whenever Christ has received a person, we should receive him. That false brethren may creep in unawares is possible. If the church be spiritual they will soon be made apparent; but as our table is the Lord's and not ours, we receive all the Lord has received, all who have fled as poor sinners for refuge to the hope set before them, and rest not in themselves but in Christ as their hope.
>
> "You say, 'Would you receive a Roman Catholic?' If a Roman Catholic really extolled Jesus as Saviour, owned his one sacrifice

of Himself as the sole putting away of sin, he would have ceased to hold the error and delusion by which the enemy has misled some souls who are still, I trust, precious to Jesus; he would cease to be a Roman Catholic in the evil sense of the word, and on those terms only would he be with us. I repeat, then, we receive all who are on the foundation, and reject and put away all error by the Word of God and the help of His ever-living Spirit."

The last clause will seem rather bombastic and conceited, but it is well to remember that Mr. Darby wrote jerkily and did not always fully express what was in his mind. Besides, he was still a young man, just thirty-nine years of age, and not yet disillusionized as to the impossibility of any company of believers putting away *all* error. His letter at least shows how different were his views from those of many today who glory in being known as his followers while forming sectarian circles of the narrowest conceivable kind.

But as to the inter-relation of assemblies Mr. Darby early taught what afterwards came to be known as exclusivism. He believed geographical distance did not relieve of responsibility to act in unison and he sought to press upon the assemblies or gatherings of Brethren their responsibility to act together in matters of discipline. This alarmed A. N. Groves, who after his return from Bagdad found what seemed to him positive evidence of the formation of a confederation of meetings which he considered would eventually put the Brethren back again on full sectarian ground. In that year he wrote a letter to Mr. Darby, whom he regarded as the leader in introducing new views, which those afterwards called "Open" Brethren have looked upon as almost prophetic, and every "exclusive" must admit it contains much food for thought. He says:

"I wish you to feel assured that nothing has estranged my heart from you, or lowered my confidence in your still being animated by the same enlarged and generous purposes that once so won and riveted me; and though I feel you have departed from those principles by which you once hoped to have effected them, and in principle returning to the city from whence you departed, still my soul so reposes in the truth of your heart to God that I feel it needs but a step or two more to advance, and you will see all the evils of the systems from whence you profess to be separated, to spring up among yourselves. You will not

discover this so much from the workings of your own soul, as
by the spirit of those who have been nurtured up from the beginning in the system they are taught to feel the only tolerable
one; and not having been led like you, and some of those earliest
connected with you, through deep experimental suffering and
sorrow, they are little acquainted with the real truth that may
exist amidst inconceivable darkness: there will be little pity and
little sympathy with such, and your union daily becoming one
of doctrine and opinion more than life or love, your government
will become—unseen, perhaps, and unexpressed, yet one wherein
overwhelmingly is felt the authority of men; *you will be known
more by what you witness against, than what you witness for,
and practically this will prove that you witness against all but
yourselves.*

"It has been asserted . . . that I have changed my principles:
all I can say is, that as far as I know what those principles were,
in which I gloried on first discovering them in the Word of
God, I now glory in them ten times more since I have experienced
their applicability to all the various and perplexing circumstances
of the present state of the church; allowing you to give every
individual, and collection of individuals, the standing God gives
them, without identifying yourselves with any of their evils. I
ever understood our principle of communion to be the possession
of the common life, or common blood of the family of God;
these were our early thoughts, and they are my most matured ones.
The transition your little bodies have undergone, in no longer
standing forth the witnesses for the glorious and simple truth,
*so much as standing forth witnesses against all that they judge
error,* has lowered them in my apprehension from heaven to
earth, in their position as witnesses . . . The position which
this occupying the seat of judgment places them in, will be this:
*The most narrow-minded and bigoted will rule, because his con-
science cannot and will not give way, and therefore the more
enlarged heart will yield.* It is into this position, dear Darby,
I feel some little flocks are fast tending, if they have not already
attained it, making light, not life, the measure of communion."
[*Italics mine*].

However, it is very evident that many Brethren were already beginning to feel the need of some clearly defined rule as to matters
of discipline, and as to this A. N. Groves and B. W. Newton
represented two extremes, while J. N. Darby seemed to take a middle

path. The latter would have the disciplinary act of one assembly ratified by all if Scriptural authority could be shown for the action. Moreover he would own as New Testament assemblies only those meetings where common principles and similar teaching was held, and where there was a definite testimony against evil in life or doctrine. At least this is what he was tending to. Mr. Groves, on the contrary, would cast each assembly directly upon God, refusing the thought of 'interference' by others. He held to the independence of each local meeting. And as to discipline he counted largely on spiritual power within repelling or else expelling unworthy intruders; a principle Mr. Darby also recognized, but not as relieving meetings of their responsibility. Mr. Newton on the other hand would organize each assembly, appoint elders and deacons, recognize pastors; and these various officers would constitute an official board to handle the affairs of the local church.

This he sought to carry out in Plymouth and in this he was ably assisted by Dr. Tregelles, and by J. L. Harris, a former Anglican clergyman of marked ability, who was recognized as co-pastor with himself.

The great majority in Plymouth were thoroughly satisfied with this arrangement, while a very small minority were very restless under it and felt that the whole principle of Brethren's meetings had been gradually given up. Looking back through the years one can scarcely escape the conclusion that it might have been better if the minority had quietly separated and begun a new meeting in another part of the city—not in antagonism to the older Brethren, but where fuller liberty could be enjoyed, and then have waited on God to show the next step. As it was they were in frequent correspondence with Mr. Darby and his co-laborers, and upon his return from the continent he was persuaded to go to Plymouth, which he did, very much to the disgust and indignation of Mr. Newton's particular friends. He denies that he was sent for, but he certainly was urged to go by many who viewed with alarm the changed conditions there. He has given a very full, and, it would seem to me, a very fair account of what followed in his *"Narrative of Facts,"* a lawyer-like document in which he tells why he acted as he did at Plymouth in the months that followed. But we must leave consideration of this until the next chapter.

In closing this very imperfect section may I add that a careful perusal of the early writings of the Brethren shows that there had been a gradual declension and lowering of the standard after the first happy years. Worldliness had crept in, with its accompaniments of pride and vain-glory. To this G. V. Wigram bore trenchant witness. Many Brethren became occupied with themselves, and commonly wrote and spoke of their companies as "the latter day remnant," "the godly residue," "the Philadelphian church," and similar self-laudatory expressions, obnoxious to a spiritual mind. They looked with supercilious contempt on saints as godly as themselves—or even far more devoted—who remained in the various organized bodies, and were not backward in claiming in some instances exclusive possession of the table of the Lord. Is it any wonder that a holy God, who loves all His people, equally, blew upon such pretension and permitted circumstances to arise which scattered and divided them, and made them a witness rather to the power of the flesh to break, than to the power of the Spirit to keep the unity He has formed?

Yet are there not lessons to be learned from the failures of the Brethren to maintain that unity in the bond of peace? Do we not, only too frequently, see devoted men of God, leaders in the present mighty work of the Holy Spirit; the protest against modernism,—arrayed against one another because of divergent views on minor details, instead of standing together against the evil they seek to combat? We may well be reminded of Nelson at Trafalgar who, coming on deck and finding two British officers quarreling, whirled them about and pointing to the ships of the adversary, exclaimed, "Gentlemen, *there* are your enemies!"

That it was the leaders who were chiefly responsible for the threatened breach of communion seems very evident. The rank and file were simple, godly Christians rejoicing in their liberty from what they regarded as sectarian bondage, and were, generally speaking, ardent gospelers going out into the streets and public places, as well as in their rented halls and chapels, to carry the glad tidings of a known salvation received by faith and evidenced by the love of the Spirit. That Satan hates this we may be sure and so he sought to destroy the testimony by sowing discord among brethren.

CHAPTER FOUR

INCREASING DISSENSION

THE VEXED question of what has since been called "the relation of assemblies to assemblies," or "the inter-relation of assemblies," was what eventually divided the Brethren into two great camps, afterwards denominated "open" and "exclusive."

As early as 1838, Mr. G. V. Wigram, one of Mr. Darby's most intimate associates, wrote:

> "MY DEAR FRIEND AND BROTHER: There is a matter exercising the minds of us at this present time in which you may be (and in some sense certainly are) concerned. The question I refer to is, *'How are meetings for communion of saints in these parts to be regulated?'* Would it be for the glory of the Lord and the increase of testimony, to have *one central meeting* the common responsibility of all within reach, and *as many meetings subordinate to it* as grace might vouchsafe? Or to hold it to be better to allow *the meetings to grow up as they may without connection and dependent upon the energy of individuals only?* I think I have no judgment in the matter, save that (as those who have the fellowship of the divine mind) our service ought to be intelligent, and whatever is done to be done wittingly. As to feeling, I do indeed long to find myself more distinctly associated with those who as brethren will feel and bear their measure of responsibility, but this is all I can say; for truly, provided there be in London some place where the wanderer can find rest and communion, my desire is met; though the glory of the Lord will of course be still to be cared for.
>
> "I am, dear brother, yours in Jesus,
>
> Oct. 6, 1838.   G. V. W."

It is very evident from the wording of this letter that up to the time it was written, there was no definite teaching among the Brethren as to the question afterwards forced upon them by unlooked-for events.

Another seven years passed with no concerted effort to arrive at the mind of the Lord in this matter. Had there been some far-sighted and influential men of God among them who would have taken the responsibility of calling a conference of accredited leaders to discuss the whole question in the light of the open Bible, division *might possibly* have been averted. I say *might possibly,* for I cannot but think the pride and self-will of many was what forced division at last and if this state had not first been judged, no amount of teaching as to "principles," however Scriptural, would have preserved the unity.

In 1845 Mr. Darby went to Plymouth, where he found, as he had been warned he would find, an entirely new order of things prevailing. Mr. Newton, as we have seen, had given up his early views, both as to Christian fellowship and as to many details of prophecy. Probably in some points he never had been in full harmony with the rest of the teachers, and his system was in part rather a development than a declension. But at any rate the Plymouth meeting was now quite at variance with the assemblies generally. There was no longer room for open ministry as the Spirit might lead. Mr. Newton and his co-laborer, J. L. Harris, were the recognized elders. They ministered turn about each Lord's day morning, their sermons largely consuming the time, and the breaking of bread occupying a secondary place. Certain persons were authorized or deputed by them to participate in minor things, even to the giving out of and the starting of hymns.

Mr. Darby found himself *persona non grata* with the leaders and their chief adherents as soon as he appeared.

Should he have simply gone away and left things to work out as the Lord might overrule, or was it best to remain and oppose the accepted pastors, whom he believed were misleading the rank and file? These questions are hard to answer. At any rate he remained and that for several months. During this time his presence encouraged a minority who were greatly distressed over existing conditions. He protested publicly and privately against what he considered to be the sectarianism and clericalism of the new order. He drew the attention of other leading men in various parts to the conditions existing there. Several conferences were held with responsible brethren, but Mr. Newton refused to be present at any such meetings and declared he would consider all such efforts to bring about an understanding as unwarranted interference. He offered to meet a few for an investigation provided he be permitted to appoint four of his friends and Mr. Darby four of his. This the latter refused, as he felt it was a matter for the whole assembly and not a personal quarrel between himself and Mr. Newton.

Finally, convinced that the Ebrington Street assembly no longer occupied the ground on which Brethren had been meeting, he withdrew from its fellowship, and with a few like-minded brethren secured another hall where a new gathering was started on the last Lord's day of the year 1845.

Mr. William Trotter writing of this says:

At first Mr. Darby's act was judged by brethren almost everywhere to be rash and premature. They had not been inside the scene, and so knew but little of the system that had been introduced. Several of those who went down to Plymouth to inquire, found things so much worse than they had any conception of, that they also separated from Mr. Newton and his party. One thing which seems to have weighed greatly with these brethren was the corruption of moral integrity, and the system of intrigue and deception which attended the evil. In April, 1846, a meeting of brethren from all parts was held in London for common humiliation and prayer, where the tokens of the Lord's presence were graciously vouchsafed to us, and from that time the eyes of brethren seemed to open to the evil. Mr. Newton and his friends were invited to that meeting but refused to attend. They printed their reasons for refusing, which were widely circulated.

Mr. Darby's *Narrative of Facts** was printed soon after, and in the autumn of that year a series of meetings was held in Rawstorne Street, London, very important in their origin, character, and results. They originated in a visit of Mr. Newton's to certain brethren in the neighborhood of Rawstorne Street and breaking bread there. He held some Scripture readings at the house of one of them, after which he stated that his errand to town partly was to meet any brethren who were wishful of information as to the charges brought against him in the *Narrative of Facts*. Most providentially Mr. Darby was at the time

---

* This is published in the collected writings of J. N. Darby.

in London. He had come to town on his way to France, and had got his passports, changed his money and was ready to depart, when brethren waited on him to detain him till efforts were made to bring about an open investigation of the whole case, with accused and accuser face to face. The brethren to whom Mr. Newton had offered to give information proposed to him this open investigation. It was proposed to him again and again by others, but steadily and invariably refused. The brethren meeting at Rawstorne street then assembled, and after united prayer and consultation concluded that Mr. Newton could not be admitted to the Lord's table there, so long as he refused to satisfy their consciences as to the grave charges alleged against him.

In connection with these events there were three documents issued by Mr. Newton and his party. One a paper by Mr. Newton himself in answer to the charges of untruthfulness. Another by his four co-rulers at Plymouth assigning reasons for his non-attendance at Rawstorne street to satisfy the consciences of saints meeting there. Also a remonstrance addressed by the Plymouth rulers to the brethren meeting at Rawstorne street on their exclusion of Mr. Newton from the Lord's table. All these were examined at large in four tracts entitled *Accounts of the proceedings at Rawstorne street in November and December, 1846.* These four tracts are very important as showing the dishonesty connected with the system of which the three papers before named were a defense. The proceedings at Rawstorne street, and the publications growing out of them, cleared the souls of many; and in February, 1847, a meeting was held in the same place, attended by many brethren from the country, in which *nearly all those who had been at all looked up to amongst brethren* gave their solemn testimony as to the evil system which had grown up at Plymouth, and as to the need of absolute and entire separation from it. The testimonies of Messrs. M'Adam, Harris, Lean, Hall, Young, and others, were all most solemn and decisive. There was scarcely a brother, whose name was well known amongst brethren as laboring in the word and watching for souls, who did not at that time acquiesce in the sorrowful necessity for separation from this evil and demoralizing system.

The entire matter was looked at from a very different standpoint by many others. Mr. Henry Groves expresses their feelings as follows:

In this melancholy year, that was to test professions of a heavenly calling made and sacred truths held (as it proved, too much in the head and too little in the heart by both teacher and scholar), Mr. Darby comes to Plymouth, and finds Mr. Newton's influence paramount. What an opportunity for grace to shine in! for Christ to triumph in the saint over self! But, alas! self triumphed over Christ on both sides of the conflict, though in different ways; and the schismatic spirit of "I am of Newton," and "I am of Darby," came in and carried all before it, but those who had been really walking before God. These could but sigh and weep for the sin and wickedness carried on in the holy name of Jesus, and keep aloof from that which so dishonored the Lord. In Corinth, Paul would take no part in the unholy strife that was going on, amongst those who contended to belonging to Paul, to Peter, or to Apollos. He was content to remain the servant, and not to become the master; for he belonged to all, and sought to raise them out of their sectarianism, by telling them that Paul, and Cephas, and Apollos, were alike theirs— theirs to serve in the bonds of the gospel; and in the same spirit the eloquent teacher, Apollos, could not be persuaded by Paul to come among them, as if to keep himself out of sight, that the crucified Lord might eclipse himself as well as Paul.

The result of this acting in grace was, that in the Second Epistle we read nothing of the divisions that marked the First Epistle — grace and forbearance had triumphed over self and schism. The grace of the teachers in Corinth was, however, wanting in Plymouth; and regardless of the unity of the body that had been boasted in, and the command to keep the unity of the Spirit that had been taught, Mr. Darby meets what he considers the sectarianism of another by a sectarianism of his own which he consummates by making a division among the saints with whom he had been in fellowship from the commencement; and *that*, notwithstanding the remonstrance of most of the brethren who came from a distance to investigate the state of things in Ebrington street, where till now all had met in fellowship. Having affected the division, he spread a table elsewhere on the last Sunday of that sorrowful and eventful year, which was in future to be exclusively "the table of the Lord," around which himself and his followers were to rally. From this meeting in December, 1845, we must date the rise of Darbyism, and its development into a distinct and self-excommunicated body, separated on grounds subversive of the great truth around which, as opposed to all sectarianism, "the Brethren" had sought to rally the saints of God; namely, that the blood of the Lamb was the basis of the union of the family of heaven: as Mr. Darby expressed it, "to receive all who are on the foundation."

The grounds of this melancholy division were, as we gather from Mr. Darby's *Narrative,* sectarianism, clericalism, and erroneous prophetic views. There was no charge of heresy; there was not one Scriptural ground on which the separation could be justified; but, as if there had been no injunction to mutual forbearance and long-suffering, and as if the blood of the Lamb no longer constituted the sure foundation of all true fellowship here, as it is of all the fellowship in the glory; we find Mr. Darby either excommunicating the saints with whom for so many years he had been in fellowship, or perhaps more correctly, excommunicated himself; in either case, rending the body of the Lord, and saying in fact, as one of old, who had no mother's heart to yearn over the child, "Let it be neither mine nor thine, but divide it." Oh, for the bowels of Christ Jesus, the heart of the loving Master, that yearned in the apostle, that would have sacrificed self a thousand times on the altar of the Lord for His body's sake! Where was the love that travailed in birth again till Christ was formed in the Galatian churches—the love that gave a mother's solicitude for the people of God that could not cut them off, though in love to them it wished that the false teachers might be even cut off for their sakes? Oh, the awful sin of schism! but a brother's sin is our own, ours to bear in priestly power before the altar. Let this be remembered, and a brother's sin will cause grief and not bitterness; and the dishonor to God and the shame to ourselves we shall seek to bear in tears before our God, as did Daniel and Jeremiah. How clearly these actings prove that real love to the Lord, and value for the unity of His body, had declined; that leaders wanted to maintain their own opinions and keep their own followers; and that these followers had made their leaders and their opinions the real bond of their union, instead of Christ Himself, who binds all into the same bundle of eternal life with Himself, the Lord and Master of them all. Alas! how had the fine gold thus early become dim, and the silver turned to dross. "To us belong shame and confusion of face."

A sober consideration of the whole matter after the lapse of nearly a century will probably make one feel that the truth is in neither extreme. Undoubtedly things were in a bad state at Plymouth. Many were sighing and longing for deliverance who did not know what to do nor where to turn.

Mr. Darby felt that Plymouth's example might be copied in other places and self-willed men might thereby shipwreck the entire movement. That he had no thought of starting a *new* movement nor of setting up a counter-system, two somewhat obscurely-worded papers of his, written about this time, make clear. They are somewhat lengthy, but I think they are of value as showing the working of his mind. He evidently desired to do the will of God at whatever cost, but he was himself in great perplexity. Nevertheless, these papers prove, I think, conclusively that he had no conception of the importance and the far-reaching effect of the step he took in separating from the main meeting on the sole charges of clericalism, sectarianism and moral condition. In conversation sometime afterward Mr. Robert Chapman of Barnstaple said, "You should have waited before acting as you did." Mr. Darby replied, "I waited six months and there was no repentance," or words to that effect. Mr. Chapman replied that at Barnstaple they would have waited six years ere taking a step that would have so divided the brethren.

The impression left on my mind is that Mr. Darby was over-zealous for what he conceived to be the glory of God and was not actuated by pride and self-will. But God alone can judge of this. He was a comparatively young man still. For less than 20 years he had been one of the recognized leaders of the new movement and it seemed to him he was called upon to save the testimony from utter shipwreck. But let the reader judge of his spirit and his views at this time from a perusal of the papers that follow:

I

I believe that the churches have been merged in the mass of ecclesiastical popular hierarchism and lost; but I believe also that the visible church, as it is called, has been merged there too.

Still there is a difference, because churches were the administrative form, while the church, as a body on the earth, was the vital unity.

What I felt from the beginning, and began with, was this: the Holy Ghost remains, and, therefore, the essential principle of unity with His presence; for (the fact is all we are now concerned in) *wherever* "two or three are gathered together in my name, there am I in the midst of them."

When this is really sought, there will certainly be blessing by His presence; we have found it so, most sweetly and graciously, who have met separately.

When there is an attempt at displaying the position and the unity, there will always be a mess and a failure; God will not take such a place with us.

We must get into the place of His mind, to get His strength. That is now the failure of the church; but there He will be with us.

I have always said this. I know it has troubled some, even those I especially love; but I am sure it is the Lord's mind. I have said: We are the witnesses of the weakness and low estate of the church.

We are not stronger nor better than others (Dissenters, etc.), but we only own our bad and low state, and *therefore* can find blessing. I do not limit what the blessed Spirit can do for us in this low estate, but I take the place *where* he can do it.

Hence, government of bodies, in an authorized way, I believe there is none; where this is assumed, there will be confusion. It was here (Plymouth); and it was constantly and openly said, that this was to be a model, so that all in distant places might refer to it. My thorough conviction is, that conscience was utterly gone, save in those who were utterly miserable.

I only, therefore, so far seek the original standing of the church as to believe, that wherever two or three are gathered in His name, Christ will be, and that the Spirit of God is necessarily the only source of power, and that which He does will be blessing through the lordship of Christ. These provide for all times. If more be attempted now, it will be only confusion.

The original condition is owned as a sinner, or as a mutilated man owns integrity and a whole body. But there a most important point comes in:—I cannot supply the lack by human arrangement or wisdom; I must be dependent.

I should disown whatever was not of the Spirit, and in this sense disown whatever was—not short of the original standing; for that, in the complete sense, I am—but what man has done to fill it up; because this does not own the coming short, nor the Spirit of God. I would always own what is of God's Spirit in any. The *rule* seems to be here very simple.

I do not doubt that dispensed power is disorganized; but the

Holy Ghost is always competent to act in the circumstances God's people are in. The secret is, not to pretend to get beyond it. Life and divine power are always there; and I use the members I have, with full confession that I am in an imperfect state.

We must remember that the body must exist, though not in a united state; and so, even locally. I can then, therefore, own their gifts, and the like, and get my warrant in two or three united for the blessing promised to that.

Then, if gifts exist, they cannot be exercised but as members of the body, because they are such, not by outward union, but by the vital power of the Head through the Holy Ghost.

"Visible body," I suspect, misleads us a little. Clearly the corporate operation is in the actual living body down here on earth, but there it is the members must act; so that I do not think it makes a difficulty.

I believe if we were to act on I Cor. 12:14 farther than power exists to verify it, we should make a mess.

But then the existence of the body, whatever its scattered condition, necessarily continues; because it depends on the existence of the Head, and its union with it. In this the Holy Ghost is necessarily supreme.

The body exists in virtue of there being one Holy Ghost. "There is one body and one Spirit, even as we are called in one hope of our calling"; indeed this is the very point which is denied here [i. e. Plymouth].

Then Christ necessarily nourishes and cherishes us as His own flesh, as members of His body; and this goes on "till we all come," etc. (Eph. 4). Hence, I apprehend we cannot deny the body and its unity (whatever its unfaithfulness and condition), and (so far as the Holy Ghost is owned) His operation in it, without denying the divine title of the Holy Ghost, and the care and headship of Christ over the church.

Here I get, not a question of the church's conduct, but of Christ's; and the truth of the Holy Ghost being on earth, and His title when there; and yet the owning of Christ's lordship. And this is how far I own others.

If a minister has gifts in the Establishment, I own it as through the Spirit, Christ begetting the member of, or nourishing, His body. But I cannot go along with what it is mixed up with, because it is not of the body nor of the Spirit. I cannot touch the unclean; I am to separate the precious from vile.

But I cannot give up Eph. 4 while I own the faithfulness of

Christ. Now if we meet (yea, and when we do meet), all I look for is that this principle should be owned, because it is owning the Holy Ghost Himself, and that to me is everything.

We meet and worship; and at this time, we who have separated meet in different rooms, that we may in the truest and simplest way, in our weakness, *worship.* Then whatever the Holy Ghost may give to any one, He is supreme, to feed us with—perhaps nothing in the way of speaking—and it must be in the unity of the body.

If you were here, you could be in the unity of the body as one of ourselves. This Satan cannot destroy, because it is connected with Christ's title and power.

If men set up to imitate the administration of the body, it will be popery or dissent at once.

And this is what I see of the visibility of the body; it connects itself with this infinitely important principle, the presence and action of the Holy Ghost on earth.

It is not merely a saved thing in the counsels of God, but a living thing animated down here by its union with the Head, and the presence of the Holy Ghost in it. It is a real actual thing, the Holy Ghost acting down here. If two are faithful in this, they will be blessed in it.

If they said, "We are the body," not owning all the members (in whatever condition), they would morally cease to be of it. I own them, but in nothing their condition. The principle is all-important.

Christ has attached, therefore, its practical operation to "two or three"; and owns them by His presence. He has provided for its maintenance. Thus in all states of ruin, it cannot cease till He ceases to be Head, and the Holy Spirit to be as the Guide and the Comforter sent down.

God sanctioned the setting up of Saul; He never did the departure from the Holy Ghost. The "two or three" take definitely the place of the temple, which was the locality of God's presence, as a principle of union. That is what makes all the difference. Hence, in the division of Israel, the righteous sought the temple as a point of unity, and David is to us here Christ by the Holy Ghost.

On the other hand, church-government, save as the Spirit is always power, cannot be acted on.

II

I suspect many brethren have had expectations, which never led me out, and which perplexed their minds when they were not met in practice. I never felt my testimony, for example, to be the ability of the Holy Ghost to rule a visible body. This I do not doubt; but I doubt its proper application now as a matter of testimony. It does not become us.

My confidence is in the certainty of God's blessing, and maintaining us, if we take the place we are really in. That place is one of the general ruin of the dispensation. Still, I believe God has provided for the maintenance of its general principle (save persecution), that is, the gathering of a remnant into the comfort of united love by the power and presence of the Holy Ghost, so that Christ could sing praises there.

All the rest is a ministry to form, sustain, etc. Amongst other things, government may have its place; but it is well to remember, that, in general, government regards evil, and therefore is outside the positive blessing, and has the lowest object in the church.

Moreover, though there be a gift of government, in general, government is of a different order from gift. Gift serves, ministers, hardly government. These may be united as in apostolic energy. Elders were rather the government, but they were not gifts.

It is especially the order of the governmental part which (I believe) has failed, and that we are to get on without, at least in a formal way. But I do not believe that God has therefore not provided for such a state of things.

I believe "brethren" a good deal got practically out of their place, and the consciousness of it, and found their weakness: and the Lord is now teaching them. For my part, when I found all in ruin around me, my comfort was, that where two or three are gathered together in Christ's name, there He would be. It was not government or anything else I sought. Now I do believe that God is faithful, and able to maintain the blessing.

I believe the great buildings and great bodies have been a mistake: indeed I always did. Further, I believe now (although it were always true in practice), the needed dealing with evil must be by the conscience in grace. So St. Paul ever dealt, though he had the resource of a positive commission. And I believe that two or three together, or a larger number, with some having the gift of wisdom in grace, can, in finding the mind of the Lord, act in discipline; and this, with pastoral care, is the mainspring of holding the saints together, in Matt. 18. This agreeing together is referred to as the sign of the Spirit's power.

I do not doubt that some may be capable of informing the conscience of others. But the conscience of the body is that which is ever to be acted upon and set right. This is the character of all healthful action of this kind, though there may be a resource in present apostolic power, which, where evil has entered, may be wanting; but it cannot annul "where two or three agree, it shall be done."

So that I see not the smallest need of submission to popery; (*i. e.,* carnal unity by authority in the flesh), nor of standing alone; because God has provided for a gathering of saints together, founded on grace, and held by the operation of the Spirit, which no doubt may fail for want of grace, but which, in every remaining gift, has its scope; in which Christ's presence and the operation of the Spirit is manifested, but must be maintained, on the ground of the condition the church really is in, or it would issue in a sect arranged by man, with a few new ideas.

Where God is trusted in the place, and for the place, we are in, and we are content to find Him infallibly present with us, there I am sure He is sufficient and faithful to meet our wants.

If there be one needed wiser than any of the gathered ones in a place, they will humbly feel their need, and God will send some one as needed, if he sees it the fit means.

There is no remedy for want of grace but the sovereign goodness that leads to confession. If we set up our altar, it will serve for walls *(Ezra 3:3)*. The visibility God will take care of, as He always did, the faith of the body will be spoken of, and the unity in love manifest the power of the Holy Ghost in the body.

I have no doubt of God's raising up for need all that need requires in the place where He has set us in understanding. If we think to set up the church, again I would say, God forbid. I had rather be near the end, to live and to die for it in service, where it is as dear to God: that is my desire and life.

Effort was made during the next thirteen months to bring about a reconciliation, but all was in vain.

Then in February, 1847, something came to light that confirmed

Mr. Darby in his judgment that he had been guided by the Lord and which led many perplexed ones to definitely side with him.

Mr. J. L. Harris had gone on with his colleague though in great distress of mind, until he became convinced that there was a positive Satanic effort in the Ebrington street meeting seeking to destroy the testimony of the Brethren. This change of attitude was brought about by his discovery that Mr. Newton was systematically propagating a line of teaching in regard to Christ that was subversive of evangelical truth.

In justice to Mr. Newton it should be pointed out that the teaching was not exactly new. In part, at least, it had been given out by Mr. Newton in an article printed in *The Christian Witness,* and edited by Mr. Harris himself several years before, and apparently had escaped censure. However, the full teaching was not set forth in this paper, nor did any suspect what it might lead up to. The doctrine in question had to do with the Lord's relationship to God as a man and an Israelite here on earth. It was a system of teaching founded on certain expressions in the Psalms and Mr. Newton first fell into it in attempting to answer Edward Irving's heresy as to "the sinful humanity of Christ." The way his fully-developed views were brought to light can best be given by Mr. Harris himself, who first drew Mr. Darby's attention to it. He says:

> "I desire explicitly to state how the manuscript came under my notice. About three weeks since one of our sisters in Exeter very kindly lent the notes to my wife, as being Mr. Newton's teaching, from which she had found much interest and profit. When my wife first told me what she had brought home, I did not pay much attention to it; but shortly after I felt it was not right in me to sanction in my house this system of private circulation, and I determined to return the manuscript unread. Accordingly I wrote a note to the sister who had lent the manuscript, thanking her for her kindness, and explaining my reason for returning it unread. It was late at night when I had finished writing, and I found in the meantime my wife had looked into the manuscript so as to get an outline of its contents, which she mentioned to me, especially the expression that "the cross was only the closing incident in the life of Christ." She thought she did not understand the meaning of the author, and referred to me for explanation. I then looked into the manuscript myself, and on

perusing it felt surprised and shocked at finding such unscriptural statements and doctrine, which appeared to me to touch the integrity of the doctrine of the cross . . .

In the law of the land there is such a thing as misprision of treason, involving heavy penalties when any one who has been acquainted with treasonable practices does not give information. In this case I believe the doctrines taught to undermine the glory of the cross of Christ, and to subvert souls; and it seems to me a duty to Christ and to His saints to make the doctrine openly known. The manuscript professes to be notes of a lecture—I suppose a public lecture. With these notes on Psalm 6 there was given, as accompanying it, notes on Isaiah 13, 14, if I recollect aright, with this notice, "This to go with Psalm 6," or something to that effect; so that it appears from this title that these manuscripts are as regularly circulated among a select few, in various parts of England, as books in a reading society.

Mr. William Trotter gives quotations from this lecture on Psalm 6, as follows:

"For a person to be suffering here because he serves God, is one thing; but the relation of that person to God, and what he is immediately receiving from His hand while serving Him, is another; and it is this which the sixth Psalm, and many others, open to us. *They describe the hand of God stretched out, as rebuking in anger, and chastening in hot displeasure; and remember, this is not the scene on the cross.*" He says, on the same page, that this—the scene on the cross—"*was only one incident in the life of Christ. . .* It was only the closing incident of his long life of suffering and sorrow; *so that to fix our eye simply on that would be to know little what the character of his real sufferings were.*"

After saying, "I do not refer to what were called His vicarious sufferings, but to His partaking of the circumstances of the woe and sorrow of the human family; and not only of the human family generally, but of a particular part of it, of Israel," he goes on to speak of the curse having fallen on them; and then adds, "*So Jesus became part of an accursed people—a people who had earned God's wrath by transgression after transgression.*" Again: "*So Jesus became obnoxious to the wrath of God the moment He came into the world.*" Again: "Observe, this is chastening in displeasure; not that which comes now on the child of God, which is never in wrath, *but this rebuking in wrath, to which He was amenable, because He was part of an accursed people;* so the hand of God was continually stretched out against Him in various ways." From this dreadful condition he represents our Lord as getting partially delivered at His baptism by John. I say partially; for elsewhere he distinctly affirms that He only emerged from it entirely by death: "His life, through all the thirty years, was made up, more or less, of experiences of this kind; so it must have been a great relief to Him to hear the voice of John the Baptist, saying, 'Repent ye; for the kingdom of heaven is at hand.' Here was a door opened to Israel at once. They might come, and be forgiven; so He was glad to hear that word. He heard it with a wise and attentive ear, and came to be baptized, because He was one with Israel— *was in their condition, one of wrath from God;* consequently, *when He was baptized, He took new ground;* but Israel would not take it," etc. Such were the doctrines promulgated by Mr. Newton.

No doubt much of this will be obscure to one who has never seriously considered the questions involved. But to an instructed Christian the teaching is most serious.

Mr. Darby at once exposed the error and even many of Mr. Newton's strongest adherents were shocked and dismayed when they learned what he really held. Pressure was brought to bear upon him to reconsider and to retract and he agreed to do so in measure, issuing a paper dated "Plymouth, Nov. 26th, 1847," and entitled *"A Statement and Acknowledgment Respecting Certain Doctrinal Errors."* In this paper he withdrew certain of his teachings for reconsideration and confessed that he was wrong in attributing our Lord's sufferings from God during His life on earth because of His connection with Adam as His federal head. The other parts of his teachings he wished to weigh further before expressing himself. He closed with the words:

> I would not wish it to be supposed that what I have now said is intended to extenuate the error which I have confessed. I desire to acknowledge it fully, and to acknowledge it as sin; it is my desire thus to confess it before God and His church; and I desire that this may be considered as an expression of my deep and unfeigned grief and sorrow, especially by those who may have been grieved or injured by the false statement, or by any consequences thence resulting. I trust the Lord will not only

pardon, but will graciously counteract any evil effects which may
have arisen to any therefrom.

                                                    B. W. NEWTON.

Messrs. J. E. Batten and H. W. Soltau, leading Ebrington street
teachers, publicly renounced the erroneous views and separated from
the Newton meeting, and with them many others left and sought
fellowship in the new gathering which Mr. Darby had started. Mr.
Batten has given a full outline of the teaching he had imbibed. It
shows how grievously Mr. Newton had been misled himself and was
misleading others.

These are the points in question:

I. That the Lord Jesus at his birth, and because born of a
woman, partook of certain consequences of the fall,—*mortality*
being one,—and because of this association by nature, he became
an heir of death—born under death as a penalty.

II. That the Lord Jesus at His birth stood in such relation to
Adam as a federal head; that guilt was imputed to him; and
that he was exposed to certain consequences of such imputation,
as stated in Romans 5.

III. That the Lord Jesus was also born as a Jew under the
broken law, and was regarded by God as standing in that relation to Him; and that God pressed upon His soul the terrors
of Sinai, as due to one in that relation.

IV. That the Lord Jesus took the place of distance from God,
which such a person so born and so related must take; and that
He had to find His way back to God by some path in which
God might at last own and meet Him.

V. That so fearful was the distance, and so real were these
relations by birth, and so actual were their attendant penalties
of death, wrath, and the curse, that until His deliverance God is
said to have rebuked Him, to have chastened Him, and that in
anger and hot displeasure.

VI. That because of these dealings from God, and Christ's
sufferings under them, the language of Lamentations 3, and
Psalms 6, 38 and 88, etc., has been stated to be the utterance
of the Lord Jesus while under this heavy pressure from God's
hand.

VII. That the Lord Jesus extricated Himself from these inflictions by keeping the law; and that at John's baptism the consequent difference in Christ's feelings and experience was so

great, as to have been illustrated by a comparison of the difference between Mount Sinai and Mount Sion, or between law and grace.

VIII. That beside all these relations which Christ took by birth, and their attendant penalties and inflictions, and His sufferings under the heavy hand of God, it has been further stated that He had the experience of an unconverted, though elect Jew.

Later Mr. Newton reaffirmed some of these teachings while confessing that others were erroneous.

Brethren generally repudiated the whole system, and Mr. Newton and the Ebrington street meeting were looked upon as defiled and leprous. While all did not agree with Mr. Darby's earlier attitude, very few dissented from his position at this time, and after a large meeting held in Bath, in May, 1848, it looked as though further division had been averted and harmony was once more to reign among the Brethren, with Mr. Newton and his followers outside.

CHAPTER FIVE

THE BETHESDA QUESTION AND THE FIRST GREAT DIVISION

MANY WHO KNOW little else about the movement of which I am writing, have heard of "the Bethesda question," and perhaps wondered what was involved in it. This I shall now endeavor to make plain.

Swete the theologian says, referring to the age-long controversy between the eastern and the western churches about "the Procession of the Holy Spirit," that "it can never be composed until justice is done to the sincerity of both parties." How often has this been true of similar differences! And most aptly do the words apply to the Plymouth Bethesda question, which rent the Brethren asunder in 1848 and still keeps them divided, though sober men on both sides decry much that then took place whether on the part of Mr. Muller and his associates or Mr. Darby and his friends.

So long as prejudice rules the mind a reasonable judgment can never be arrived at. If each can see but self-will or indifference to Christ's glory on the part of the others there will never be a healing of the breach.

I desire to recognize the integrity and devotedness of the leaders on each side of the unhappy affair. To question Mr. Muller's love for Christ and desire to glorify Him is as foolish and sinful as to charge Mr. Darby with selfish ambition and the spirit of Diotrephes. Both were men of God, greatly used in their respective spheres. Their differences were as sad as those that separated the Wesleys and Whitefield in the previous century.

George Muller was a German Baptist minister who had settled in England, and Henry Craik was a Baptist pastor in Devonshire, where the two were near neighbors in the later twenties of the 19th century. God had been leading both along the same road that he was opening up to Dr. Cronin, J. N. Darby, and others in Ireland. At Teignmouth Mr. Muller had begun a weekly meeting for the breaking of bread under the direct guidance of the Holy Spirit, he himself refusing to preside. This was but a few years after the work began in Dublin, and some months before there was any meeting in Plymouth, or in any other part of England, so far as is now known. Even earlier than this Mr. Henry Craik had been a guest of Anthony Norris Groves in Exeter, and they often spoke together of the fallen state of the church and the advisability of proceeding on simple, Scriptural lines. Mr. Henry Groves, son of A. N. Groves, relates in *Darbyism* that Mr. Craik said to him on one occasion "It was not at St. Andrew's; it was not at Plymouth; it was at Exeter that the Lord taught me those lessons of dependence on Himself and of catholic fellowship which I have sought to carry out."

It is important to note this for there has been an effort by some to exalt Mr. Darby as though he were the prophet of the movement, whereas it is evident that there was a distinct work of the Spirit along the same lines in a number of different places at about the same time.

Mr. Craik and Mr. Muller often conferred together and were of one mind as to their principles and sought to carry them out so far as they had light while still in Devonshire, refusing a stipulated salary and endeavoring to lead the saints into the knowledge of their priestly privileges and of the heavenly calling of the church.

In regard to the establishment of Bethesda chapel I cannot do better than quote Mr. Henry Groves who was thoroughly familiar with the facts. He says:

"While Mr. Muller was at Teignmouth, Mr. Craik was at Shaldon, a village close by, where for some years he had been laboring for the Lord. It was there that they were first drawn together; and when in 1832 it was proposed to Mr. Craik to come to Bristol, he only consented to do so on the condition that his brother and fellow-laborer would go there too. Bethesda chapel was at that time for hire, and was taken for them by a gentleman who had heard Mr. Craik preach; and entering on its bare walls, they labored together during a period of more than three and thirty years. This circumstance is mentioned because of the false assertion often made, that the church at

Bethesda was originally the remains of a Baptist congregation. These brethren belonged to no denomination, but brought to Bristol with them those views of church-fellowship and of faith which had marked them in Devonshire, and which led to their being considered by both churchmen and dissenters as occupying the anomalous position of belonging to no party, and who without personal resources were content, as it was said at the time, 'to minister without salary, and to accommodate their hearers without pew rents.' But the Lord whom they served has these many years showed that 'those who honor Him He will honor.' The Lord has so caused the light of the saints gathered in fellowship to shine abroad that persons from Holland, Sweden, France, Portugal, and other places far and near, have come to learn the way of the Lord more perfectly, and to know the secret of that *order, harmony* and *fellowship* which has for so many years characterized them.

"It is further an interesting fact, that there are many assemblies meeting in the north of Ireland, the fruit of the late revival there, which owe their present liberty of church communion and ministry to reading Mr. Muller's *Narrative;* and one who is now with the Lord, and was used as the instrument in the Lord's hand of the awakening in those parts, acknowledged to the writer when he met him at Kells, in 1858, as he did subsequently in Bristol, that the sense of the reality of prayer which he had obtained from reading Mr. Muller's *Narrative,* led him to seek for that faith in reference to the conversion of sinners, which resulted in that remarkable revival which then began in the north of Ireland.

"In 1832 the first seven members were received into fellowship in Bethesda. That year cholera broke out, and the Lord wonderfully blessed the ministry of the Word to the conversion of many a poor sinner; and from that small commencement has the Lord been adding continually to the church, till the number in fellowship at present stands about twelve hundred. It will not fail to be noticed by those who have much intercourse with these saints, particularly with the poorer class, how much the paths of practical godliness and of living faith that have been taught and lived have been owned of God, in leading them to follow in the footsteps of those who have sought to be examples to the flock in daily life, not only 'in word,' but also 'in behavior, in charity, in faith, in purity.' Such was the position occupied by Bethesda; and Mr. Wigram, after the disruption, writing in reference to this time, says: 'Time was once when Bethesda was Nazarite in character, and derided by the world and by dissenters, and I gloried in fellowship with her reproach.' "

At first there was a question in Mr. Muller's mind as to whether unimmersed believers should be received to communion. Were such to be considered as walking disorderly? This probably gave rise to the idea that Bethesda was an independent Baptist congregation.* But upon consulting the saintly Robert Chapman of Barnstaple he became convinced that difference of judgment as to the ordinance of baptism ought not to constitute a ban to Christian fellowship, and so, ever afterwards saints were received at Bethesda as such and not because of like views on an ordinance.

George Muller's great work of faith and labor of love in connection with the Ashley Downs orphan houses marks him out as one of the spiritual giants of the 19th century. This is too well known to require lengthy notice here. But I draw attention to it because of the shocking way in which carnal men on the exclusive side have referred to one whose shoes they were not worthy to bear. Of one thing there can be no question. The prayer-hearing God who so marvellously honored Muller's faith in him never refused fellowship with him when others branded him as contaminated with moral leprosy and with indifference to Christ because he differed with many as to how the Plymouth matter should be handled. One trembles to think what it will mean to answer at the judgment seat of Christ for casting aspersions on a man of God like Muller and personally I would rather cut off my right hand than pen one word of ungracious criticism, though it is my sincere judgment that a mistake was made at Bethesda the results of which have been far-reaching indeed.

The matter was forced upon the assembly at Bristol in this way. When the difficulties at Plymouth came to a culmination and Mr. Newton and those remaining with him were considered under the ban of excommunication some from the Newton meeting went

* The Bethesda congregation was not originally a Baptist church. This error has been repeated over and over again, and many imagine they see in it the root cause of the whole after trouble, in that the church as a whole is said "to have been received into fellowship, instead of insisting on individual examination." But this is all a mistake, and altogether wide of the mark.

to Bristol and applied for fellowship at Bethesda. This at once
aroused a minority, headed by a Mr. Alexander, who protested
against their reception on the ground that "a little leaven leaveneth
the whole lump." They felt that to receive persons from Ebrington
Street was virtually to undo the discipline at Plymouth and besides
was introducing the evil into the meeting at Bristol. Against their
protest the overseeing brethren decided that the persons in question were not involved in Mr. Newton's errors and might after
examination be received, which they were, with the result that
Mr. Alexander and the other protesters withdrew from fellowship. That this was hasty action on their part I think any thoughtful person will recognize, while on the other hand few will
condone the action of the overseers in ruthlessly overruling their
objection and admitting the friends of Mr. Newton until a thorough
inquiry could be made. Doubtless the Bethesda elders desired to
avoid perplexing the simple and raising needless questions as to the
exact character of the teaching of Newton. But their action only
served to spread the flames, so to speak, instead of putting out
the fire. There was much agitation and considerable correspondence
between Mr. Alexander and Mr. Darby, and the Bethesda meeting
was greatly disturbed thereby.

Finally a meeting of the elder brethren was called and after
considerable discussion a letter was drawn up setting forth their
reasons for acting as they did. This historic document I give in
full. It is known as "The Letter of the Ten":

"DEAR BRETHREN: Our brother, Mr. George Alexander, having printed and circulated a statement expressive of his reasons
for withdrawing from visible fellowship with us at the table
of the Lord; and these reasons being grounded on the fact
that those who labour among you have not complied with his
request relative to the judging of certain errors which have
been taught at Plymouth; it becomes needful that those of
us who have incurred any responsibility in this matter should
lay before you a brief explanation of the way in which we
have acted.

"And first, it may be well to mention, that we had no
intimation whatever to our brother's intention to act as he has
done, nor any knowledge of his intention to circulate any letter,
until it was put into our hands in print.

"Some weeks ago, he expressed his determination to bring his views before a meeting of the body, and he was told that he was quite at liberty to do so. He afterwards declared that he would waive this, but never intimated, in the slightest way, his intention to act as he has done, without first affording the church an opportunity of hearing his reasons for separation. Under these circumstances, we feel it of the deepest importance, for relieving the disquietude of mind naturally occasioned by our brother's letter, explicitly to state that the views relative to the person of our blessed Lord, held by those who for sixteen years have been occupied in teaching the word amongst you, *are unchanged*.

"The truths relative to the divinity of his person, the sinlessness of his nature, and the perfection of his sacrifice, which have been taught both in public teaching and in writing, for these many years past, are, through the grace of God, those which we still maintain. We feel it most important to make this avowal, inasmuch as the letter referred to is calculated, we trust unintentionally, to convey a different impression to the minds of such as cherish a godly jealousy for the faith once delivered to the saints.

"We add, for the further satisfaction of any who may have had their minds disturbed, that we utterly disclaim the assertion that the blessed Son of God was involved in the guilt of the first Adam; or that he was born under the curse of the broken law, because of his connection with Israel. We hold him to have been always the Holy One of God, in whom the Father was ever well pleased. We know of no curse which the Savior bore, except that which he endured as the surety for sinners—according to that Scripture, 'he was made a curse for us.' We utterly reject the thought of his ever having had the experiences of an unconverted person; but maintain that while he suffered *outwardly* the trials connected with his being a man and an Israelite—still in his feelings and experiences, as well as in his external character, he was entirely 'separate from sinners.'

"We now proceed to state the grounds on which we have felt a difficulty in complying with the request of our brother, Mr. Alexander, that we should formally investigate and give judgment on certain errors which have been taught among Christians meeting at Plymouth.

"1st. We considered from the beginning that it would not

be for the comfort or edification of the saints here—nor for the glory of God — that we, in Bristol, should get entangled in the controversy connected with the doctrines referred to. We do not feel that, because errors may be taught at Plymouth or elsewhere, therefore we, as a body, are bound to investigate them.

"2nd. The practical reason alleged why we should enter upon the investigation of certain tracts issued at Plymouth was, that thus we might be able to know how to act with reference to those who might visit us from thence, or who are supposed to be adherents of the author of the said publications. In reply to this, we have to state, that the views of the writer alluded to could only be *fairly learned* from the examination of his own acknowledged writings. We did not feel that we should be warranted in taking our impression of the views actually held by him from any other source than from some treatise written by himself, and professedly explanatory of the doctrines advocated. Now there has been such variableness in the views held by the writer in question, that it is difficult to ascertain what he would now acknowledge as his.

"3rd. In regard to these writings, Christian brethren, hitherto of unblemished reputation for soundness in the faith, have come to different conclusions as to the actual amount of error contained in them. The tracts, some of us knew to be written in such an ambiguous style, that we greatly shrunk from the responsibility of giving any formal judgment on the matter.

"4th. As approved brethren, in different places, have come to such different conclusions in reference to the amount of error contained in these tracts, we could neither desire nor expect that the saints here would be satisfied with the decision of one or two leading brethren. Those who felt desirous to satisfy their own minds, would naturally be led to wish to peruse the writings for themselves. For this, many amongst us have no leisure time; many would not be able to understand what the tracts contained, because of the mode of expression employed; and the result, there is much to fear, would be such perverse disputations and strifes of words, as minister questions rather than godly edifying.

"5th. Even some of those who now condemn the tracts as containing doctrine essentially unsound, did not so understand them on the first perusal. Those of us who were specially requested to investigate and judge the errors contained in them, felt that, under such circumstances, there was but little probability of our coming to unity of judgment touching the nature of the doctrines therein embodied.

"6th. *Even supposing that those who inquired into the matter had come to the same conclusion, touching the amount of positive error therein contained, this would not have guided us in our decision respecting individuals coming from Plymouth. For supposing the author of the tracts were fundamentally heretical, this would not warrant us in rejecting those who came from under his teaching, until we were satisfied that they had understood and imbibed views essentially subversive of foundation-truth;* especially as those meetings at Ebrington Street, Plymouth, last January, put forth a statement, disclaiming the errors charged against the tracts.

"7th. The requirement that we should investigate and judge Mr. Newton's tracts, appeared to some of us like the introduction of a fresh test of communion. It was demanded of us that, in addition to a sound confession and a corresponding walk, we should, as a body, come to a formal decision about what many of us might be quite unable to understand.

"8th. We remembered the Word of the Lord, that 'the beginning of strife is as the letting out of water.' We were well aware that the great body of believers amongst us were in happy ignorance of the Plymouth controversy, and we did not feel it well to be considered as identifying ourselves with either party. We judge that this controversy had been so carried on as to cause the truth to be evil spoken of; and we do not desire to be considered as identifying ourselves with that which has caused the opposer to reproach the way of the Lord. At the same time we wish distinctly to be understood that we would seek to maintain fellowship with all believers, and consider ourselves as particularly associated with those who meet as we do, simply in the name of the Lord Jesus.

"9th. We felt that the compliance with Mr. Alexander's request would be the introduction of an evil precedent. *If a brother has a right to demand our examining a work of fifty pages, he may require our investigating error said to be contained in one of much larger dimensions; so that all our time might be wasted in the examination of other people's errors, instead of more important service.*

"It only remains to notice the three reasons specially assigned by Mr. Alexander in justification of his course of action. To the first, viz., that by our not judging this matter, many of the Lord's people will be excluded from communion with us"—we reply, that unless our brethren can prove, either that error is held and taught amongst us, or *that individuals are received into communion who ought not to be admitted, they can have no Scriptural warrant for withdrawing from our fellowship.* We would affectionately entreat such brethren as may be disposed to withdraw from communion for the reason assigned, to consider that, except they can prove allowed evil in life or doctrine, they cannot, without violating the principles on which we meet, treat us as if we had renounced the faith of the gospel.

"In reply to the second reason, viz., 'that persons may be received from Plymouth holding evil doctrines,'—we are happy in being able to state, that ever since the matter was agitated, we have maintained that persons coming from thence—if suspected of any error—*would be liable to be examined on the point;* that in the case of one individual who had fallen under the suspicion of certain brethren amongst us, not only was there private intercourse with him relative to his views, as soon as it was known that he was objected to, but the individual referred to—known to some of us for several years as a consistent Christian—actually came to a meeting of laboring brethren for the very purpose that any question might be asked him by any brother who should have any difficulty on his mind. Mr. Alexander himself was the principal party in declining the presence of the brother referred to, on that occasion, such inquiry being no longer demanded, inasmuch as the difficulties relative to the views of the individual in question had been removed by private intercourse. We leave Mr. Alexander to reconcile this fact, which he cannot have forgotten, with the assertion contained under his second special reason for withdrawing.

"In regard to the third ground alleged by Mr. Alexander, viz., that by not judging the matter, we lie under the suspicion of supporting false doctrine, we have only to refer to the statement already made at the commencement of this paper.

"In conclusion, we would seek to impress upon all present, the evil of treating the subject of our Lord's humanity as a matter of speculative or angry controversy. One of those who have been ministering among you from the beginning, feels it a matter of deep thankfulness to God, that so long ago as in the year 1835,* he committed to writing, and subsequently printed, what he had learned from the Scriptures of truth relative to the meaning of that inspired declaration, 'The Word was made flesh.' He would affectionately refer any whose minds may be now disquieted, to what he then wrote, and was afterwards led to publish. If there be heresy in the simple statements contained in the letters alluded to, let it be pointed out; if not, let all who are interested in the matter know that we continue unto the present day, 'speaking the same things.' (Signed)

HENRY CRAIK,	EDMUND FELTHAM,
GEORGE MULLER,	JOHN WITHY,
JACOB HENRY HALE,	SAMUEL BUTLER,
CHARLES BROWN,	JOHN MEREDITH,
ELIJAH STANLEY,	ROBERT AITCHISON."

I do not hesitate to say that it seems clear to me that far more importance has been attached to this document than it deserves, or than the signatories ever expected it to receive. It was manifestly never intended for widespread circulation nor as establishing a precedent which other assemblies were to follow.

It was simply a declaration by the leaders at Bethesda of their judgment at the time and of their reasons for acting as they did. Persons might or might not agree with them but there is certainly no ground to question their motives, nor is it brotherly to charge them with lack of conscience and with neutrality as to Christ because in their judgment the Newtonian question should not be forced upon hundreds of simple believers. Mr. William Trotter, author of *The Whole Case of Plymouth and Bethesda,* boldly accuses the signers of want of uprightness, because one of them, Robert Aitchison, afterwards seemed to swing over completely to Mr. Newton and left the Bethesda fellowship. But this is uncharitable to say the least, and while he was ever an admirer of Mr. Newton there is no evidence so far as I have been able to discover that would prove he held Mr. Newton's views

* *Pastoral Letters,* by H. Craik.

when he signed the paper, He is not the first man who repudiated at one time what he accepted at least in part, later on.

The *crux* of the whole matter is paragraph 6. Mr. Darby felt this was a most dangerous principle, as undoubtedly it is, if it be not qualified. He considered that it opened the door to all manner of defilement in the shape of evil teaching and wicked principles. It was like receiving infected persons, or suspected ones at least, from a plague-stricken house. His soul revolted from it with horror as a most grievous evidence of indifference to Christ. He, the Holy One, had been attacked. Bethesda would put peace before righteousness and would not take the trouble to guard the assembly from such fearful errors as had been made manifest at Plymouth. His sincerity cannot be rightly questioned. The pity is that he failed to realize that Messrs. Muller and Craik were undoubtedly as desirous of honoring Christ as he. The question was how best to do it?

And it should be emphasized that again and again it has been shown that the Ten at Bethesda did not mean to commit the assembly to intercommunion with assemblies holding false doctrine, but rather sought to so act as to deliver souls by receiving them in hope that they would not have any further fellowship with their former teacher. Mr. Muller and his associates were thinking of the saints. Mr. Darby was thinking of Christ. His stern hatred of any system or doctrine that detracted from the glory of the Holy One of God filled him with indignation toward what seemed to him to be neutrality and indifference. He never wavered in this judgment to the day of his death, but on the other hand he never contemplated the wholesale refusal of brethren who did not see eye to eye with him, that many of his followers and associates insisted on. His later letters prove this conclusively.

It is to be regretted that there was so much correspondence by letters and that the leaders on both sides did not get together in brotherly conference after the letter of The Ten was written that they might carefully go into it together, but doubtless neither party had the slightest realization of how widespread the division would become over this vexed question.

Stripped of all unnecessary details it simply simmers down to this: What should be the attitude of Scripturally-gathered assemblies of saints, to persons themselves properly under sentence of ex-communication, or to those associated with them? Bethesda and those of like mind practically said, "Examine them individually and receive such as have not inbibed the teaching or wilfully endorsed the evil." These were called "Neutral" or "Open" breth-ren by the others, who maintained that inasmuch as it is written "a little leaven leaveneth the whole lump," an assembly tolerating known evil is like a leprous house and any intercommunion with it, receiving from or commending to it, is but to spread the defile-ment. Association with evil necessarily defiles the otherwise clean and sound believers. Therefore they would refuse all fellowship with any church or assembly tolerating moral or doctrinal evil. They maintained also that if one were excommunicated for Scrip-tural reasons by any company of Christians, he was by that act properly excluded from every assembly of saints on earth until by repentance and confession he was re-instated. These were known as "Exclusives."

Thus it will be seen that the terms "open" and "exclusive" have no reference to the Brethren's attitude toward Christians not reg-ularly meeting with them or holding denominational membership, but they relate solely to these matters of internal discipline.

Reverting to the question under discussion, it may help to get the exclusive point of view if I quote verbatim from William Trotter's *Whole Case*, in regard to events immediately following those already delineated. He writes:

"A meeting was held in Bethesda, October 31st, 1848, in which Mr. Muller gave his own individual judgment of Mr. Newton's tracts, stating that they contained a system of in-sidious error, not here and there, but throughout; and that if the doctrines taught in them were followed out to their legitimate consequences, they would destroy the foundations of the gospel, and overthrow the Christian faith. The legi-timate consequences of these doctrines he stated to be 'to make the Lord need a Savior as well as others.' Still, while recording so strong an individual judgment as this, Mr. Muller said that he could not say Mr. N. was a heretic, that he could not refuse to call him brother. And he was most care-ful in maintaining that what he said was not the judgment of the church, but his own individual judgment, for which he and he alone was responsible. As to the paper of 'the ten,' and all the steps connected with it, he justified them entirely, and said that were they again in the circumstances they would pursue the same course. And what, I ask, is the natural effect of such a proceeding as this? On the one hand the individual judgment against the evil lulls to sleep consciences that are beginning to awake. People say, surely there can be no danger of unsoundness where such a judgment against evil is recorded as this. While on the other hand the door is left as wide open to the evil as ever; and Satan is quite satisfied if you will only let it in, whatever strong things you may say against it."

Bethesda, however, indignantly repudiated the charge of neutrality, indifference to Christ, and of leaving the door open to the evil.

Meeting after meeting was held to see what more could be done. Mr. Newton's tracts were more carefully examined by the leaders, and finally so decided a pronouncement was made against them that all of his friends withdrew from the meeting. This, in the eyes of "open" brethren cleared Bethesda completely. And it is related by Mr. Muller himself that in July, 1849, Mr. Darby made him a personal call and acknowledged this. That interview was so brief and unsatisfactory, however, that it accomplished nothing toward reconciliation, but rather widened the breach,

Mr. Muller's letter is self-explanatory.

"BRESLAU, GERMANY, April 30, 1883.

"DEAR SIR: On my way back from a missionary tour in Russia and Russian Poland to England, your letter—of April 6—has been forwarded to me to this place. The reply to your question is this: In July, 1849, Mr. Darby came to me to the New Orphan House No. 1, on Ashley Down, Bristol, and said, 'As you have judged Newton's tracts, there is no longer any reason why we should be separated.' My reply was, 'I have this moment only ten minutes time, having an important engagement before me, and as you have acted so wickedly in this matter I cannot *now* enter upon it as I have no time!' I have never seen him since.

YOURS truly,
GEORGE MULLER."

There is no way now of getting Mr. Darby's side of this regrettable incident, as he had departed to be with Christ two years before the letter was written. It is known, however, that he never acknowledged having declared that Bethesda had cleared herself of complicity with the evil. But he would be a bold man who would question the veracity of so godly a brother as George Muller, though some allowance should be made for prejudice and intervening years, as nearly thirty-five years had elapsed between the event itself and the letter relating it.

One wonders if these two men of God would have permitted any engagement, however important, or prejudices, however strong, to keep them from arranging a full brotherly conference, if they could have foreseen the years of strife and sorrow, the heartbreaks and family estrangements, the bitterness and dissension, and above all the stumblingblocks thrown in the way of others seeking after the truth, which resulted from leaving this sad affair unsettled. It would almost seem as if these two men of God had it in their power to end the division then and there and both missed the opportunity.

To go into further details here would only weary the reader and be without profit to anyone. Suffice it to say that everywhere that Brethren met — on mission fields and in the home lands — the Bethesda question was carried and they were thus torn asunder into two conflicting camps — yet holding the same truth.

Newtonianism never again lifted up its head among them. And as for Mr. Newton himself he had no further place in their assemblies, whether open or exclusive. He lived to be 93 years of age, and in all his later teaching there is no hint of the views he held at the time of the strife. Neither have his early teachings "leavened" the brethren of either class, for as intimated above it is everywhere repudiated, yet the division continues and men unborn when it occurred take sides for or against Bethesda and walk apart from one another still; though there are not wanting evidences that the Spirit of God is moving in many quarters toward the revival of first principles, which may in time lead to restoration of fellowship between brethren long separated.

The many divisions among both branches, of which I have yet to write, have in themselves contributed toward this much-to-be-desired end.

CHAPTER SIX

FURTHER DEVELOPMENTS

THE THIRTY-ODD YEARS following the break over the Bethesda questions were, in spite of much internal strife, owing to growing ecclesiastical pretension and an ever-increasing emphasis on discipline for minor details of doctrine or behavior, years of marked blessing in many ways. This was, strange enough as it must have seemed to many "exclusives," particularly true in connection with those so ruthlessly spurned as neutral or loose brethren. Even J. N. Darby owned that "God in His sovereignty has given them much blessing in the gospel." Their assemblies multiplied and through the labors of earnest evangelists vast numbers were saved. Tract depots turned out gospel papers by millions and itinerant gospelers went far and wide proclaiming the glad tidings of a present salvation through faith in Christ alone. Hundreds more, leaving all for Him who had saved them, went forth to the regions beyond to establish missions among the heathen. In China, India, the Straits Settlements, Africa and among the aborigines of New Zealand and the islands of the seas, they lifted up the standard of the cross, unsupported by salaries, and unsustained by mission boards at home. Their trust was in the living God who, through His own people, ministered to them, as "for his name's sake they went forth, taking nothing of the Gentiles." F. S. Arnot, the pioneer of the Zambesi country in Central Africa, and later on Dan Crawford of the "long grass country" were among those whose names shall be in everlasting remembrance.

While the exclusive wing of the brethren turned more to occupation with truth for believers, yet they too had many ardent gospel preachers, such as George Cutting, author of "Safety, Certainty and Enjoyment" (which has had a circulation in many languages of about seven million copies) ; Dr. W. T. P. Wolston, a physician of Edinburgh, Scotland, for years editor of the *Gospel Messenger* and author of many books; Charles Stanley of Sheffield, the well-known tract writer; and a host of others. But the exclusives shine as teachers. It was in these years that William Kelly started the *Bible Treasury* and edified thousands by his clear Scriptural expositions. C. H. Mackintosh and Andrew Miller founded *Things New and Old*, and Mr. Mackintosh wrote his *Notes on the Pentateuch*, which D. L. Moody, Major Whittle and others found so helpful. J. B. Stoney edited *A Voice to the Faithful* and *Food for the Flock*, periodicals of a somewhat different type, decidedly introspective and subjective, which paved the way for what afterwards came to be known as Ravenism. Others there were of equal note, too numerous to mention.

This Branch of the movement had its missions also, though never in so large a way as the "open" section. But they began and have maintained missionary work in the West Indies, Egypt, South and Central Africa, the Guianas and parts of India, Burma and Japan. On the continent of Europe, in America and the Antipodes the movement spread in a remarkable way, but it is noteworthy that the farther removed assemblies were from British influence the more they prospered. I know some will resent this, but the facts speak for themselves.

There seemed a determination on the part of some to centralize the movement in England and particularly in London, and this has ever proven a source of trouble and weakness.

An independent work of the Spirit of God sprang up in the northeastern part of Scotland after the great revival work of Duncan Matheson; and Donald Ross, Donald Munro, John Smith and many more were literally forced outside of denominational lines and began meetings very similar to those of the earliest brethren, though entirely apart from them. A great wave of blessing swept over Aberdeen and adjoining shires extending to the north of Ireland, and through emigration to Canada, Australia and New Zealand.

About 1870, meetings such as these were held in the house of my grandfather, William Ironside of New Deer, Aberdeenshire, and a little later my uncle, Henry W. Ironside, came out to Canada and was the means of interesting his elder brother John, afterwards my father, in the movement. At this time Donald Munro and John Smith came to Ontario.

My father's uncle by marriage, John Rae, was pastor of a Baptist church in Scotland, when the revival reached his parish and, finding himself in hearty accord with it, he came out to the name of the Lord alone. I have heard him tell how tidings of this work, and the fact that the breaking of bread had begun on simple Scriptural lines among the northeast coast meetings, reached the ears of "Exclusives" at Edinburgh and elsewhere. Rejoicing in this evident work of God, yet fearing anything that looked like "independency," they sent representative brethren to the place where Mr. Rae and others were ministering, in order to confer with them as to the possibility of full fellowship. But to the eternal shame of these unwise and shortsighted messengers, be it said that they had no more sense than to bring before the leaders and the newly-gathered converts the necessity of judging the Bethesda question ere they could commune together! This demand to judge a matter of which most if not all, had never heard, was indignantly refused and the discredited representatives of a narrow sectarianism and rigid unscriptural exclusivism returned to their homes to warn their assemblies against the new movement as already defiled! What mistakes good men make when tied up to narrow principles and bound by carnal prejudices! It was like the Erskines fighting George Whitefield and declaring his work to be of the devil because he refused to own their confederated churches as "the people of God in Scotland." I believe it was Mr. Donald Ross who refused to listen to anything reflecting on the character or soundness of George Muller (of whose piety and labors he knew something by report), and thereby brought the matter to a head. George Muller must be judged as a defiled man or the Edinburgh brethren would have nothing to do with Mr. Ross or his associates! What humbling facts are these, to be faced at the judgment seat of Christ!

Sometime later it came to the attention of these men of God that a believer's conference was to be held in Glasgow and, yearning for fellowship, a number of them, including Mr. Ross, decided to go down and see if the meetings were along the lines they had been learning from the Word of God. Instead of suspicion and a demand to judge a question of which they knew nothing, John R. Caldwell and others warmly received them, feeling that they were already commended by the reports that had reached Glasgow of the gospel they preached and the way they had been used of the Lord. Without any questions as to their attitude in regard to disciplinary matters elsewhere, they were welcomed to communion and accorded the platform, to teach and preach the Word. Thus they became unconsciously linked up with "open-brethrenism." Had the "exclusives" shown anything like the same common sense and brotherly love instead of meeting them with suspicion their whole after-history might have been different.

In the 70's many of these preachers from Scotland and the north of Ireland came to America and labored with great blessing, particularly in the province of Ontario and in nearby eastern states. Later the movement extended all over the two countries. Alexander Marshall, author of *God's Way of Salvation,* started a paper in Orillia *The Gospel Herald,* and traveled far and wide, leading hundreds of souls to Christ. Donald Ross was ever a pioneer and spent many years in Canada and the States, until taken home.

Through immigration "exclusive" meetings were also started on this side of the Atlantic and so the division was continued in America that had begun in England. J. N. Darby, G. V. Wigram and others came over to minister the Word, and American and Canadian teachers and preachers left all to go out proclaiming the Word of life and truth. Numbers of clergymen getting in touch with the movement became definitely identified with it, renouncing all ecclesiastical titles and preferment. Of these I may mention Malachi Taylor, Frederick W. and Robert T. Grant, A. H. Rule, and E. S. Lyman; to which list could be added many more.

In Iowa, Paul J. Loizeaux, a French Huguenot by birth whose family had emigrated to America, was awakened and saved, and almost immediately began preaching the grace of God to others. A college professor, cultured and of magnetic personality, he became a spirit-filled and flaming evangelist and went everywhere proclaiming the Word, in self-denying dependence on the Lord. Hearing of Mr. Darby, he arranged to meet him and finding himself already in happy agreement with him, he was received into fellowship and almost immediately afterwards other members of the family followed. One wonders what would have been the result if Mr. Darby (like some of his misguided followers) had insisted that he "judge the

question" before he would have anything to do with him! Many
know of P. J. Loizeaux as the author of *The Lord's Dealing with the
Convict Daniel Mann,* a remarkable record of the grace of God
to a condemned murderer, whom the beloved author met and led to
Christ in Kingston penitentiary. It is a marvelous story of sovereign
mercy and has been circulated by hundreds of thousands and I dare
say blessed to myriads of anxious souls. The evangelist and his
brother Timothy founded the Bible Truth Depot, first at Vinton,
Iowa, and later removed to New York, where Loizeaux Brothers'
publishing plant has been turning out fundamentalist literature for
the past fifty-odd years.

The Grants were both Church of England clergymen in Canada
and were men of culture and piety. They at first were much
opposed to the Brethren and considered their teachings subversive of sound theology and proper ecclesiasticism. But through
the literature they were led to change their viewpoint and both
resigned their parishes to take their places henceforth among
these despised brethren who gave no recognition to clerical titles
and looked with disdain on costly ornate houses of worship and
set forms of service. R. T. Grant eventually settled in Los Angeles
and began tract work and preaching among the Mexicans, out of
which developed under God's good hand what is now known as the
Grant Publishing House. The founder never so designated it, but
after his departure to be with Christ Mr. W. H. Crabtree, to whom
the work was committed, felt it but a fitting tribute to the venerable
pioneer to use his name. From the first it was a work of dependence
upon God, and marvelous were the stories Mr. Grant could tell of
answers to prayer for supplies when none but God and himself knew
the circumstances. From the unpretentious establishment out on the
western hills have gone forth millions of pages of books and tracts
in Spanish, Italian, French, Portuguese, Chinese, Japanese, Russian,
Filipino dialects, English and possibly other languages. While a
nominal charge is made to those who are able and willing to pay,
the great bulk of it has gone out free and has been supplied as
heavenly ammunition to missionary soldiers representing all denominational boards or none. Many who criticize the Brethren for
lack of interest in missions little realize how much the mission fields
of the world are indebted to them for literature that has brought
light, life and liberty to many who were in darkness, dead in tres-

passes and sins, and bound in cruel fetters of ignorance and super-
stition. Under Mr. Crabtree's direction the work is constantly in-
creasing.

But I realize I am anticipating. I was to tell of the events of
the years from 1850 to 1880 and I have in my enthusiasm run along
on some lines to the present time.

During these years the exclusive wing of the movement was
hardening and crystalizing in an ominous way in Great Britain. Mr.
Groves' prophecy was proving terribly and pathetically true. The
early Scriptural principles were being displaced by a rigid humanly-
devised sectarianism which if left unchecked, would have made the
Brethren the narrowest and most bigoted denomination outside the
church of Rome. In spite of great activity in preaching and teaching,
and widespread circulation of sound literature the spirit of judging
one another wrought havoc among the local assemblies. Excom-
munications for the most trivial things were frequent. Discipline became the great question of questions. Claims were made regarding
it that, today, seem almost ludicrous, if one forgets how terribly in
earnest these brethren were. Then they become sorrowful indeed.

In one such instance (what was known as the Sheffield case at the
time) relative to a man adjudged a trouble-maker and therefore excluded from a local gathering, but who wished to commune elsewhere,
Mr. Darby wrote a letter, often referred to since, in which he said:

> I understood the breach arose between you and Rotherham
> by reason of your rejection of Goodall. With the main facts
> of his case, I am acquainted, for I took part in what passed, and
> now allow me to put the case as it stands as to him. I put it
> merely as a principle. He (or anyone else) is rejected in Lon-
> don. The assembly in London have weighed, and I with them,
> the case and counted him as either excommunicated or in schism.
> I put the two cases, for I only speak of the principle. I take part
> in this act, and *hold him to be outside the church of God on
> earth, being outside* (in either case) *what represents it in Lon-
> don;* I am bound by Scripture to count them so. I come to
> Sheffield; there he breaks bread, and is—in what? *Not in the
> church of God on earth,* for *he is not of it in London,* and there
> are not two churches on earth, cannot be, so as to be in one and
> out of another. How can I refuse to eat with them in London
> and break bread with him in Sheffield? I have one conscience
> for London, and another conscience for Sheffield? It is con-

fusion and disorder. I do not apprehend I am mistaken in saying you received Goodall without having the reasons or motives of the Priory or other brethren in London. If you have had their reasons, the case is only the stronger, because you have deliberately condemned the gathering in London and rejected its communion; for he who is outside in London is inside with you.

The letter was addressed to a Mr. Spurr of Sheffield and is dated Feb. 19, 1864. At the time of writing Mr. Darby was on an evangelistic and teaching tour in the south of France. Referring to the letter Mr. Henry Groves exclaims with much feeling:

> Beyond the pale of an anti-Christian communion, no such arrogant assumption has been made; and it has been reserved for Darbyism to develop a system, which, upon the smallest basis, should erect the most tremendous superstructure — a superstructure which, in the intolerance of its claim and the boldness of its assertion, reminds us of the days of papal power in the middle ages. How has the humble gathering of the two or three in the name of Jesus, from a "church in ruins," been forgotten and set aside by this new dogma! and instead of it a position taken which is destructive of Scriptural standing. Can it be believed possible, that those who started with the acknowledgment of the individual responsibility of all saints to Christ, should dwindle down into the position here taken, so as to assert, that being outside their small assemblies in London is "outside the church of God on earth?" That original principles could be so openly repudiated, and former testimony so entirely forgotten! But so it is. These progressive steps in ecclesiasticism it is important to notice, as showing how soon one who excommunicated Mr. Newton in 1845 on the ground of clericalism, should fall into an ecclesiasticism that embodies in itself worse evils than those condemned in another.

But a fairer judgment of the letter will be arrived at if it be borne in mind that Mr. Darby never for a moment held or taught that the little assemblies among which he moved *were* the church of God on earth. What he did hold most tenaciously was that every assembly of believers should always act as representing the whole church in that particular place. If such a company acted in righteous discipline therefore, the person put away, should, he believed, be debarred from communion everywhere until restored. This would hold equally true if the Christians putting the evil-doer away, in obedience to the Word, were known as Baptists, Wesleyans or by any other name; as well as in the case of an assembly of Brethren.

This principle seems fair and sound, though I recognize it is one that needs to be most carefully guarded, as further chapters will abundantly prove. It is a very easy thing to find an assembly or church moved by prejudice or stirred by false accusations ignorantly excommunicating the wrong party and then just as ignorantly insisting that its action be recognized by all. But I fear it will be said that I am trying to teach principles where I set out only to narrate facts, so I forbear.

In the year 1866 a breach occurred between Mr. Darby himself and some of his most intimate friends, over his matured views on the sufferings of Christ. He published sometime before this various papers purporting to examine into the depths of Scripture's teaching as to this most solemn of all themes whose mystery grows the more one meditates upon it. Ever since the Newton controversy the extent and nature of Christ's sufferings had been more or less to the fore in the teaching of the Brethren. Mr. Darby's book on the subject is still available and I refer any really earnest inquirer to the volume in question. It gave great offense to many at the time of publication. W. H. Dorman and Captain Percy Hall called upon Mr. Darby to disavow its teachings, and as he refused they withdrew from fellowship, followed by Mr. Thomas Newberry (afterward editor of *The Englishman's Bible*). These brethren wrote vigorously against the author of *The Sufferings of Christ*, charging him with having fallen into practically the same errors as Mr. Newton. Captain Hall definitely wrote:

> So like are they to Mr. Newton's doctrines, that even had they not been as bad in themselves as I judge them to be, I should be quite unable to maintain the place of what is called testimony against Mr. Newton while connected with those who hold what I think to be as bad.

Mr. Dorman and Mr. Newberry charged him with positive heterodoxy in teaching a third-class of sufferings that were not atoning, and insisted that he had taught that atonement was made by "wrath-bearing" rather than by "blood-shedding."

Yet as one goes over the whole subject afresh it seems plain that each of them completely misunderstood Mr. Darby. On the other hand it must be confessed that his language was most ambiguous, so that it is difficult for another to make clear exactly what he really did teach. But the three classes of suffering are practically these:

(a) Christ suffered pre-eminently when He poured out His soul unto death, to make atonement for our sins. In this He was absolutely alone. In the nature of the case no one could share it with Him. He was the antitypical ark going on ahead into the river of judgment to turn back its waters that His people might pass through unscathed.·

(b) He suffered as a martyr for righteousness' sake — and this of course was *not* atoning. It was what man laid upon Him and in which others have suffered with Him before and since.

(c) But He also suffered in His deep and holy sympathies, entering into the anguish and sorrows of His people — especially of the remnant of Israel in the last days, beneath the sense of God's displeasure because of their sin. He entered into this as feeling for them anticipatively. This last is the "third-class, non-atoning sufferings" which caused the charge of fundamental error to be hurled at Mr. Darby. I may have awkwardly expressed it, but it is what I gather from reading his book.

As to the charge that he taught atonement by wrath-bearing and apart from blood-shedding it seems plain to me that only one who overlooked the great mass of his writings on the subject could ever make such a claim.

One might almost as well declare the same of Isaiah because in his great atonement chapter (the 53rd) it is the truth of Christ's soul being "made an offering for sin" that is dwelt on and nothing mentioned about the actual shedding of blood. The same might be said of Psalm 22.

The controversy became most heated, and Mr. Darby offered to withdraw altogether from fellowship rather than be the means of dividing brethren again, but the other leaders refused to listen to this, and he was prevailed upon to remain. As a result Mr. Dorman left the "exclusives," declaring that they were now in the position that Mr. Newton's followers were in 1848. But as the years have passed and Mr. Darby's doctrinal views on this much-discussed and most sacred subject have become better understood there are few indeed of those who really investigate the matter who do not see in it precious truth to be accepted with reverence and adoring love rather than dangerous error as Mr. Dorman thought.

Had Mr. Darby been less vehement in his denunciation of others he might not have been subjected to such a severe grilling himself. But he bore it with remarkable meekness, his adversaries themselves being judges. As he grew older he mellowed considerably and it is evident that he began to look with dread upon the high exclusive pretensions of many of his followers. One thing he always insisted on; the title of every godly believer to a place at the table of the Lord. The Bethesda split made it difficult to act on this, as it led many to say, "If we cannot receive from assemblies very similar to our own, how can we receive from churches where much that we value is altogether repudiated?" But Mr. Darby never insisted on the refusal of all "open" brethren as such. His letters show that he always tried to distinguish between leaders and those led. That this seems hardly consistent with the "leaven" theory does not alter the fact. The following letter gives his views as to reception; it was written just a few years before his death:

> The question is, as to reception of saints to partake of the table of the Lord with us, whether any can be admitted who are not formally and regularly amongst us. It is not whether we exclude persons unsound in faith or ungodly in practice: not whether we, deliberately walking with those who are unsound and ungodly, are not in the same guilt—not clear in the matter. The first is unquestionable: the last, brethren have insisted on, and I among them, at very painful cost to ourselves. This is, to me, all clear and plain from Scripture. There may be subtle pleas to get evil allowed, but we have always been firm, and God I believe has fully owned it. The question is not these: but suppose a person known to be godly and sound in faith, who has not left some ecclesiastical system — nay, thinks Scripture favors an ordained ministry, but is glad when the occasion occurs — suppose we alone are in the place, or he is not in connection with any other body in the place, staying with a brother, or the like; is he to be excluded because he is of some system as to which his conscience is not enlightened — nay, which he may think more right? He is a godly member of the body, known as such. Is he to be shut out? If so, the degree of light is title to communion, and *the unity of the body is denied by the assembly which refused him.* The principle of meeting as

members of Christ walking in godliness is given up, *agreement*
with us is made the rule, and *The Assembly becomes a sect with
its members like any other*. They meet on their principles, Baptist or other—you on yours, and if they do not belong to you
formally as such, you do not let them in. The principle of
brethren's meetings is gone, and *another sect is made,* say with
more light, and that is all. It may give more trouble, require
more care to treat every case on its merits, on the principle of
the unity of all of Christ's members, than say "You do not belong
to us; you cannot come." But the whole principle of meeting
is gone. *The path is not of God.*

I have heard, and I partly believe it, for I have heard some
rash and violent people say it elsewhere, that the various sectarian
celebrations of the supper are tables of devils. But this proves
only the unbrokenness and ignorance of him who says it. The
heathen altars are called tables of devils because, and expressly
because, what they offered they offered (according to Deut.
32:17) to devils, and not to God; and to call Christian assemblies by profession, ignorant it may be of ecclesiastical truth,
and hence meeting wrongly, tables of devils is monstrous nonsense, and shows the bad state of him who so talks. No sober
man, no honest man, can deny that Scripture means something
totally different.

I have heard — I do not know whether it be true — that it
has been said that the brethren in England act on this ground.
If this has been said, it is *simply and totally false.* There have
been new gatherings formed during my absence in America
which I have never visited, but the older ones, long walking
as brethren, I have known from the beginning have *always* received known Christians, and everywhere I have no doubt the
newer ones too, and so in every country. I have known individuals take up the thought, one at any rate at Toronto, but
the assembly always received true Christians; three broke bread
in this way the last Lord's day I was in London. There cannot
be too much care as to holiness and truth: the spirit is the Holy
Spirit, and the Spirit of truth. But ignorance of ecclesiastical
truth is not a ground of excommunication, where the conscience
and the walk is undefiled. If a person came and made it a condition to be allowed to go to both, he would not come in simplicity in the unity of the body; I know it to be evil, and cannot
allow it, and he has no right to impose any conditions on the
church of God. It must exercise discipline as cases arise accord-

ing to the Word. Nor indeed do I think a person regularly going from one to another systematically can be honest in going to either; he is setting up to be superior to both, and condescending to each. That is not, *in that act,* a pure heart.

May the Lord guide you. Remember, you are acting as representing the whole church of God, and if you depart from the right as to the principle of meeting, separating yourselves from it is to be *a local sect on your own principles.* In all that concerns faithfulness, God is my witness, I seek no looseness, but Satan is busy to lead us to one side or the other, to destroy the largeness of the unity of the body, or to make it mere looseness in practice and doctrine; we must not fall into one in avoiding the other. *Reception of all true saints is what gives force to the exclusion of those walking loosely.* If I exclude all who walk godily as well, who do not follow with us, it loses its force, for those who are godly are shut out too—there is *membership of brethren.* Membership of an assembly is unknown to Scripture. It is members of Christ's body. If people must be all of you, it is practically membership of your body. The Lord keep us from it. That is simply dissenting ground." (Italics largely mine.)

It is interesting to know that while in Chicago on one occasion Mr. Darby was invited by D. L. Moody to give a series of Bible readings in Farwell Hall. These were attended by many lovers of the Word of God, but unfortunately suddenly came to an abrupt end as the two clashed over the question of the freedom of the will. Mr. Darby held to what Mr. Moody considered extreme Calvinism on this point, affirming that so perverted was man's will he could not "will" even to be saved and he based his contention largely on the texts "Which were born not . . . of the will of the flesh . . . but of God"; and, "It is not of him that willeth . . . but of God that sheweth mercy." Mr. Moody insisted that man as a responsible person was appealed to by God to turn to Him and would be condemned if he did not. "Ye *will* not come to me that ye might have life," said Jesus to those who refused His message. "Whosoever will" is the great gospel invitation. The controversy became so heated one day that Mr. Darby suddenly closed his Bible and refused to go on, thus losing one of the great opportunities of his life, as it will seem to many.

In after days he and F. W. Grant clashed, though not openly, over the same subject.

Separating from Mr. Moody, Darby did not hesitate to condemn Mr. Moody's work in his characteristic way. In his letters he warned his followers against it as likely to bring a great increase of worldliness into the church. It is a striking instance of how prejudice can blind and mislead an otherwise great man. Were he living today how surprised he might be to see the work begun by the great warm-hearted evangelist a veritable bulwark against both worldliness and apostasy. Mr. Moody ever confessed his indebtedness to the writings of the Brethren for much help in the understanding of the Word, but it was C. H. Mackintosh and Charles Stanley who had the greatest influence. The writings of the former he always highly commended.

Another American leader whom Mr. Darby met was Dr. Daniel Steele, the great Methodist divine, and advocate of Wesleyan perfectionism. He was at first greatly delighted with Mr. Darby's downright earnestness of purpose and vast knowledge of the Word and attended many of his readings in Boston. But he could not accept the doctrines of grace and considered Mr. Darby's teaching on the two natures and the believer's eternal security utterly false.

One day when Mr. Darby was expounding I John 1:7 showing that the subject dwelt on there is *"where* you walk, not *how,"* Dr. Steele interrupted with the question, "But, Brother Darby, suppose a real Christian turned his back on the light, what then?" "Then," replied Mr. Darby, "the light would shine upon his back!" Later Dr. Steele wrote a book against the brethren, called *Antinomianism Revived, or Plymouth Brethrenism Exposed.* This was ably answered by F. W. Grant in *Christian Holiness: Its Roots and Fruits,* which is now out of print.

CHAPTER SEVEN

"PLAYING CHURCH"

THE THIRTY YEARS following the Bethesda break were, as we have seen, the flood-tide for the Exclusive section of the Brethren. The ebb was bound to come but few expected it to come so soon. Yet keen observers inside the fellowship had, for long, predicted disaster as they saw the ever-increasing evidences of weakness, — the growing ecclesiastical pretension, spiritual pride, and scarcely-concealed contempt on the part of many for less-instructed believers; all of which had resulted slowly but none the less surely in a gradual narrowing-down of the fellowship and restricting of communion. Mr. Darby's early thought that he only desired to see "what would serve as an available mount of communion where all godly believers could meet," had, despite his frequent protests, been superseded by a system of teaching that the fellowship of saints was largely a fellowship of meetings governed by the same principles and recognizing one another's disciplinary acts.

Mr. R. T. Grant told me in 1898 that G. V. Wigram, ere he died in 1879, bitterly lamented the fact that Brethren had been "blowing ecclesiastical bubbles" and "playing church," and that he felt God could not go on with them in such folly. He passed away just as his prophetic words were in course of fulfilment.

It is noteworthy that Dr. Cronin, the first of the Brethren so-called, was the one who unwittingly brought about the crash. In the year 1876 the exclusive assembly at Ryde in the Isle of Wight, fell into a most grievous state as a result of bickering and strife over the question of the rightfulness of marrying a deceased wife's sister. According to English law, such a marriage was within the prohibited decrees, and condemned alike, at that time, by church and state. (The ban has since been removed.) In France such a marriage was recognized as honorable and in every way legal. One in the

Ryde assembly, whose wife had died, crossed the Channel and married his sister-in-law. Upon his return to England a storm of protest was raised. It is needless to dwell upon the details, but as is ever the case when the unruly members gets its unhallowed work in, the assembly was soon in a wretched state. So bad was its internal condition that Mr. Darby refused to visit it and emphatically described it as "rotten."

In Ryde there was an English Church clergyman, Finch by name, a friend of Dr. Cronin's, who was deeply interested in and exercised by the teachings of the Brethren. Attending a convention or conference in London he was received at the communion, and returned to Ryde fully determined to leave the establishment and take the Brethren's position. But he found that most of his congregation were prepared to take the same step so all withdrew together from the established church, and were ready to begin meeting simply as Brethren. Immediately a difficulty arose. It seems that it was one rule of the solemn game of "playing church," to use Mr. Wigram's expression, that there could be only one church in a city. There might be many meetings, as in London and elsewhere, but all must be recognized as one, and it was held necessary that Mr. Finch and his friends should all disband and apply individually for fellowship in the already-recognized Ryde meeting.

This Mr. Finch firmly refused, knowing well the condition of the local gathering. One wonders how any true under-shepherd, with a real heart for Christ's sheep and lambs could have done otherwise than to refuse to be a party to the bringing of a company of earnest believers, anxious to walk in New Testament truth, into a meeting almost torn in pieces by unseemly gossip and un-Christlike wrangling. Accordingly they broke bread as a separated company as all brethren had done at the first. In this they had the counsel and advice of Dr. Cronin who doubtless recalled early days as he saw the way these saints were being led on. He visited Ryde and tried to help the local assembly but felt it was impossible, and so he notified them that he was perfectly free to break bread with the new company, which he did; an action that was looked upon as a fearful sin in the eyes of those who put the new game above the souls of saints.

Upon the aged doctor's return to his home assembly at Kennington, he learned that his act had been construed by many as a definite overt attack on "the ground of the one body." Kennington, it was said, was one body with the "rotten" assembly at Ryde. It could not be one body with the new gathering, however godly and fragrant with Christian love and devotion. But many saw otherwise and for about six months it was impossible to get concerted action at Kennington. Finally the patriarchal offender was excommunicated and for months set back with the tears streaming down his face as his brethren remembered the Lord, and he, the first of them all was in the place of the immoral man or the blasphemer. Finally he promised that, although unable to confess his act as sin, he would not offend in the same way again out of deference to the consciences of his brethren but still he was kept under the ban. Is it any wonder that some critic said of the Brethren that they are "people who are very particular about breaking bread, but very careless about breaking hearts"?

But lest my account seem to be prejudiced and one-sided I think it best to permit one of Dr. Cronin's opponents to tell the story as it appeared to him, so I quote here from a pamphlet, published anonymously, and widely-circulated after the division had actually been consummated. It may seem to be anticipating to use a part of this document here, but I want to make clear the results of Dr. Cronin's act in participating in the sacred observance of the Lord's Supper with what was considered an independent meeting, by brethren who had all been looked upon as independent by other godly believers a few years back:

Is not a True Judgment of the Independency at Ryde, and the Conduct of Kennington Essential to Discovering a Right Path as to Ramsgate?

There would have been no division amongst us, on this matter surely, if we had been adequately sensible of the real character of the *attack* made three years ago on the testimony of God as to the "one Body—one Spirit," and if there had been faithfulness to Christ in dealing with the offender. How many of us were not clear about it. Strange to say, the attack was not merely *schismatic* (in this case, fellowship with a meeting not recognized), *it was also the usurpation by a single brother* (in a place far removed from the sphere of his *local* responsibilities) *of the Lord's authority (only rightly exercised) in and by the Assembly* (Matt. 18:18-20; 1 Cor. 5:4, etc.).

The attempt was virtually *to excommunicate a whole Assembly* gathered on divine ground, with which brethren were avowedly in fellowship, and have remained in fellowship to this hour; and, in the same town, to form another Assembly in opposition, without the fellowship of brethren.

IF *the Assembly sought to be dealt with had deserved excommunication, it would not have affected the principle involved in the attack.*

This being so, we need not repeat here the charges brought against the Ryde Assembly and the answers to them.

The *instrument* used of the enemy was well calculated to darken our vision—a venerable and greatly esteemed brother, one of the earliest identified with this testimony of God!

The *motive,* too, was the deliverance of saints by an exercise of power alleged to have been used for God in righteousness. For a time even some long known as spiritual, intelligent, and godly were deceived *(Prov. 9:15).* Their love and veneration for this brother surely it was which blinded them.

His previous career, and recognized position, gave additional force and importance to his course, and it really acquired a deeper character of evil, causing wider disaster in consequence *(Lev. 4:22; Acts 20:17 and 30).* After more than five months' delay at Kennington, he was excommunicated; but have we even yet fully seen what his assumption really involved?

Our endeavor to clear ourselves of his act and course cost us dearly.

What contentions there were, *disintegrating us to the very core!* . . .

Was this attack "a mistake," a "blunder" merely, as suggested by some? It was no *single* mistaken act of Dr. C. It was a deliberate *course* of unscriptural independency on his own individual responsibility on the lines mentioned, viz., disowning the Ryde assembly and setting up an independent Table. It extended over a period from May, 1877 (when, on his own individual responsibility, he judged and disowned the Ryde Assembly by not breaking bread, and going into their room at the close of the meeting, stating that he could not own the Table to be the Lord's, and that "Ichabod" was written on it), to February and March, 1879 (when he consummated fellowship with the new meeting he had helped to start). All this was in violation of the remonstrances and consciences of the saints of God, and of the judgments expressed by those most esteemed amongst us for spiritual discernment. It is *not* the fact, therefore, that Dr. C. thought he had, or expected to have, the approval of his brethren. He admitted this himself. He knew he was acting in direct opposition to the principles of God for the rule of the church of God, owned by brethren, and ultimately said that, according to the principles, he ought to be declared out of fellowship. On his return from Ryde, after his first breaking bread with the new meeting on the 9th and 16th February, 1879, brethren in London remonstrated with him; but he told the brethren at Kennington, on the 10th March, that he knew he had acted contrary to brethren's rules, but he did not own the cordon of brethren! At a meeting of brothers at Kennington on the 13th March, 1879, it was unanimously decided that they had no fellowship with Dr. C.'s act in setting up a Table at Ryde. Dr. C. had, in the meantime, again gone down to Ryde, so on the 14th March a leading and elder brother at K. wrote him and told him of the judgment of the brothers at K., and entreated him not to break bread again at Ryde, but he did so, in spite of this letter and of the judgment of his brethren. Again, when he called on Mr. F., at Ryde, on 8th February, preparatory to breaking bread with his meeting next day, he said, "I've come, *without any letter,* to be with you tomorrow." Further, in his written statement of his proceedings at Ryde, prepared for a few brethren on his return, he says, "I felt free to cast my lot in with them, *disorderly as it must have seemed, and disowned as it may be.*" But he went to Ryde on 8th February for the express purpose of breaking bread with Mr. F.'s meeting, having beforehand written him that he should, if in Ryde, ask to break bread with his meeting, and he inquired the direction of the Johnstreet Room, where he thought Mr. F. was breaking bread. He had also previously written to Mr. F. to encourage him in starting the new meeting, whilst at the same time the Assemblies in the Isle of Wight and elsewhere still owned the Ryde Assembly, and they told Mr. F. that they had no confidence in his independent action. Individual brethren also wrote and warned him (Mr. F.) in the strongest way as to the result of independency. In Dr. C.'s letter to Mr. F. of 17th December, 1878, he says, "I have made a note of the direction of the Upper Room." There were other painful features attending this matter, to dwell upon which would make this paper too long. No amount of gracious waiting and entreaty subsequently to confess the wrongness of his (Dr. C.'s) course — not the heart-rending state of things consequent upon it, not even the condemnation of his act by Kennington brothers on 13th March had any real weight with him.

It was therefore a deliberate intentional act, expressive for him of a principle, held at all cost, for which he claimed divine guidance and sanction.

A year ago he scorned the suggestion that he should confess his act as wrong with a view to restoration, and (to adopt his own recent phrase) he does not consider himself as "excommunicate of God." That is what he thinks of the solemn judgments of Assemblies everywhere excluding him. Those most friendly (if there is any difference amongst us towards him) say in extenuation that "he never saw the truth of the 'one Body.'" Well, if so, I Cor. 14:38 is surely the Word for us in such a case. Let us be clear at all cost.

But why dwell upon this *now*?

For two reasons:—

1. Because it is needful still to be clear as to the origin of our deplorable division, on account of the activities known to be going on to undermine the action of 1879.

2. Because much observation and long, anxious consideration has produced the deep conviction that, in proportion as we are now clear as to the Ryde attack *in conscience before God* (not an assent merely to the judgment of others), shall we be *helped* to a right judgment as to the *Ramsgate* sorrow. There is only one test. How does the Lord—the Head of the Body—the Church—view all this?

Do we consider the point involved *vital,* necessitating a faithful stand?

Without controversy, the cause of the present divisions lies here. But this is not said to ignore concurrent causes on which others have dwelt, though they have been sometimes referred to, as if this matter were not enough to demand a decisive judgment.

Have we the slightest doubt that what has been and is going on *is a deadly assault of Satan on the precious truth of God— "One Body—One Spirit"?* These words are often uttered as a formula, but alas how feebly held! That which is most precious to Christ in this world will be the object of the special malice of Satan. "It [a work of Satan] will be ever founded on practically setting aside the power of that truth which has been in any given case, the gathering principle, and the testimony of

God to the world." (J. N. D. copied in Bible Treasury Jan. 7, 1882, p. 7.) Do we think we escaped by our course in 1879? No:—Satan is our persistent foe. There is a continuity in the assault from 1879 to 1881.

The Lord's prerogative in the Assembly, the "two or three gathered to His Name" is also again lightly called in question in another form. Hence confusion and every evil work, with a view to disintegrate and scatter that which we trusted the Lord had gathered. Surely what we are going through is unmistakably an attack of Satan.

Doubtless such pretentious words carried great weight with many, but read thoughtfully after the lapse of fifty years they seem almost grotesque, and would be actually so if they were not so bad, in their amazing declarations and reckless charges of wickedness and defiance of Scriptural principles.

While the matter was still up for discussion at Kennington, other assemblies were greatly roused and were trying to hurry them to definite action.

At Ramsgate a majority party, led by a fiery zealot, Mr. Jull, proceeded to excommunicate the entire Kennington Meeting for its dilatoriness in dealing with the "wicked old doctor." Because the minority refused to go with them in this hasty action they disowned them in like manner and went out to start a new meeting "on divine ground." The majority met in Guildford Hall and the minority at Abbott's Hill, and these two names were destined to become well known in the months and years that followed. Owing to an oversight about procuring the key to the Hall, the Abbott's Hillers did not get in to break bread the first Lord's day after the division and so were later considered off church ground altogether. This is an important point to bear in mind in view of what happened in Montreal a few years later.

The whole matter was referred to London when a letter was presented at a London assembly from Guildford Hall. This was held to necessitate an investigation to decide whether Guildford Hall or Abbott's Hill was in schism. A course of meetings were held at Park Street, London, and the whole matter was thoroughly canvassed. It soon turned out that William Kelly was not likely to acquiesce in any extreme measures. He had long viewed with alarm the encroachments of ecclesiasticism, and he could see no wickedness in Dr. Cronin's action. Mr. Darby, now in his 81st year and a very sick man, pleaded vainly that no *ultra* severe measures be taken, and declared that if questions like these were made tests of fellowship he "would not go with such wickedness." Particularly did he plead that nothing be done that would result in a separation from Kelly, the man whom Spurgeon said had "a mind made for the universe, narrowed by Darbyism." But another question had for a long time caused friction between W. K. and many on the other side, namely, his open and pronounced opposition to infant-baptism, or as they preferred to call it, household baptism. The result could therefore readily be anticipated.

At the last meeting the London leaders upheld the seceders at Ramsgate, though not endorsing all their acts and declared Abbott's Hill out of fellowship, because they refused to own the others unless they came back individually confessing their sin. As J. B. Stoney and others left Mr. Darby's bedside to go to this meeting he pleaded that grace be shown and begged that Kelly be not turned out.

But things had now gone so far it seemed impossible to avert division, and when they returned they told him that Kelly had refused to act with them in regard to Ramsgate and was now outside! Darby was greatly agitated, but too feeble to resist. He muttered, "It must be the will of the Lord!" and made no further protest. Stoney, and the "high church" party had triumphed. All who refused to accept the Park street decision were henceforth looked upon as schismatics and refused the privilege of communion. Andrew Miller, J. A. Von Poseck, Dr. Neatby, and many other well-known leaders, together with a large number of assemblies in the British Isles and many in the West Indies, were "off the ground of the church of God."

The reader will, I judge, be interested, if he has followed me thus far, in William Kelly's own statement, showing why he refused to bow to the London decision. It is entitled,

WHY MANY SAINTS WERE OUTSIDE THE PARK STREET OF 1881

While Dr. Cronin's matter was before Kennington, Park Street sent out (in 1879) an independent and sectarian Declaration, on which Mr. Jull and others left the Ramsgate meeting.

The rest there waited for London's decision, declining as in duty bound to prejudice a case still pending. The Jull party went out, several brothers "one by one declaring that they withdrew from the assembly as then constituted." It was they who sought to reconstruct or revolutionize. The rest were content to act like as all others, save a very few small meetings full of the same fanaticism which actuated the seceders. This was ecclesiastical independency, a breach of unity subversive of the church.

Not content with groundless secession of itself demanding repentance and of course condemned by all the meetings that did not so act, the seceders after one day's interval set up a counter meeting outside recognized fellowship, and gave plain proof of "new-lumpism" by rejecting summarily and clerically some of their own following. This was what Scripture calls "heresy" or "sect" (I Cor. 11:19; Gal. 5:20). He who was thus active is (in Titus 3:10, 11) branded as "heretical" and "self-condemned."

Claiming that "they broke bread together on the alone divine ground of one body, one Spirit," they quickly ceased nevertheless. Too self-confident to see or judge the real evil of their proceedings, yet finding out their mistaken policy, they seized on flaws in their Brethren who remained, both to deny their standing and to reintegrate their own pretensions. Hence (in 1880) they repeated their party effort, with the bold assumption that "the Lord would own and protect" their second table. This the Lord did not; nor was it long before they themselves dropped it.

Then came their third and too successful renewal (in 1881) after private encouragement. It was Brethren now who sunk low enough to ask if they were never to break bread. Was this a right or godly question then? Had they truly condemned their party work throughout, all would have rejoiced; but justifying themselves as they did in the main, how in this state could it be allowed without compromising the Lord's honor and Word?

The Park Street meetings followed. It is idle to say that no other course was open. Who can gainsay that Scripture teaches us to localize mischief by dealing with evil on the spot of its outbreak? It was the enemy's snare to precipitate division, long sought by fiery zealots everywhere, of whom H. J. Jull was one. Park Street then intervened, where was a known predisposition, not to say determination, to at length endorse the seceding

party, still impenitent as to their gravest offenses, though ready
to own other failures—a blind for themselves and their sup-
porters. It is false that they there cleared away, as was pre-
tended, their open wrongs against the Lord's name in the assembly. "Haste and errors of judgment" were confessed, but
neither independency nor heresy, of which thousands of saints
knew them to be guilty; nor were they asked to confess either,
as far as was shewn. But chief men among Brethren, who of
late lent secret countenance, led Park Street into public sanction
of their third start; and other subordinate men were glad to
push it on: yet these knew that J. adhered to the Park Street
Declaration which led him into the ditch, though J. N. D. had
got it withdrawn. For *he* thought *it* independency, as he told
J. H. B. who at once reported this to J.

This was the evil deliberately committed by Park Street in
the Lord's name, and sought accordingly to be imposed upon
all. Its acceptance was not left as usual for the Lord to vin-
dicate if sound, or disannul if wrong. It was speedily required
on pain of forfeiture of fellowship, in the face of known, wide,
and deep disapproval. This meant nothing short of separation
forced through on a question of discipline. What could those
do who were sure that the entire procedure was unscriptural and
a party snatching a triumph for party? They could not agree
to what they judged unrighteous and untrue, cleaving the more
in their weakness to His name and Word, as all once used to
do together. They neither went nor sent to Park Street or its
allies, but were in sorrow, humiliation, and prayer, if per-
adventure the Lord might purge through sense of a false position, and of the previous evil that brought it about. We at
Blackheath acted as was done at Plymouth in 1845-6, when a
small minority left Ebrington Street, after it got wrong ecclesiastically as well as morally, before the heterodoxy of
B. W. N. when known gave it a far darker character; we did
not reject souls from Park Street, though not going there.
Crying to the Lord for His gracious interference, we had suspicion and insult for our forbearance. We wrote plainly when
challenged for receiving several of Lee, our neighbors, who
could not more than ourselves subscribe a decree we believed
to be sinful.

Some blame us, notwithstanding our common and solemn
convictions, for not refusing those despised little ones. We
think it would have been justly despicable, as well as error, if

we had not received saints suffering for a godly protest, in order to retain a fellowship no longer true to the Lord's name. By letting them break bread with us, we well knew that our adversaries rejoiced to have the occasion they desired. Surely our Lord has said, when the preliminaries are done in obedience, "Hear the church"; but is this His voice when they were not? Has He not also called him that has an ear "to hear what the Spirit saith unto the churches?" To idolize assembly judgments as necessarily right is condemned by His Word.

But we may come still closer. The more that episode of sin, shame, and sorrow is weighed, the clearer it will be that ecclesiastical independency had unconsciously and extensively infected those who talked loudly of "one body and one Spirit." This was evident in the discredited Park Street Declaration. This carried away, not only H. J. J. and his companions in their secession and even worse, but the numerous party that might blame but aided and abetted them, at last bent at all cost on having them back without confession of their evil acts which betrayed false principles. Had they honestly been ashamed of their heretical or party ways the third time more than the first or the second? They themselves strenuously denied their guilt in this kind; yet no intelligent believer acquainted with the facts, and without strong personal predilection, can doubt it. Therefore, till repentance for those public wrongs was known to give them the right hand of fellowship was both to become partakers of their sins, and to part from all unprepared to join in that universally imposed unrighteousness. Far from penitence on that score, they indignantly and uniformly repudiated every charge of independency, or even schism, to say nothing of heresy. Yet it is as certain as can be that they were thus guilty, and that those who knew it as surely as ourselves joined at Park Street to condone it in their reception.

Therein ensued the strange and grievous fact of Park Street, judging for itself, and leading each company in London to judge for itself, independently of others. Thus through influence were enticed many with a conscience defiled, as also the fear of being "cut off" alarmed no fewer into acquiescence. For the advocates of division, without check somehow from those that knew better, applied to an ecclesiastical question the extreme measure, which we in obedience to Scripture had hitherto confined to Antichrists and blasphemies. Who could anticipate a *great* and *good man*, that had written "I shall never be

brought into such wickedness," drawn by inferiors into that very
stream? We know how strongly he resisted it for years, alas!
beguiled at length into what he had ever hated when left to
himself with the Lord. Witness, only a little before, his letter
to Jull, which it was sought to hide; as they did shamefully
a postscript of his on a critical occasion previously.

It would have been evil if (not Park Street and other self-
isolating fragments, but) the assembly in London had acted
independently of a known widespread conviction elsewhere, that
its proposal was utterly wrong, and must if confirmed demoral-
ize, *or* repel, saints all over the world. How much worse when
the independency of Park Street gave the signal to every other
part of the same city, and then to the country meetings, as well
as everywhere, to follow that fatal course! In the new departure
truth was forgotten, and grace prevailed quite as little. Nor
(apart from the wrong change of venue to London, perhaps
above all to Park Street for a reason already given) was there
the least excuse for failing to act in the unity of the Spirit and
obedience of the Word. A proposal might have been submitted
to all the gathered saints, and action taken or refused, as
judged due to the Lord. It was the more to be heeded when
passion was letting in disorder. But dissolving for the time,
and for this matter only, into independent assemblies, each
judging for itself, was to adopt the human device of a voluntary
society, and to ignore the ground of God's church, abandoning
for the nonce our divine relationship and its duty. God thus
allowed an evil movement of party to fall into a flagrant contra-
diction alike of his principle and of our own cherished practice
in faith. Could it be for anything else but the worldly and
rather vulgar end of catching votes? A sad fall for saints who
for many a year walked together in faith, if but "two or three"
here and there, and rejoicing to suffer for the Name, whatever
the show or scorn of enemies! It caused heart-breaking to not
a few that were hustled out, and that for the Lord's sake rather
than their own: has it ever been matter of grave self-judgment
to many prominent in those days, when good men were too
often swayed by the more unworthy?

Nor can plea be more hollow than claiming heaven's sanction
of a measure so begun, carried on, and completed. A com-
mendatory letter to one meeting or another was no valid reason
for shifting the place Scripture indicates for a decision without
prejudice or favor, even if all had to wait in our weakness ever

so long. How shocking to take it up hotly where partiality was rife, notorious, and violent—where was the expressed desire for a division to get rid of all but "the spiritual" *i. e.* their own sort! Acts of the assembly done in obedience, without bias or connivance, all are bound to accept, even if individually one regretted over leniency or over severity, as may be sometimes. Just before indeed was a case in London, closely related to the Ramsgate rupture, by which the party of division hoped through unprecedented rigor toward one in error but greatly beloved, to drive out largely of their Brethren. But grace prevailed. Almost all bowed, though in grief. The ill-wishers were sorely disappointed, and grew more relentless and overbearing. So Park Street took up the Ramsgate question; with what character and result we too well know. Since then God has permitted many an object-lesson, last and worst of all in the heterodoxy as to Christ and eternal life,* before which even party is comparatively a small thing. Some there are who, if they had been entangled more or less by the divisionist party in the past, have by grace cleared themselves from that worst evil. But if they can neither deny nor justify the fact here stated (and I believe truly), are they not in an unsound ecclesiastical position? May faith and love work deliverance to the praise of the Lord's name.   W. K.

When the news of the division reached Canada and the United States it was generally accepted that Mr. Kelly was now in independency, and the assemblies on this continent went wholesale with Park Street. In Toronto about 50 persons whose consciences revolted against such pretentiousness, were declared out of fellowship. The letter setting forth the position of the majority follows:

TORONTO, CANADA,
OCTOBER 2ND, 1882.

To the Saints gathered to the Name of the Lord Jesus throughout Canada:

BELOVED BRETHREN, — At a meeting of the Assembly in Toronto, on the 13th September, 1882, to consider our position with respect to the decision of Park Street, London, England, on the "Ramsgate Question," after patiently waiting upon and remonstrating with a few Brethren who refused to accept the

---

* This refers to the development of what came to be known as "Ravenism" which will be discussed later.

judgment, we were forced in deep sorrow of heart to withdraw from them, in order to affirm and maintain the principles of the Church of God (Eph. 6; I Cor. 11:19; II Tim. 2:19).

Our acceptance of the judgment of the Park Street decision is *not based on a knowledge of the facts* and circumstances connected with it, but upon the ground that "there is one body and one Spirit." This decision we fully receive as having the sanction of the Lord, and must therefore be binding upon us, for "whatsoever ye shall bind on earth shall be bound in heaven, and whatsoever ye shall loose on earth shall be loosed in heaven" (Matt. 18:18). We adopt this course in order to preserve fellowship with our Brethren who are "endeavoring to keep the unity of the Spirit in the bond of peace"; otherwise we should deny the very foundation of the church of God, and the truth of the one body as a principle of gathering.

Among the many signatories to this amazing letter we find F. W. Grant, who was destined within a very short time to have a rude awakening in regard to the seriousness of the principle for which he here stood sponsor.

But there seemed to be a spell upon the minds of Brethren generally. Even the godly and enlightened C. H. Mackintosh (author of the "Notes," etc.) wrote: "All we have to do is thankfully to accept the judgment of our Brethren gathered at Park Street. If that judgment be wrong, God in his own time and way will make it manifest."

Henceforth there were two Exclusive parties, and, singularly enough, Mr. Kelly's associates became, many of them, as stiff and rigid in their views as any they had separated from, despite the fact that their revered leader W. K. ever advocated the reception of all godly saints, except of course from other sections of Brethren! The following extracts from his writings give his principles in no uncertain way:

"We receive every Christian walking as such, without reference to their connection with Nationalism or Dissent; we rejoice to have communion with them, whether privately or publicly. They may join us in worship and the supper of the Lord. They are as free as any of us to help in thanksgiving, prayer, or a word of edification, if so led of God; and this without stipulation either to leave their old associations or to meet only with us. Where is this done save only with 'Brethren?' With us on the contrary, if any godly Churchman or Dissenter thought fit to come when we remember the Lord together, he would be quite in order if he did any or all of these things spiritually; and this, not from any permission on our part, but as a matter of responsibility to God and His Word."

Extracts from a letter on "OPENNESS IN RECEIVING AND FREEDOM IN SERVICE":

BLACKHEATH, August 31, 1875.

My dear Brother . . . Individuals among Brethren may urge their private views on evangelists or others; but all such narrowness is censured by every wise man in our midst; and, what is more important, it is dead against that return to keeping Christ's Word and not denying His name which characterizes the work. The question has often arisen as to fellowship as well as service; and as often those who are entitled to speak have resisted the tendency to a restrictive school. If some have sought to require intelligence in those received my own answer has been that it is vain and unscriptural; that they themselves when received were the very reverse of intelligent; that if intelligence is to be anywhere, it should be in those who receive; and that those who require it in the received fail in the intelligence they demand from others; else they would not expect it where it could not be . . . Hence *Scripture knows nothing of keeping outside a godly-walking member of Christ.*

As little does it countenance the church's interference with the Lord's work, and especially in the gospel. To set the servant in the simplest dependence on the Lord, to foster his immediate responsibility to the Lord, without the intervention of the church is what every brother holds as a sacred duty and principle . . . This maintains the evangelist intact in his liberty and responsibility to his Master. Ever yours, W. K.

But, alas, Kelly like Darby was not strong enough to control the zealots in his party! Soon the same rigid principles were seen in many of the so-called Kelly meetings as in those they had left.

Chapter Eight

THE MONTREAL DIVISION

In 1882 J. N. Darby died "old and full of years." His life began with the 19th century and he lived through more than four-fifths of it. He was the great outstanding figure of "Brethrenism," though he never accepted the "Darbyism" of many who professed to follow him. Dr. James H. Brookes, in whose church Mr. Darby held two weeks' meeting while in St. Louis in the 70's, considered him one of the greatest Bible scholars of his generation. His published writings in English, including three volumes of letters, comprise 44 volumes. He wrote voluminously also in German and French and to a lesser extent in Italian. He translated the New Testament into Italian and the entire Bible into French, German and English, (except the later Old Testament Books, which not being completed in English at the time of his death were translated from his French and German Bibles by his helpers in the work). His style of writing is not easy to read, though he could, on occasions write the purest of English. In a letter to C. H. Mackintosh, commending his "Notes on the Pentateuch," he said, "You write to be understood. I only think on paper."

Mr. Darby was not, however, a good judge of human nature. He was easily imposed on by designing men and often used unconsciously to further schemes of which he did not at heart approve. "All my pets turn out badly," he said on one occasion.

In his later years he was largely under the influence of J. Butler Stoney, a man of undoubted piety and ability but whose subjective teaching was considered by many as being anything but healthful spiritually. We have seen how he was persuaded to acquiesce in the Park Street decision that resulted in the Kelly Division. Many believed that had he withstood that piece of ecclesiastical folly the divisions that followed might never have occurred.

In America F. W. Grant had become by 1880 the leading figure among the exclusive Brethren. His platform gifts were not of a high order but as a teacher he was unexcelled. Many consider him, to this day, the superior of Darby himself in accuracy and spiritual insight, but he always held himself as but a disciple greatly indebted to J. N. Darby. Up to the last, the two were fast friends, though for a number of years there had been slight doctrinal differences between them. But they were in no sense fundamental, although resulting in division after Darby passed away. They concerned the exact application of the 7th of Romans, the sealing of the Spirit, the impartation of life and other minor details. Undoubtedly on these subjects there was wide room for diverse views and there had been different schools of thought among the Brethren for years. But after J. N. Darby died there was an effort made by English leaders to force this particular teaching on all, which resulted in disaster.

Several years before the Montreal or Grant Division there was considerable friction in Canada over the question of "Sealing." When is a believer sealed with the Spirit? Mr. Darby and his adherents answered, "When he believes the gospel." Others said, "When he trusts in Christ." To the ordinary mind there might not seem to be any difference between the two answers. But to the theologian (and all Brethren seemed suddenly to become theologians) the difference is immense!

Let me illustrate by an actual occurrence—the earliest of which I can get any record:

F. W. Grant was editing a periodical called "Helps by the Way," about the year 1879 or 1880 and was living in Toronto. R. T. Grant, his brother, was there on a visit. On Lord's day it was mentioned in the assembly that a young man, who had been converted on what proved afterwards to be his death-bed had expressed a desire to partake of the Lord's Supper ere he passed away. This was made much of and it was decided that he must be examined as particularly as though he were to be actually received into the now rigid Toronto meeting, so far had these brethren drifted from their first principles.

Two brethren were deputized to call on him and report to the gathering. He was very weak but they catechized him most unmercifully. Finally he said wearily, "I can't answer all your

questions, but I know I am trusting Jesus, Is not that enough?"
"Not at all," one replied. His aged father (a Baptist) was sitting
by the bedside and indignantly asked, "Pray what more is required?" "He must be sealed by the Spirit ere he can be
permitted the communion, and he cannot be sealed till he sees
the finished work of Christ," they replied. And so he was refused the hallowed privilege of obedience to his Saviour's request, "This do in remembrance of me." For ere this wretched
meddling could be rectified by wiser and more gracious Brethren,
he was absent from the body and present with the Lord. R.
T. Grant was at the weekly celebration of the Lord's Supper
when they gave their report. His soul was filled with holy
indignation and he expressed his abhorrence of such supercilious
conduct in stern language. Returning to his room, he wrote a
paper for his brother's magazine on "When is the Believer Sealed?"
pointing out that nowhere is it said that sealing is dependent
on a certain understanding of the gospel scheme but that the
Spirit seals all who believe in Christ at once and until the
day of redemption. This drew down upon him the ire of
English Brethren who thought they saw in it a direct attack
on J. N. Darby's views. Lord Adelbert P. Cecil, a brilliant but
eccentric young nobleman who had become an earnest and able
evangelist (but who was in no true sense a teacher), wrote
the editor, who on his part returned it saying that if purged from
its abusive expressions he would publish it but not otherwise. Cecil
rewrote it and it was published, and with it a note from F. W.
Grant inviting comment and explaining that he was not himself clear
on the subject. All this was related to me by R. T. Grant himself.

From Mr. Darby's sickroom in England there came forth a pamphlet entitled "The Sealing of the Spirit" to which F. W. Grant
gave much thought and attention, but the aged leader had died ere the
editor of "Helps" could prepare his own statement. Never dreaming
of its being construed as a personal attack on a dead man, F. W.
Grant finally published his matured convictions. These being challenged by many he prepared a larger booklet, entitled, "Life in
Christ and Sealing with the Spirit," which became the immediate
cause of division.

Let me digress long enough to say that even this difference did not alienate the two great teachers. In Feb. 1881 Mr. Darby wrote F. W. Grant the following which proves the contrary:

Thank you for your very kind letter. We both believe that the blessed Lord is at all times sufficient for His church, both in love and faithfulness and power. Nor does the state of the saints expose them by the departure of any one to what it was at the first. The church is not a concentrated whole as it was then. Still I believe my going would make a change; not that I have an idea that anything depends on me. God forbid it should. How could it? Depend on what?

A man can receive nothing except it be given him from above. But the last link with the first start of this truth would be gone. If it does come may it only link them more together. But I am much better. I was as low as I could well be, and the bad fall I had at Dundee shook me, I do not doubt, more than I thought. My heart and lungs were a feeble spring to my body, but this, like all the rest, is in the Lord's hand. Last night I did not even sit up any part of the night. At first I had to sit up all night, though propped up and sleeping. I take a little food, too, at night. I had long felt my place was to be quiet here, so the Lord in His wisdom kept me here. Thank God my mind is as clear as ever and I enjoy the Word and the Lord's goodness, I suppose more than ever. At first I could not long find to work. Now I do as much as usual, only I don't hold meetings save one reading for laborers at the house. I went last Lord's day morning. My lungs are the most sensibly weak. I have not been ill, but knocked up and overworked. There is a great desire for the Word, I may say, everywhere, and blessing, too, in the way of conversions in a good many places. The shake has done the Brethren a great deal of good, though we are far from what we ought to be, but there is more healthfulness of tone and regards towards God. A great effort in South London to make a party, but none active in it. I think that anybody who knows them respects them, and they labor on under God's hand to bring about His judgment concerning themselves. And the rest go on quietly and leave it all to Him, and so I trust they will. I am sure He is faithful and true. What a comfort it is to think he watches over us and condescend to take notice of all our need and to order our ways.

I work morning and afternoon as far as I can, and in the evening let the strain go and indulge in the Word and feed on His own love. One of my present studies is *Adonai.* Please tell Robert (I sent a message) that I will write when I can, though I answer some daily, I have still an arrear of close on thirty letters, which are a pull on me. The Lord be with you and guide you in your work. Love to the brethren.

Affect, yours in the Lord,

J. N. DARBY

The original of this is in possession of the Grant family.

With F. W. Grant it was purely a question of truth. In his booklet he taught that divine and therefore eternal life was the possession of believers in all dispensations, "Life in the Son," who was ever the fountain of life. But that in the present age of grace the knowledge of eternal life is given through the Word and that all who receive Christ possess it and are immediately sealed by the Spirit. The man in the 7th of Romans had both life and the Spirit but did not have experimental knowledge of either till he saw his place in Christ risen, as set forth in Romans 8.

All this was attacked by Cecil and others as heterodoxy of a virulent character. It was said that F. W. G. taught that Old Testament saints were in the Godhead a monstrous misconception. Many, however, who were favorably disposed toward Mr. Grant thought it would have been wiser if he had been less pronounced, and particularly advised him not to publish his pamphlet. He sent it in manuscript to a number of teaching brethren, asking for a candid consideration of his positions on the controverted points. Many agreed with him. Others were neutral. While as mentioned above the strict Darbyites (I do not mean to use the term offensively) thought it very dangerous propaganda and not only counselled him not to make it public but predicted division if he did. He replied, "If the truth will divide us, the sooner we are broken to pieces the better." This was construed to mean that he was determined to head a schism.

But I think it best to let a brother tell the rest of the pitiful story, who passed through it himself. I quote from a statement by Wm. Banford of La Chute, Quebec:

I have been seeking to know, for my own satisfaction at least, when the first abberations as to eternal life began. It was admitted to us in England by a leading brother that J. N. D. held during part of his ministry, the same views in the main as F. W. G. on eternal life and sealing. As near as I can find the modification of these views came in at the end of the 60's, and in connection with Rom. 7, 8:1-9. This was the question of Deliverance, of course: but the new views gradually necessitated the bringing in also of a difference between the life received at new birth and eternal life received at some later time, the former characterizing the one in Rom. 7 — the latter that of one in the full Christian place as in Rom. 8. It has never been made clear by those who held these strange views, whether one must receive the Holy Spirit and eternal life to be delivered, or be delivered to receive either or both. F. W. G. took the whole question up in the full teaching of Scripture and put it before his Brethren. None among those who opposed him have ever attempted this. They have never put forth any consistent teaching of Scripture for the new views. There are only detached expressions on certain passages relating to eternal Life and sealing which run directly contrary to the teaching of many other portions, and there is no attempt to bring out a consistent line of truth or to explain the differences.

For us since Christianity was established our being born again is under the shelter of the blood of Christ, and being so is sealed by the Holy Spirit, as in the type the oil was put upon the blood. For us the types of the passover, Red Sea and Jordan coalesce. Under the shelter of the blood of the Lamb of God we are (not only safe but) saved from the judgment of God: — pilgrims in the wilderness, and in Christ in the heavenlies. This is our standing in Christ by sovereign grace. The knowledge and experience of all this glorious portion is all learned gradually from the Word of God, and we need to have the Holy Spirit indwelling in us to lead us into all this. But all is ours from the first moment of faith, and it is now fully admitted (which was denied 28 years ago) that faith cannot be separated from new birth—a born-again believer and a believer has eternal life and the Holy Spirit.

The effect of the new teaching, however, was to turn souls in upon themselves to learn whether they had received the Holy Spirit yet or no. J. N. D. referred frequently to these conditions as coming out everywhere in the 70's, although he attributed them to an entirely wrong source. "No matter where we begin our readings," he would say, "it is not long before we are in the seventh of Romans." It also developed the thought of a class among believers (I don't forget the new teaching that a merely born-again person cannot be called a believer, though this is being largely modified)—who had eternal life in contrast with another which had only new birth.

Along with this error as to "life" and "sealing" came in another and these two were very rife in the 70's. I refer to the teaching as to the church which became so exaggerated that it largely threw into the shade the true ministry of Christ. The central error of this was (more or less modified by one or another) that it had such wonderful place, such wonderful authority and power—that whatsoever it bound or loosed on earth was bound and loosed in heaven whether right or wrong. Many were the discussions arising over these things among young and old during many years preceding the fatal days of '80 to '85. The moral sense revolted against the view, but it carried many of us along who wanted, doubtless, to be considered in the advanced class. I was myself quite along with these doctrinal and ecclesiastical views.

When Lord A. P. C. came to Canada from England several months before the culmination of his course, he visited many of the gatherings in the large centers of Canada and the eastern states and continuously carried on a deliberate campaign of attack on F. W. G. Thus far F. W. G. had only put out an edition of about 80 copies of his small tract, entitled, "Life and the Spirit." He sent these to leading brothers in Britain and America, drawing attention briefly to errors coming in and developing among us. A. P. C.'s attack came on because of this. F. W. G. had not yet put out his large tract "Life in Christ and Sealing with the Spirit." It is true (though I have not seen it used as a reason) that he had also earlier written openly against the "Unity of Church in a City" such as existed in London, because of its unscripturalness and the dangerous influence thus given, and sort of metropolitanism. This roused leaders over there into great bitterness against him. But the public attack began because of the small tract, which being for the leading brothers alone, showed how above-board this servant of God was. This is not the way of a heretic. If there were heresy (that is in the sense of division making) A. P. C.'s whole course during those many months indicate that he was a heretic. But we make no charge. He has to do with God about that. And no charge was made against him for this, though it might well have been. The whole line of attack came from him. He constantly quoted and read from letters from English Brethren, as being behind him. He also publicly threatened F. W. G. with penalties at a general meeting, if he put out his larger pamphlet which went more into details, and which was already prepared, entitled "Life in Christ and Sealing with the Spirit." But why should not a servant of the Lord put forth the word which he firmly holds to as the truth? We are all too prone to keep back the truth lest others should be offended, but would he be a faithful servant of God who would do so? Who is it who says: "He that hath my Word let him speak my Word faithfully" (Jer. 23:8); and again, "Let the prophets speak two or three and let the others judge" (I Cor. 14:29). Would he be fitted to be a servant of God in such a world as this who would quail before any threat of church penalties and withhold the truth given of God? It is said: "he might have waited till the storm had passed over!" Then he would have waited forever, I believe, for truth must always force its way here. Faith looks up to God its source, and not to man or even "the church." Where would early Christianity have been if God's servants had waited for the south wind to blow softly? Or the Reformation? Or any movement of the Spirit of God at any time in old days or new? The time to give out truth is when God gives it, . . . and when the time comes when "the church" says to God's servant: "You shall not put out what you have under penalties" that order of things has about reached its limit in the holy government of God. J. N. D.'s voice comes in here as the voice of a man of God indeed; that was already well forgotten 28 years ago. "Do not mind the whole church (they are but chaff) when they interfere with our responsibility to the Lord. Exercise the gift in subjection to God's Word, and those who will judge let them judge" (Coll. writings, Vol. 31, page 459). F. W. G. put out his pamphlet, the publishers assumed the responsibility of it in spite of threats from England, and how many since have thanked God for the edification they found in it!

In the meantime, for local reasons doubtless, Montreal was found by A. P. C. to be a congenial place to bring his work to a head, with the assistance of Mr. Mace who was having gospel meetings in Albert Hall, and Mr. Baynes, the aged gospeler beloved by the rank and file of the gathering. Both were popular on the gospel's account. There he carried on his agitation until the news reached F. W. G. from different sources that there was grave danger of division. This brought him rightly to Montreal, for if division had taken place, those who blame him for going would probably have been the first to blame him for not going. All such questions must be left with God and His servant. He went avowedly to prevent any such thing as division, and pressed repeatedly that there was no reason for it in the differences between A. P. C. and himself, or other Brethren who were claimed to be behind A. P. C.

A strong party was formed at Montreal and there was great secrecy. The paper of the 38 rejecting the ministry of F. W. G. was signed and read at a meeting called. Few of the signers knew anything about what they signed, and young persons and simple people signed this paper, calling upon the Lord's people and His servants everywhere to reject his ministry, who scarce could have any spiritual exercises or knowledge of these things.

Brethren hoped the agitation would end with this, but not so. Emboldened by evident success, and a majority of the meeting assured, they pressed on and soon this party assumed to be the assembly. Under the new ecclesiastical practices this was easily accomplished. Protests of godly men were quietly ignored, letters from Brethren and assemblies elsewhere were not allowed to be read and it was announced that no outside interference would be allowed. Another meeting was called, the last of many, and in spite of a large number of protests, representing 40 persons, the action was taken, and F. W. G. was an excommunicated man.

The paper prepared beforehand was read by Mr. B. and several brothers protested moderately and sorrowfully, and it was evident there was no power to carry it through. It was read a second time, and again several brothers protested, many more than spoke in favor of it, and it was plain the conscience of the assembly was against it. It could not go through. How was it going to be done then? Mr. B. read his prepared paper a third time, and called on those in favor of it to stand up. Very few were present that night—the poor sheep were frightened and scattered, but it was declared carried, and Mr. Hart read Matt. 18:18. They didn't call for the "Nays." That would be too low ground for the church to take! A brother asked if this action was final. Mr. B. replied that it was. A brother from Hamilton who dropped into the room that night not knowing what was on said: "I cannot accept this as an assembly judgment." Mr. B. replied—"I cannot help that."

Let it be remembered that this scene was the finale of an indescribable period of many months duration, that many of the protesting brothers were already "silenced" by authority of this party, that outside Brethren were publicly notified they would be allowed no voice, that it was promised publicly that other gatherings would be attended to when they were through with Montreal, that they refused to allow letters from other gatherings to be read, that all was being done deliberately and in fellowship with others elsewhere already worked up by A. P. C. and Mr. Mace, that A. P. C. claimed he represented English Brethren, that by his canvas he knew he could depend on many in the leading centers in the states, that Mr. Mace was already away working in Ottawa and Toronto, that the gathering for months knew only constant attack, and denouncement of F. W. G. and all who did not fall in with A. P. C.; that it was intimated they were going to deal with others one by one or in lots in the meeting; and we can realize the hopelessness of continuing a protest which had already gone on so long. It was as useless as protesting to a hurricane. I was a silent witness at most of the meetings after F. W. G. came. He of course was away at Ottawa and elsewhere for some time before the last act.

This culmination of the whole movement, this final rejection of a servant of Christ along with the formal deliberate rejection of him as a minister of the Word of God, and so the truth for which he stood, the assumption of a party to be the Assembly, the assumption of Eldership, the violence, the attaching the Holy Name of the Lord to this solemn iniquity, give for all who want the will of God, the character now fastened upon this meeting. Up to this final act our protesting Brethren rightly bore all, including the act of the 38 rejecting and refusing the precious ministry of F. W. G. an act the consequences of which remain still most disastrously for all who endorse it. But now an overt act is committed putting away unrighteously in spite of all protests, and these Brethren who have gone on thus far can go on no longer. They must either endorse this action of a party assuming to be the assembly and join in this act, or separate from it to keep a good conscience and communion with God. They were hitherto willing—pleaded—for continuance with N. H. H., with F. W. G. but they would listen to nothing.

It is necessary to explain some things in this statement. Lord Cecil went to Plainfield, New Jersey, where F. W. Grant then lived (having moved from Toronto shortly before) and where there was a large assembly. He tried to prove that the "new teaching" was heretical and demanded that the booklet be withdrawn and not published. But others felt he had no right so to act and reproved him for his violent language and insisted that the book be published that all might consider the teaching. Cecil then went to Montreal where he forced a division. Henceforth, there were in America two kinds of exclusives: one known as the Natural History Hall party (from the name of the meeting-place in Montreal) affiliated with the Park Street party in England, and the other known as the Grant party. Approximately three-fourths of the exclusives in Canada and the states refused the Natural History Hall judgment and sided with Mr. Grant, not necessarily endorsing all he taught but as protesting against such high-handed methods as those employed by Cecil and his associates.

These insisted that the Lord's authority was behind their action and it must be bowed to. If any refused to own the judgment as of God they were excommunicated.

Thus the game of "playing church" went ruthlessly on to the scandal of the godly and the delight of the carnal.

In the course of years the Brethren of the so-called Grant party have attempted again and again to heal the breech, but thus far it seems hopeless, though many individuals and assemblies have thrown down the barriers erected in 1884.

Lord Cecil was drowned shortly after the division was consummated, in the Bay of Quinte, off Lake Ontario. He was an earnest man, of rare devotion, but not fitted by natural gifts nor by grace for the place he assumed. Upon getting news of his death F. W. Grant wired to R. T. G. (who was in California): "Dear Cecil is drowned and with him goes all hope of healing the division."

Sixty years have gone by and it still exists. In the meantime the London party has broken into six or more fragments while the Grant party has been added to each time by distressed and exercised individuals and whole assemblies returning to it, or as some would say amalgamating with it.

F. W. Grant put forth much written ministry, notably "Facts and Theories as to the Future State" which Charles H. Spurgeon said gave "the last word on the right side of every question discussed"; the "Numerical Structure of Scripture" and the "Numerical Bible" an exceptionally helpful commentary taking cognizance of the spiritual meaning of Scripture numerals, which however, he did not live to complete. He was never strong physically and died a comparatively young man in 1901, at his home in Plainfield.

I called on the veteran "Open" brother, Donald Ross, in Chicago just after word came of F. W. G.'s demise. Mr. Ross was a patriarchal figure with long flowing beard. He sat in a big chair and when his son Chas. Ross mentioned that I was with the exclusives he asked sharply "which branch?" I replied, "With those who refused the judgment against F. W. G." "Oh," he said, "I'm glad of that." Then after a moment or two of silence, he exclaimed, "Frederick Grant is in heaven!" "Yes," I replied, "He is with the Lord."

"Frederick Grant is in heaven!" he declared a second time with peculiar energy. Again I answered as before. Almost fiercely he exclaimed, "I tell you Frederick Grant's in heaven! Aye—and they were glad to get him there! A little clique of them tried to cast him out of the church of God on earth. They let him die, so far as they were concerned, in the place of the drunkard or the blasphemer. But oh, what a welcome he received up there! And he's with Cecil now and the two are reconciled. Soon I'll be there too— and we'll all have fellowship together at last." Then musingly, he added, "Aye, aye, Frederick Grant was cast out himself, and yet he would not have had fellowship with me down here. But we'll all be together up there!"

A few months passed by and Donald Ross had also joined "the choir invisible" whose one song shall ever be, "Unto him that loved us and hath made us kings and priests."

What a pity persons destined to such glorious privileges misunderstand one another so sadly on earth!

CHAPTER NINE

INCREASING DISSENSION

THE READING DIVISION

THE LATE REV. Dr. W. H. Griffith Thomas, who held tenaciously to much for which the Brethren stand, said on more than one occasion, "The Brethren are remarkable people for rightly dividing the Word of truth and wrongly dividing themselves." It was in no spirit of unkindness that he made this remark but rather as lamenting what has ever caused pious souls among themselves deepest grief. Yet the remedy seems most elusive. Organization has not precluded division in the various Protestant denominations, nor for that matter in what proudly calls itself the Catholic church; even as lack of organization has not kept the assemblies of Brethren united in one fellowship. All Christians know that division cures nothing. It only puts off the evil day, leaving questions for a later generation to settle that have not been properly faced when they first demanded attention.

While the Grant division was being perpetrated in America another equally groundless, in the judgment of many, was forced through in Great Britain.

While Mr. Darby lived his strong influence and dominant personality held the conflicting elements within the London exclusive party in check. When he was called home it seemed as though dissension was to be unchecked both in Britain and abroad. Walter Scott, one of the most prolific writers among the Brethren, has written of him:

> It has been the experience of most men brought into personal contact with Mr. Darby, that the influence exercised over them has been almost overwhelming. His marvelous power in grappling with principles and tracing their application to their legitimate results; his simple and unaffected piety, combined with the ripest scholarship and unequalled ability in expound-

ing the Word of God, accompanied by a generous appreciation of the good and excellent outside the ecclesiastical sphere in which he moved, fitted him to become, as he undoubtedly was, a recognized leader in the church of God.

The same writer has given an account of the funeral of this man of God which I am sure will have a tender and pathetic interest to such of my readers as shall peruse the balance of this book, therefore, I give it in full.

The Funeral of John Nelson Darby at the Cemetery in Bournemouth 2nd May, 1882

J. N. D. had been brought to Bournemouth some weeks before his death, to the house of Mr. Hammond, an ex-clergyman of the Church of England.

On the morning of the funeral there had been a prayer meeting at Sunbridge House (Mr. Hammond's), at which a farewell letter of Mr. Darby's to Brethren was read, and which was subsequently copied for private circulation.

The time fixed for the interment was 3:30 p. m., and within about five minutes of that time the hearse was at the cemetery gate.

There the coffin was placed on a bier, under which, at either end, a long pole was placed transversely, so that, while a brother held the handles of the bier at each end, other brethren took hold of the pole on either side; and as the distance from the gate to the grave was considerable, the bearers were changed several times, so as to give as many brethren as possible the privilege of carrying the body to the grave.

No regular procession was formed, but brethren—and there was a good sprinkling of sisters as well—followed the body en masse. The effect at this point was striking. Every voice was hushed; and nothing was heard but the tread of many feet, almost as regular as the measured tread at a military funeral.

Many friends had already congregated around the grave, whither the body was at once taken.

After about a minute's silence, Mr. M'Adam gave out the Hymn 229 in *The Little Flock Hymn Book,* "O Happy Morn," sung to *Praise.* Just as the last note of this hymn died away, a lark rose from the greensward close by, and poured forth its joyous notes. Perhaps many did not notice it—to the writer's ear it was quite in harmony with the scene.

Mr. C. E. Stuart, of Reading, read from Matt. 27:57-60, and in a few words pointed out the contrast between the burial of the Master and the burial of the servant. To the few around the Master's grave it seemed that all their hopes had been cut off. How different was it to us today in committing the servant's body to the grave, through the death of the Master. We were not there to eulogize the servant, but we could speak of the Master.

Mr. Hammond prayed.

Dr. Wolston, of Edinburgh, then read from Gen. 48, part of verse 21: "Israel said unto Joseph, Behold I die but God shall be with you"; Phil 2:12, 13; and Rev. 1:17, 18, and said a few words suggested by the passages.

Mr. Blyth gave out the one-verse hymn, 286, "Soon thou wilt come again," sung to *Indian*.

Mr. C. Stanley read from John 14:1-3, and I Thess. 4:14-17, "The Father's House and the Rapture of the Saints," and in a few words referred to our departed brother as having been the means of reviving the truth as to the Lord's coming.

"Lord Jesus Come," Hymn 324, was then given out by Dr. Christopher Wolston, and sung to *American*.

The coffin was lowered into the grave by Brethren.

Mr. Roberts, of Worcester, prayed.

"Brightness of Eternal Glory" was then sung to *Alma*, followed by the Doxology, "Glory, Honor, Praise and Power," which closed the meeting.

The coffin was of polished oak, with a brass plate on which was engraved:—

JOHN NELSON DARBY
Born 18th Nov., 1800
Died in the Lord
29th April, 1882

There was a very large number of friends present from all parts of the country — from eight to ten hundred.

The S. W. Railway ran a "special" to London in the evening to take back those who had come from the city.

There has been erected a large plain stone to mark the resting place of the richly-gifted servant of the Lord, on which is carved an inscription of 11 lines as follows:

JOHN NELSON DARBY
"As Unknown And Well Known"
Departed to be with Christ,
29th April, 1882
Aged 81
2 Cor. 5:21
Lord let me wait for Thee alone,
My life be only this,
To serve Thee here on earth unknown,
Then share Thy heavenly bliss.

J. N. D.

The Mr. C. E. Stuart mentioned above was one of J. N. D.'s old friends. A courteous and courtly gentleman, of independent fortune, a man of culture and refinement, a Christian of deep piety and transparent character, he had early identified himself with the movement and was an honored and beloved servant of Christ whose ministry, both oral and written was of an invaluable character.

At Reading, his home, he was held in most affectionate esteem by the large assembly in which he ministered to edification. But he had long foreseen certain tendencies against which he mildly protested, which brought him into conflict with the subjective school. At the time of the Kelly division he sided with London, feeling that "Abbott's Hill had not a leg to stand on," because of their refusal to receive the Guildford Hall Brethren as a body. This blinded him to the greater evil of condoning the ecclesiastical pretension of Park Street, from which he, as F. W. Grant, was to suffer so soon aftrwards.

It is pathetic to have to record that in less than three years from the time he preached at Mr. Darby's funeral, he was himself branded as an heretic and declared excommunicated by the London party.

There were two issues involved in the Reading trouble. One was a moral question involving a charge of untruthfulness which was sifted to the bottom and shown to be groundless, when investigated by the local assembly. The graver matter was one of doctrine and though his home assembly looked into this also and cleared him, their judgment was ruthlessly set aside by London and the stigma of heresy fixed upon Mr. Stuart and all who continued in fellowship with him.

The supposed heresy was contained in a booklet entitled "Chris-

tian Standing and Condition" which was construed as a direct
challenge to views taught by J. B. Stoney and others in two
periodicals denominated, "Food for the Flock," and "A Voice to
the Faithful." In his treatise C. E. S. distinguished between "Standing" and "Condition" as follows:

Standing, he said, invariably has to do with the ability to stand
before the throne of God. It is a forensic, or judicial term and
"a Christian can have no higher standing than to be justified
before the throne of God." His condition or state is the new
place God has given him in Christ. His old condition was "In
Adam," his new condition is "In Christ." Practice flows from the
apprehension of these truths. The doctrine is quite fully developed
in his *Exposition of the Epistle to the Romans.*

J. B. Stoney declared this teaching was a complete giving up
of Christianity and a reversal to Judaism. With him standing
involved "the removal of the First Man from under the eye of
God." While condition was the Spirit's work forming Christ
within. It will be seen that both used the terms somewhat differently to most teachers among the Brethren before and since the
trouble that developed.

Refusing the decisions of the Reading assembly, which according to their own teaching were "bound on earth and therefore
bound in heaven," London undertook to re-try the case. Once
more the ecclesiastical machinery was set in motion and almost
before the Reading Brethren realized the seriousness of the opposition, a meeting was called at Park Street and, though absent and
therefore not permitted to speak for himself, C. E. Stuart was
declared out of fellowship and the Reading assembly with him,
unless they acquiesced in the London judgment, which was solemnly
affirmed to be the voice of the Lord in the midst of his assemblies, and from which there could be no appeal.

So for the third time in five years division swept through
the ranks of the exclusives, until some eighty assemblies in Great
Britain and many in New Zealand, Australia, and other parts, were
cut off as schismatic, and, for the time being Stoneyism had again
triumphed. The ostracized meetings became known as the Reading
or Stuart Brethren.

Those with Mr. Grant in America saw in the high-handed action
against C. E. S. a repetition of the Montreal schism and hands

were stretched out across the sea to their distressed Brethren and fellowship cemented between them. There was also a desire for intercommunion with the Kelly brethren but differences between W. K., and C. E. S. hindered this; though the American Brethren have always freely received from either of these two parties whenever they presented themselves. In fact they have always taken the ground that inasmuch as London and Montreal made the divisions, the doors of the so-called Grant meetings were open to any from the various exclusive parties whenever they desired communion with them. Later this was modified in regard to the Raven party where strange teaching was soon manifest.

F. W. Grant completely repudiated the principle of assembly judgments being binding on the consciences of the saints even though there was no proof of their Scripturalness. Had he seen this at the time of the Kelly division he would not have signed the Toronto letter.

The following extracts from one of his papers will serve to make his position clear when fully awake to the pretentiousness of the London party:

> To all whose hearty endeavor is to keep the unity of the Spirit in the bond of peace:—
> BELOVED BRETHREN:—
> That the hand of God is upon us is but too evident. Our shame is public. It requires no spirituality to see that exactly in that which we have professedly sought we have failed most signally. The unity of the Spirit in the bond of peace is just, most surely, what we have not kept. It is easy, of course, to reproach each other with this, and to protest that we of any one particular section are free from the responsibility of this. It is not possible to escape, after all, the reproach which God has permitted to be against us all,—the reproach, not of here and there some local divisions, but of division from end to end; and not where separation from manifest evil has been a divine necessity, but upon points of ecclesiastical discipline or of doctrine confessedly in no wise fundamental, — too minute, in fact, to be made a ground of division by the narrowest and most sectarian of sects around us! Yet we all disclaim as injurious the accusation of being sects.

Some of us have separated from the doctrine that "in Christ" is state, not standing!

Some, from the doctrine that the Old-Testament saints had life in the Son!

Some, because they differed as to the judgment of an assembly with regard to fellowship with one of the divisions of a divided gathering!

And on account of such things, those who could receive Christians freely from the denominations around, refuse absolutely and decidedly, saints with whom in every other respect they are in the fullest accord, and whom they do not charge with anything else they would call ungodly!

And more, one of the greatest and most decisive arguments used and admitted to uphold these divisions is that we are to "endeavor to keep the unity of the Spirit in the bond of peace!"

Alas! who hath bewitched us, that such things should be possible at all,—that we should not be able to recognize the true character of an endeavor to keep the unity of the Spirit by such means as cutting off all who differ from us, and building the wall of separation highest where the real differences is in fact the slightest?

I know, of course, the fact will be disputed. They are too condemnatory, seen simply in the light, for one to care thus to face them. Yet is it not better at once to face them, than to leave them to be met for the first time where we must each one of us give account of himself to God? . . . Are there no *principles* which have been accepted as truth, and which have worked disastrously? Is there not reason for testing afresh by the Word our ecclesiastical principles, as, for example, those of fellowship and discipline, in view of the course to which they have led? If "by their fruits ye shall know them" is a test recognized in Scripture, is not the fact of three divisions in five years enough to beget suspicion that all is not right here? especially when, as already said, we find the plea of unity urged constantly for division, and most efficacious (strangely enough) in producing this.

Many at the present time are involved in deeper trouble than would be found in answering the question, Which of these divisions has truth and righteousness upon its side? And it is little to be doubted that many are deprived of energy to act for God by the palsy of fear that some fundamental error must be somewhere in principles which they had believed divine. Can it be of God, they ask, that questions which can scarcely be made intelligible to many a simple soul must be forced upon all, under the severest ecclesiastical penalties, with the certainty, at any rate, of being broken up by them; and that those who, attracted by the plea that the church of God is one, seek for something in principle as broad and catholic as this implies, should be confronted with the Park-street judgment and much else, as problems needing to be solved before they can discern which of several conflicting yet kindred bodies can justify a claim to this?

Is there, then, left no plain path in which the feet even of the lame may not be turned out of the way—may even be healed? At one time, as we all know, we *had* something easily defined and easily maintainable by Scripture,—carrying true consciences, not perplexing them. Have we suffered this to be taken from us? Could we have lost it without being ourselves in some way guilty for the loss? Was it not *while we slept* we lost it? Assuredly, the way of the Lord is still and ever a way not needing great intellect or attainments for its discovery, but a way in which the wayfaring man, though a fool, should not err. Would it be like our God if it were otherwise? . . .

The method has been to appeal to the local assemblies around for a new decision, and thus to initiate a division which might extend far and wide. Thus, in fact, have we been again and again broken up. For one assembly has, in fact, no jurisdiction over another,—no title to be heard more than another. And the same is true of any number of such assemblies. It would be merely the principle of a majority upon a large scale,—a principle, we are all clear, is not sanctioned by the Word. By this counter-action, then, of local assemblies, we are committed at once to division.

Yet it is where the actual gathering to Christ's name is there is He in the midst, and whatsoever they bind on earth is bound in heaven. This neither insures the infallibility of those so gathered, nor implies—as so many apparently now suppose— that to deny the righteousness of their action is to deny Christ to be in their midst. Where in Scripture is the warrant for such a thought? What they *"bind* on earth" is indeed "bound in heaven"; but can any "bind" unrighteousness in the Lord's name? Surely not: such an act cannot be "bound" by any

body of men whatever. *The character of the act is necessarily
implied in the word used by the Lord* . . .

But if the assembly fail, or appeal be made against its decision, to whom now is the appeal? and in what way should this be carried out? As to the first question, it is easily answered. For the reason already stated, to the local assembly it is not, but to that which the local assembly represents—the church at large. This is the only alternative, and it is as simple as instructive to consider that at this point the assembly as a whole takes the place of any local assembly when judging of any ordinary case. There is more difficulty, more gravity, no doubt, but the application of the very same principles in the one case as in the other. To see this, helps us also in whatever necessary differences result from the larger sphere . . .

As to fellowship in its open expression at the table of the Lord, it is with all Christians, truly such, with only this limitation in Scripture, that we put out from among ourselves a "wicked person" (I Cor. 5:13). . .

Three characters of wickedness the Word specifies: *moral* evil, the leaven of I Cor. 5; *doctrinal* evil, the leaven of Galatians and Matt. 16; and *willful association with this,* as in II John 10, 11. I do not need, for those to whom I am speaking, to insist more on these. But there is need to ask, Can we Scripturally refuse any of the Lord's people except on one of these grounds? Perhaps most would agree we cannot, while many, however, would so indefinitely extend the idea of these as to narrow their fellowship practically much more than this.

These extracts are from "The Relation of Assemblies to Assemblies," a perusal of which in its entirety will prove most illuminating to those who may be further interested, but for which there is not space in the present chapter. There can be no question but that the principles therein taught would if consistently carried out, soon put an end to division, but consistency is a rare plant and does not often come to full flower even in Christian assemblies.

C. E. Stuart, always an independent thinker, refusing to be subject to any defined creed, written or unwritten, put forth some views on propitiation as one element in Atonement shortly after the 1885 division, that caused quite a furore at the time. W. Kelly thought he detected positive heresy and attacked him strenuously, but as the atmosphere cleared it became evident there was nothing fundamental at stake. But for a time a five-sided debate went on in Brethren's periodicals and from their lecture-platforms. The question at issue was the exact meaning of propitiation and the time when it was effected.

C. E. Stuart taught that Christ became High Priest to make propitiation (Heb. 2:17). He maintained that He was never Priest on earth (citing Heb. 8:4 as a proof-text) and that, therefore propitiation was but one element in atonement and must have been made by our Lord after death. He held that in the disembodied state He entered the heavenly sanctuary and there made propitiation by presenting His blood, upon and before the mercy seat.

This W. Kelly refused as a slight upon the work of the cross. He agreed with C. E. S. that Christ was not a Priest on earth, but held that He acted as Offerer on the cross when He offered up Himself and there made an available propitiation for all men, though He was only the Substitute for all who believe on His name. This distinction between propitiation and substitution was one on which J. N. Darby had dwelt in his writings at considerable length.

R. T. Grant felt W. Kelly was begging the question raised by C. E. S. as to propitiation being priestly work, and agreed with C. E. S. that Christ was not a Priest on earth, therefore, propitiation must have been made in heaven—but he held that in the disembodied state our Lord could not be considered as High Priest for it was necessary that His manhood be complete ere He could act as Priest and therefore propitiation could not have been made until as the resurrected man, at His ascension, He passed through the heavens in the power or value of His own blood.

E. C. Pressland, an English teacher of some ability who was in the Reading fellowship, sought to reconcile the divergent views by holding that, inasmuch as there are three heavens—atmospheric, starry and the divine abode—our Lord when lifted up on the cross was in the heavens and therefore could act as Priest and so make propitiation, which was all completed when he cried, "It is finished."

It remained for F. W. Grant to offer the fifth suggestion, namely that Heb. 8:4 does not deny that Christ was a Priest while on earth but simply states that He was not of the Aaronic order. That as Priest He offered up Himself to make propitiation and, that the terms propitiation, expiation, and atonement are identical in meaning, as all are translations of the same Greek word, as used in the

Septuagint and the New Testament. He held that propitiation is by substitution.

For several years the controversy went on and even after C. E. Stuart had been taken home there were not wanting some to charge him with vital error, while many who accepted his views felt as strongly in regard to W. K. and F. W. G., being convinced that they both rejected vital truth.

Still the examination of Scriptures was helpful and opened up new lines of truth to many, as is often the case. What is needed is brotherly confidence and the spirit of humility with readiness to learn one from another and an honest desire to know the truth for its own sake, for it is written, "We can do nothing against the truth but for the truth." Scripture leaves room for large differences of opinion where fundamental truth is not called in question, and it is always wrong to endeavor "to make a man an offender for a word."

As the years have passed the Reading meetings, so-called, have dwindled until at the present time there are very few left of any size in Great Britain, though they are somewhat stronger numerically in New Zealand.

CHAPTER TEN

"RAVENISM" AND LESSER DIVISIONS

IN RETRACING the experiences the Brethren have passed through, an impartial observer cannot but be struck by their apparent inability to deal with a crisis when it actually arrives, even though their literature abounds with the most careful and minute instruction as to the methods of disciplinary action according to Scripture. The principles consistently carried out would have kept them from division and averted their multiplied schisms from the first, but the weakness of the movement has been in its lack of coherence and therefore of anything like unanimity of action when a grave crisis has arisen. Even where good and godly men believed the same things and were in agreement that evil ought to be dealt with, they seemed incapable of acting together. This has been clearly demonstrated in the four divisions already noticed and it is equally apparent in the so-called Bexhill-Greenwich, or Raven schism of 1890.

Less than five years after the Reading trouble, disastrous results of wrong principles were again manifested in the London party, which eventually culminated in another world-wide separation. To make plain what led to this, it is necessary to make the reader more fully acquainted with a unique figure, whose teaching was indirectly responsible for what took place at this time. J. Butler Stoney was one of the young men attracted to J. N. Darby in the thirties. He was a brilliant and wealthy youth, educated as a barrister, and seemingly had the world at his feet when the attractive power of the cross brought him to the place where he saw the emptiness of all earth's dazzling prospects, and Christ became henceforth the absorbing passion of his soul. In the new movement he found just what he delighted in: unworldliness, and a fellowship with spiritually-minded believers that his soul craved. He gladly threw aside splendid opportunities for advancement down here to "lay hold on that which is life indeed." His affection for Mr. Darby was almost extravagant—yet not to be wondered at—so much did he see of Christ in his servant in those early days, and so eager was he to learn the truth that was being unfolded.

For some sixty years Stoney was an outstanding figure among the Brethren. He edited several monthly papers, notably *Food for the Flock,* and *A Voice to the Faithful* (the latter envelope size), and was a frequent contributor to the other periodicals. Perhaps no finer expository and pastoral ministry was put forth by him than his *Discipline in the School of God,* though most of his books are of a very high order and are edifying to a degree. On the other hand their intensely subjective character requires that they be read with great care and with due regard to the other side of the truth, developed by the objective teacher.

His mind was of the character of that of Fenelon or, perhaps more aptly, that of Tauler, although without a trace of asceticism. This comes out very manifestly in his written ministry, as noted above.

As most of the Brethren's teaching was decidedly objective, it may be that this particular line was given by God in grace to preserve the balance of truth—but, as is so often the case, soon it became apparent that there were two rival schools among them, the majority following the objective teachers, and a minority delighting in the subjective, which ministry soon considered itself "the remnant testimony," led by Stoney and a few others whose mental processes were similar in character. These developed what came to be known as "The Brethren's Perfectionism."

J. B. Stoney died on May 1, 1897, having been confined to his room from October, 1895, with a severe illness. It is blessed to note how preciously he entered into the realities of spiritual things during those months in which he was shut away from all outside activities: months, too, in which the movement with which he had been so long connected was passing through a severe trial, the direct result of the perversion of his own teaching.

A. E. Knight summarizes those sickroom experiences in a way that will refresh the souls of those who know Christ. He says:

> In those October days of 1895, physical weakness and suffering were a new thing to Mr. Stoney, and soon after being con-

fined to his room he was heard reviewing before the Lord these unfamiliar experiences. "I am learning a new road in dependence upon Christ . . . He has fought the battle and we get the good of it. Thank Thee, glorious Lord!" His thoughts go out to beloved fellow pilgrims traveling the same road, and he communes helpfully; "The reason people find their path so difficult is that they have not a single eye for a single Person." How fully the Lord was his own object at this time may be gathered from the admission so remarkable in its utterness and finality, "I have learnt to do without anything or anyone but the Lord. He is enough without letters, or friends, or anything else." All his springs were in God.

The affections of this beloved saint of God were indeed set on things above, the things where Christ is (Col. 3:2), and he realized more than ever in those first days of his illness how clean must be the cut with the world ere full attainment of his quest could be realized. "There is a great gap between God's things and man's things," he was heard saying . . . "I began with, 'I will delight in the Lord,' and it brought me to the end of all things here." Anon he asks—and the goal of his affections seems nearer than before — "Do we belong to the scene where the brightness is, or to the scene where blindness is? It is not the scene only that is bright, but the Person in it. *He* belongs to it. Wonderful way to open heaven . . . by a Person!" He did not pretend, of course, that earthly things had no beauty—his mind was keenly alive to the beauties of the old creation; but the more excellent beauty of "things above" eclipsed them all, and they became by comparison of no account. "If a man would only dwell on the divine reality of God's world," he soliloquizes, "he would see that this is only man's world. In God's world *all* is divinely beautiful. This is a beautiful world, but it is only like a flower. In God's world all is according to God. I am roaming in beautiful worlds, and I rouse up and find myself in this world." Then, as he poises the one against the other—man's world against God's world—his soul exclaims, "How small everything is in contrast to eternal things!" Small, indeed, and how transitory! Does not the prophet say, "All flesh is grass, and all the goodliness thereof is as the flower of the field; the grass withereth, the flower fadeth; because the Spirit of the Lord bloweth upon it" (Isa. 40:6, 7)? Death and decay are here; that is the trouble. Yonder there is no decay, no death; "There everlasting spring abides, and never-withering flowers."

He is still engaged with this study of contrasts in the following meditation, wherein his experience is not so much a condition of ecstasy as the peace of communion, a holy tranquil resting in Christ. "There is a great contrast between things outside this scene and the things here; but no matter what they are, you must look up to the Lord for small matters as well as for great. My rest is, that I am not conscious of anything here until I open my eyes; I am above the things here in the sense of His power; *that is rest* even in the night. Outside of everything with the Lord, that is communion, that is what I call rest—the great thing is to stay in it. Make the Lord your delight and not any circumstance; when lost in Him, *that is rest."* Weighty words, as emanating from a bed of weakness and pain, where the speaker was practically cut off from all creature streams save the ministrations of a devoted daughter, his companion to the last. Ripe for glory, it needed but a very brief experience of the sickroom to reconcile him to the new conditions; indeed he was heard saying on the very first day: "A day's experience in bed. I began with grace and I came to praise. Then I came to see what service is. I see that the great lack in the servant is that *the purpose of God is not his ideal.* If it is not, if he does not know the purpose of God, he cannot lead souls to glory. You must begin with grace in order to end with glory. Your knowledge of the glory is according to the measure of your knowledge of the grace." . . .

At times he must have had memorable entrance into the experience described in II Cor. 3:18, "beholding as in a glass the glory of the Lord," and the reflected glimpses we get of these experiences are very sweet. "I had a wonderful night," he told his daughter somewhere in February, 1896. "The whole sky seemed lighted up; the light circling around, and the Lord in the midst, immensely great, surveying the earth. I was there too. It seemed as if He were showing it to me, or at least there it was for me to see at a distance, and I was but a speck looking at it." "The whole sky seemed lighted up and the Lord filling the whole space," he said on another occasion, alluding to the same experience; and doubtless this "beholding with open face the glory of the Lord" (II Cor. 3:18) was still in his mind when he declared, "I have been in the courts of glory. What do you think is the first thing you learn when you get there?

You find that glory is your destination."

Sometimes these visions of the night were of a less tranquil character, but the record of them is vivid and stimulating. "I think you would like to hear of my experience last night," he writes to a friend in March, 1896. "I awoke in the night with great fervor, occupied with a verse, 'saved by the mighty power of God.' I had been contending for it in my sleep, but the people were making such a rant of it, and I was panting like a hunted hare. I tried to explain to them that salvation was effected on the cross, and that the believer is given the power of God to enjoy it. My great text for myself was, 'I sat under his shadow with great delight'; but that only in the Spirit of God could I enjoy it. The moment I went to sleep the rant began again, and I awoke in excitement. I looked to the Lord to establish the fact to myself, that it is only in the Spirit of God we can get clear of excitement in the flesh, and the Lord in a marked way made me know that I was free from the flesh, and could enjoy it all in the Spirit. When I awoke this morning I felt like a man after a race; and in reviewing it, my meditation was, that the first great thing is to overcome the man that was removed in the cross, and the next great thing is to walk in the power of God—to walk in the Spirit. Those I was contending with were all imaginary people whom I did not know, but you can imagine the sort of night I had." . . .

In October one seems to mark a further step. Six months before he had spoken sweetly of enjoyment found in the Lord's shadow; now he remarks to a friend: "When I last saw you I was sitting under His shadow with great delight. Now I am with Him in heaven. I could not express what He brings before me—the sense of His love and favor . . . Keep yourself in the love of God—*in the love of God* . . . I *delight* in the love of God . . . In the beginning of my illness I used to say that my body is the Lord's. Now I say that I am a member of Christ" (I Cor. 6:15).

It would be of profit to quote more at length but space forbids. One of Mr. Stoney's most intimate disciples was Mr. F. E. Raven, an English gentleman, who until his retirement held a position under the government. His mind was even more mystical than that of Stoney, and he was greatly valued as an exponent of the subjective school; but his unguarded utterances soon exposed him to much criticism from the rest.

In a special meeting held at Witney, near Oxford, about Easter, 1888, certain of Mr. Raven's teachings were called in question by a number of laboring brethren, led by Mr. J. H. Lowe, who objected seriously to statements made that seemed plainly to deny the believer's present possession of eternal life. Mr. Raven at that time insisted that he meant nothing more than what J. N. Darby had taught in connection with life and sealing. But the teaching in question seemed clearly to deny the believer's present possession of eternal life. He spoke in a vague way of eternal life as a sphere of blessing, and a condition of soul, rather than as something communicated to the believer in new birth. He was also very confused as to the hypostatic union of the divine and human in the Person of the Lord.

In November, 1889, some one hundred and fifty Brethren in London, who had been looking into the teaching considered questionable, felt the matter so seriously that they were much relieved when Mr. Raven stated: "In view of what happened at the last meeting, I do not want to set myself in opposition to Brethren. I am not conscious of having taught anything contrary to the truth, though I do not wish to justify expressions. But in present circumstances, out of respect to Brethren's consciences, I will abstain from ministry in London. Further, if Brethren wish it, I will abstain from attending these meetings." While this relieved the tension temporarily, it settled nothing, as "F.E.R." was as active as ever in disseminating his teaching elsewhere.

In essence, the teaching objected to can be given in F. E. R.'s own words as published in 1890. (There are lengthy footnotes which for brevity's sake are omitted, though of importance):

GREENWICH, March 21, 1890.

I have thought it well, I trust before the Lord, to reprint, on my own responsibility, the text of my letter to Mr. O. of December 6th, 1889, adding some notes in explanation of points that in the text may not be quite clear, or may appear open to question. The text remains unchanged, save that the last paragraph is omitted for the reason that I believe some of the thoughts therein referred to have been withdrawn or modified. I take the opportunity of avowing in the most distinct and emphatic way that I never had in my mind the thought of separating eternal life from the Person of the Son of God, or of asserting that eternal life, is, for a Christian, any other than Christ. I would add that I have not been nor am without exercise of heart or sorrow before the Lord in regard to the strained and painful state of feeling existing amongst us; and I regret, on my own part, the measure in which it has been contributed to by obscure or defective expressions of mine which have gone abroad, taken from letters to individuals, or reports of readings. I can only say I wrote or spoke according to the light I had, and I have since sought to make all the amends in my power, without sacrificing the truth, by rendering explanation, I trust in patience, to all who desired it, both publicly, privately and by letter. Believing that what I have sought to maintain is substantially the truth as to Christianity in its proper heavenly character, such as it has been brought before us by those most highly esteemed, I have confidence that the Lord will care for the simple who desire God's will, and assure their hearts as to what is or is not of God. (Signed) F. E. R.

The key to almost all that I have said lies in my objection to apply in an absolute way to the believer in his mixed condition down here statements in Scripture which refer to what he is, or what is true of him, viewed as in Christ. Such a practice results in the statements becoming mere dogmas, conveying little sense of reality. This may be seen in regard to divine righteousness as spoken of in II Corinthians 5:21. The believer is in Christ, and as there, is become God's righteousness in Christ: but besides this, he still is in a condition here, in which the existence of sin and the flesh are taken account of (the Spirit lusts against the flesh), and this is wholly distinct from our state in Christ, to which divine righteousness in its fullest sense applies. Christ in glory is the full expression of divine righteousness, and to be there as he is, is that into which grace introduces us in Christ. Hence, Paul looked to be found in Him having the righteousness which is of God by faith. The above in no sense weakens or sets aside the reality of the believer's present standing in Christ; it is his true position according to grace; but it needs to be borne in mind that it is the position of the believer before God, distinct from his actual condition here with the consciousness of the existence of the flesh in him.

I may add a word of explanation as to the use of the word "state." I have commonly used it as indicating that which is true of us as new-created in Christ (as seen in the new man) apart from any question of the Christian's walk here.

Next, as to eternal life. It was God's purpose in Christ from eternity; it was, in essence, with the Father in eternity, but has now been manifested in the only begotten Son of God, who came here declaring the Father, in such wise as that the apostles could see it, and afterwards declare it by the Spirit—but I regard it of all importance to maintain, clear and distinct from any purpose of blessing for man, the true deity, the eternal Sonship of the Word. Eternal life is given to us of God, and is in God's Son—for us it is the heavenly relationship and blessedness in which, in the Son, man is now placed and lives before the Father, the death of Christ having come in as the end before God of man's state in the flesh. "He that has the Son has the life"; the testimony he has received concerning the Son is, by the Spirit, the power of life in the believer, he having been born of God to receive it. He has also eaten the flesh of the Son of man, and drunk His blood. But at the same time, the believer still has part in seen things here (which the Son has not) and all that is seen is temporal, and will come to an end. It has no part in eternal life, though it may be greatly influenced by it. As to eternal life being a technical term, it simply referred to the fact of its having been a term in common use among the Jews without any very definite meaning. They frequently came to the Lord with questions as to it, and thought they had it in the Scriptures . . .

I may add a few words in regard to new birth. It is an absolute necessity for man, if he has to do with God in blessing. It lies at the beginning of all—without it a man cannot see, much less receive any saving testimony. It is the sovereign act of the Spirit of God. Peter and John both recognize that those who were really in the faith of Christ were born again of the Word of God, or born of God—a seed of God has been implanted in them from the outset. None the less, new birth of itself does not conduct into heavenly relationship or blessing. For this, something more was needed, namely, redemption, which in its full power, sets man in Christ in glory, and the renewing of the Holy Ghost, which fits man for the new order of things. Of course, these are now, through grace, the portion of the believer.

(Signed)   F. E. R.

The objection to this was that eternal life was made a state or condition—not a new life imparted. New birth, too, was in order to believe, not through believing. The more Mr. Raven labored to make his position clear, the more he seemed to involve it in obscurity. Finally, at a large convention in Greenwich, in 1890, there was open dissension over it and when some who sided with Mr. Raven went from Greenwich to Bexhill (where there was a very small assembly), their letter of commendation was refused. Bexhill and Ealing assemblies acted together and in June of that year definitely declared Greenwich out of fellowship. Messrs. J. H. Lowe, W. T. Whybrow, Major H. M. McCarthy and others insisted that Bexhill's action be accepted as the judgment of the Lord. C. Stanley died just as the division was being pressed through. He stood with the opponents of Mr. Raven. C. H. Mackintosh on the other hand went with Park Street which exonerated F. E. R. and refused Bexhill's action as schismatic. His stand is peculiar, inasmuch as he never taught in all his ministry the vagaries advocated by Mr. Raven. But it was a time of great confusion, and C. H. M. was wearied out by constant bickerings and separations. He wrote J. A. Trench as follows:

DUBLIN, IRELAND, November 29, 1890.

I feared that you would have to encounter a good deal of trial in consequence of the sad and humiliating condition of things amongst us. I have never known anything like it during the fifty years I have been on the ground. Only think of some who have walked for years in ostensible fellowship with us, now charging us with being identified with heresy, blasphemy and attacking the adorable Person of the Son of God; mark the bitterness of feeling, the diligent effort to gather up in all directions dirt to fling back upon their brethren; where is the spirit of Christ in all this? Where the broken heart and weeping eyes at the terrible thought of our being involved in such evil? Alas, there is what looks much more like a malignant effort to extract heresies out of papers, which if read with an unprejudiced mind would yield profit and edification. It is all most deplorable.

As to the charges brought against Mr. Raven of heresy, blasphemy, and attacking the Person of the Son of God, they are simply monstrous, there is no foundation for them. Some seem possessed with the idea that there is behind and underneath a regular system of doctrine subversive to Christianity. I ask such, what have we got to do with what is behind and underneath? We can judge what is before and above and they have utterly failed to produce adequate evidence to sustain their charge, but beloved C. . . . I am persuaded that we needed all this terrible sifting, else the Lord would not have allowed it to come upon us, and further I believe that the Lord will bring rich blessing out of it all to individual souls, indeed I see it already in many; I see more earnestness; more reality; more knitting of hearts in true brotherly love, instead of cold, formal, nominal fellowship. For myself I am conscious of feeling a real spring in the inner man, a more profound sense of love of God; the preciousness of Christ and authority, majesty, fulness and loving depths of Holy Scripture, and I look for much more for myself and others through the infinite grace of Christ. I do trust that we may soon be done with this heart-sickening, soul-withering discussion and strife and be allowed to go on heart to heart in communion and worship shoulder to shoulder in service and testimony, that is what I long for, nothing else has any charm or interest for me. This is what I have been seeking for in my poor way to realize and promote for the last fifty years, and by the grace of Christ shall never accept anything else.

C. H. M.

His hopes, however, were vain, for trouble followed upon trouble as the years went on.

Shortly after the division was consummated, Mr. Raven came out with what savored of Apollinarianism, declaring of our Lord that in incarnation "He was not personally man. He was personally the Logos, in human condition." It is this that C. H. M. refers to above. This aroused William Kelly, who after a minute examination of Raven's doctrines, declared him to be "heterodox as to eternal life, but above all, as to Christ's person." F. W. Grant reviewed his teaching in a booklet entitled *Re-tracings of Some Truths* and concluded he had definitely departed from the teaching current among Brethren from the beginning. Many feel that it was the refusal of F. W. G.'s teaching as to eternal life and sealing of the Spirit that had opened the door to a great host of erroneous conceptions.

In 1902, the Raven party divided again over a question of how to treat simple believers when an assembly had been broken up by the ill-behavior of its guides. This resulted in the Glanton party as distinct from the London party. Nearly all the evangelical men that were left sided with Glanton assembly in the reception of the scattered ones at Alnwick, a nearby town. London actually put Glanton away for thus caring for Christ's bewildered ones! Dr. W. T. Wolston tells the story in a trenchant manner in *Hear the Right*.

The Glanton Brethren shortly afterwards made certain confessions to the Stuart and Grant brethren (who on their part confessed haste and a low state resulting in division), which have resulted in the partial re-establishment of fellowship—save that a few on both sides are still demanding fuller confessions of one another as to failures in the past.

The Bexhill party was also divided in 1906 over a question of the jurisdiction of an assembly in regard to silencing a teacher whose ministry was considered unprofitable in Tunbridge Wells and was enjoyed in Acton, England. The one assembly declared the man unfit either to minister or to break bread—the other endorsed him fully—and assemblies everywhere in the Bexhill fellowship were called to side with one or the other.

More recently the so-called Raven meetings have been divided over the teaching of an American leader who denied the truth of the Eternal Sonship of Christ. This most serious error caused many to take a definite stand against it and led to another separation. But sadly enough by far the greater majority saw nothing wrong in such views and have gone on with the promulgator of them. This puts these meetings entirely off the ground of the early Brethren who considered a true confession of Christ the very first consideration.

It has been an unpleasant task seeking to present in some measure of detail the grounds of these various divisions, yet I am persuaded the consideration of them will not be without profit, if other Christians learn thereby to avoid the snares and pit-falls which caused such grief and sorrow among the brethren whose cry was "Unity" but whose practices wrought such widespread schism among believers.

CHAPTER ELEVEN

THE OPEN BRETHREN

THE PREVIOUS CHAPTERS have shown, unhappily, how the rigid application of the exclusive principle of disciplinary action has wrought dividing this particular wing of the movement into eight clearly defined companies. First, into the Darby and Kelly schools; then in America, into what are generally known as The Natural History Hall (or Cecil) and Grant Companies. Then, as we have seen a little later, the Darby branch in Great Britain divided into the Park Street and Reading (or Stuart) fellowship. The Grant and Stuart meetings, however, were very shortly afterwards united, recognizing the fact that both were now on practically the same ground; namely that of the refusal of arbitrary assembly judgments when such are manifestly without any Scriptural basis. This did away with one of the divisions. Effort was made at about the same time to amalgamate the Kelly Brethren with the Grant Meetings, and Mr. Kelly came to America to negotiate with leading Brethren on this side. But two things came up to hinder full fellowship. In New York, there was trouble at that time over the teaching of Malachi Taylor, a very much beloved brother who, rightly or wrongly, was reputed to deny worship to the Lord Jesus Christ, teaching that worship should only be offered to the Father through the Son by the Spirit. It is difficult to determine at this date just exactly what Mr. Taylor's views were at that time. Certainly in all the years afterward ere he was taken home to be with the Lord, he taught clearly and distinctly that the Lord Jesus was, to use his own language, "worthy of all worship, praise and adoration now and for evermore." However, he and his friends were set aside and on Mr. Kelly's arrival from Great Britain Mr. Taylor met him and presented his side of things. As a result, it became quite impossible for Mr. Grant and his friends to convince Mr. Kelly that it would be unscriptural for him to go on with what was called the Taylor meeting. Shortly afterwards, as we have seen, Mr. Stuart's peculiar views on propitiation were published and these Mr. Kelly not only refused but in his usual intense way violently attacked them as setting forth a "ghostly theory of the atonement." In America, however, any Brethren coming commended from Kelly Meetings have always been received by the Grant Meetings. Mr. R. T. Grant was firmly convinced that had all American Brethren taken their stand definitely with Mr. Kelly against ecclesiastical pretension in 1881 it would have saved the Exclusives from a vast amount of trouble afterwards. He felt to the day of his death that the Ramsgate question was God's controversy with the Brethren.

Pursuing the chain from which we were turned aside by this digression, we note that just as the Reading and Grant Meetings became one, so through Park Street's endorsation of the Natural History Hall judgment at Montreal the two extreme companies of England and America were also one. Afterwards, the Park Street party divided over the Raven question, those who refused Mr. Raven's teaching as unscriptural becoming known as the Lowe or Bexhill party and the others generally bearing the name of their principal teacher. The Raven branch again divided over the Alnwick question, those refusing London's excommunication of the Glanton assembly for showing kindness to the distracted saints at Alnwick becoming known as the Glanton Brethren. These latter have, generally speaking, agreed to freely receive their formerly separated Brethren from the Grant and Reading Companies as they recognized when their own difficulties arose that they were the victims of the same high church ecclesiastical tyranny that had so ruthlessly cut off thousands of saints in Britain and America who could see no evil whatever in the teaching and principles of F. W. Grant and C. E. Stuart. It is only fair to say that some Glanton Brethren have not been prepared to go the whole length, and a number of the Reading Assemblies insist that the Glanton people have not fully judged the sin committed when Mr. Stuart was excommunicated for teaching what they believed to be precious truth. Therefore, there has been here and there division among the Reading Brethren over the question of the reception of those with Glanton. In America, too, a very few of the Grant Meetings refuse anything like the thought of amalgamation with the Glanton Brethren, while generally receiving individuals from them after making certain that they are not in any way identified with the vagaries of what is generally called Ravenism.

The Bexhill party also divided into the Tunbridge Wells and Acton branches, each of which still claims to have the only table of the Lord on earth and to be "the original company of Brethren." Many of those in the Acton meetings individually repudiate such pretension, and individuals in many cases have sought fellowship in the Grant Meetings in America. But others refuse to recognize these Brethren as on divine ground until they confess what they call the sin of setting up another table when they went on with Mr. Grant after the Montreal judgment.

The following incident will give the conception of some of these, though it occurred before the Tunbridge Wells and Acton break. A Bexhill brother explaining the various divisions used the following simile: "The Brethren may be likened to a biscuit. A large piece was broken off. That represents the Open brethren. Other pieces also were broken off: namely, the Grant, Reading, Kelly and Raven Brethren; but, thank God," he piously exclaimed, "we remain the middle of the biscuit." Could conceit and self-complacent narrowness go farther? Yet in some degree each off-shoot of the London party with the exception of the Glanton companies would take that very ground. With three different "middles of the biscuit," though, it is a little difficult for simple souls to distinguish the original center from the broken pieces.

But now having seen how rigid Exclusivism has utterly failed to do the very thing it was supposed to effect; that is to enable believers to keep the unity of the Spirit in the bond of peace, it may be well to ask: Has Open Brethrenism fared any better? The answer may be both Yes and No.

Yes—for no such worldwide divisions have taken place among these assemblies as among the Exclusive Brethren. No—because actual organic unity is as far from being manifested among the Open Meetings as among the Exclusives.

Starting with the idea of the independency of the local assembly and the rejection of the Exclusive view of the ground of the one body, the Open Meetings have become largely congregational in character. While this in itself militates against widespread schism and localizes division, it has really fostered the spirit of disunion and independency.

Now, in using the latter word, I do not wish to be offensive, for I fully recognize that what Exclusives call independency, Open Brethren think of as immediate dependency on God, rather than the recognition of a union of meetings. Nevertheless, the fact remains that assemblies holding this principle break up into warring fragments very often on the slightest provocation; and where they do go on unitedly in happy fellowship and active gospel testimony, it is generally because of the individual spiritual energy of some leader or leaders in the local meetings whose influence over the rest is so strong that others yield to such leadership and so division is averted.

But it is no uncommon thing to find in one given locality several meetings, all recognized as Open, which have no real fellowship with each other; although if a conference is held in a distant city, representatives of all these meetings might be there who would break bread together at the time and share alike in the ministry and fellowship; but on returning home they would not in some instances so much as enter one another's halls or meeting rooms. Illustrations of these unhappy conditions could be given, but it seems better simply to state the fact rather than to draw attention to particular places, for one realizes that the brethren in all such meetings doubtless mourn over the separations and misunderstandings; but the difficulty is how to rectify them. Nor do I mention such things here with the thought of advertising the failures of Brethren, but rather with the hope that a fair, plain statement of conditions might lead to the recognition of a Scriptural way out.

Often these divisions are simply the result of some one individual's energy or eccentricity. Possibly some leader cannot get on with the rest; so he goes out, takes a certain number of followers with him, and rents a new hall beginning another meeting, not as hiving off from the older one and in full fellowship with it, but as advocating somewhat different principles, as a result of which the older meeting immediately closes the door on the new one and refuses to receive from it, unless persons returning utterly repudiate the more recent gathering. Or, it may be that some prefer an organ or other musical instrument to guide in the singing in the Sunday school or gospel meetings, and to legal Brethren this is ever taboo. So one company goes out and puts in an organ or piano, while the others go on without such help, but are equally content to go on without their Brethren too, even charging the latter with lack of conscience because in this matter they desire to become all things to all men if by any means they may save some. Singularly enough, those refusing to have any fellowship with their Brethren who use musical instruments in gospel work will perhaps have a piano or organ in their own homes; and while with amazing inconsistency they denounce their Brethren as going in the way of Cain (whose son invented the harp and organ) because they use music to aid in Christian testimony, yet these same Brethren will gladly avail themselves of many another product of Cain's world such as modern inventions, like the automobile for instance, which is the result of Tubal-Cain's inventive genius, for personal use; while perhaps, as I have known in some instances, bitterly protesting against so much as sending a Ford car to a missionary for use in his work, on the ground that it is an unapostolic method of reaching the masses, as there is clearly no Scripture that indicates the apostle Paul or any of his co-laborers ever toured the ancient world in an auto!

Again, some meetings are much freer in communion than others or in reception of ministry for other companies of believers. Gatherings where people are put through a rigid process of examination ere being allowed to break bread, and where it is insisted upon that they should separate from all denominations and possibly be baptized by immersion before they can sit at the Lord's table are generally spoken of as "tight" meetings. Others having various degrees of fellowship with Christians not formally with them are spoken of contemptuously by their "tight" Brethren as "loose." Yet it will generally be found that meetings so stigmatized seldom if ever receive believers of whose Christian character and soundness in the faith there is any reasonable doubt. It may be said of Brethren as a whole, taking in all shades and distinctions, that they stand for the reception of converted people sound in the faith at the table of the Lord, and of none others.

In regard to ministry, there are some Open meetings, and it has to be acknowledged some of the very best of them, who have a stated preacher, perhaps not exactly serving on a salary basis, but to whom regular monthly or weekly remittances are given that he may pursue his work without distraction; while other meetings would not even permit the arrangement beforehand as to who is to declare the gospel on a given night. They come together without any prepared program and wait upon the Lord after the meeting starts, looking to the Spirit to guide the right man to take the platform, if indeed a platform there be, for more than one meeting has been torn to pieces over the question as to whether the brother addressing the meeting should be raised a few inches above his fellows in order that all may see and hear better. The platform has been looked upon as a badge of clerisy, and the attempt to introduce it has marred the harmony of the meeting, if it has not led to actual division.

In certain quarters, the plan above mentioned of having no stated preacher but carrying on gospel testimony in dependence on the guidance of the Holy Spirit has worked out well when there were spiritually minded Brethren possessing evident gift and sensitive to the Spirit's guidance. But in other cases, it has proven a dismal failure, the most illiterate and ignorant men often pushing to the front and insisting on being heard, while godlier and better instructed servants of Christ shrink into the background and keep in retirement. As a result of this fleshly activity it has come to pass that in most of the Brethrens' conferences and other gatherings for public testimony, speakers are now selected beforehand in order to avoid confusion and waste of time. Even among the Exclusive Brethren this is generally the case as well as in the Open Meetings.

It will be seen from the above how very difficult it would be at the present time to get anything like unity in judgment upon any particular question among the assemblies of Open Brethren. This makes it exceedingly hard for Exclusives who are so accustomed to act organically to understand their Open Brethren who act locally. It also calls for a good deal of consideration when one remembers that thousands of these Open Meetings have been formed in complete independence of what may have transpired in past years. While Exclusives as a rule are fairly well read on questions of division, the Open Brethren generally avoid such questions and seek to act as local meetings before the Lord. Possibly Mr. William Shaw of Scotland who for years edited a little periodical called *The Believers' Pathway,* puts the open position as clearly as anyone could.

I quote from an article entitled, "Fellowship Among Saints," which was published many years ago:

> When we came out at first our path was simplicity itself. Our eyes had just been opened to the great beauty of the gathering name of our Lord Jesus Christ, and to the truth that we were *one* with every saint that loved His name . . . A great tide of joy arose in the hearts of the saints as they beheld that "goodly land" into which the Lord had brought them, and their union, not only with Christ the Head in heaven, but with every member of His body on earth! We had no call to found "a church." We were *in the church;* we realized that we were bound up, with every believer, in the bundle of life with the Lord our God; and we found it blessed to be in the bundle. Neither had we any call to found a form of church-government. The Lord Himself had already furnished us with the New Testament pattern. Recognizing our *oneness* with all the people of God, we saw and rejoiced to see that the place we occupied was the birthright place of every believer. We perceived that *the Lord's table was for the Lord's people,* and that the qualification for sitting there was simply this, that you are a believer in Jesus and walking godly.
>
> Many believers did not see that their true place was there; but that was their responsibility, not ours. What we were to see was simply that the principles on which we gather would include every child of God on the face of the earth who was sound in faith and practice. That is, that the constitution of the assembly would include all whom the Lord included, and exclude only those He excluded. We therefore acted on the Scriptural precept, "Receive ye one another, as Christ also received us to the glory of God" (Rom. 15:7). We found believers who had very little light upon "separation truth." But that was no reason why they should be rejected. We felt that the measure of a brother's light could not be made "a test of fellowship," provided he was sound in the great fundamentals of the faith. Indeed, in those days many a believer in the earliest twilight of his "learning the ways which be in Christ" was wonderfully helped and established by being welcomed as a member of the great family of God.

Thousands of the believers who so gathered had never heard of Bethesda or Plymouth. The names of Darby, Kelly, Grant, Stuart, Raven, Cecil or Lowe would all have been strange to them. They did not even know that there ever had been any other meetings similarly gathered. Yet when such Christians presented themselves at meetings of the various Exclusive parties for reception, they were refused until taken over the entire ground of the Plymouth Bethesda controversy and forced to take sides. Of course, this was only true if they fell into the hands of legal or ignorant men. The more spiritually minded and better instructed of the Exclusives have always sought to receive such brethren in their simplicity without raising questions of which they knew nothing.

But as the years went on, among the Open Meetings themselves many questions arose that led to another type of Exclusivism, and Mr. Shaw refers to this in the following remarks, though he does not by any means seem to understand what was originally meant by the term Exclusivism:

> Such was the divine simplicity of the principles on which we gathered at the first. The question then that comes here is simply this—Are these the principles on which we are gathered today? In many cases we fear the answer must be a decided "No!" While professing to be as "open" as ever, we cannot disguise the fact that in the course of the past twenty years a tightening process has been at work. We may not be able to explain how it has come to pass. But we have to do with the fact. It stares me in the face. The leaven of Exclusivism has been at work among the assemblies—yea, among those who abjure Exclusivism and all its works.

This tightening process, as he calls it, at last led to the development in Great Britain of the Needed Truth Party, a company maintaining that only those gatherings that acted together upon questions of reception, recognition of elderhood, believers' baptism, separation from all sects and denominations, including even other companies of Brethren, could be recognized as churches of God. Some of the statements of the Brethren who advocated these views are almost beyond belief. They took up the terms "within" and "without" used by the Apostle Paul in I Corinthians, the fifth chapter, and made the "within" apply wholly and solely to their particular meetings while the "without" referred, so they say, not to the ungodly but to Christian people, members of the body of Christ, who were not in the Needed Truth meetings. As it may seem almost incredible that such teaching could ever have become current, I give

a few quotations that will make it clear. J. A. Boswell, writing
on the "Kingdom Present," in *Needed Truth,* Volume 4, 147, says:

> It seems to us that it has in great measure been lost sight of,
> that God has a purpose not only through the individual testi-
> mony of His children—by their lives or the gospel from their
> lips, but also by the collective testimony of His gathered to-
> gether saints in accordance with His will. As we have already
> said, it is in the house of God, and in it we believe alone,
> that the government of God can be carried out in this age,—
> or in other words, the kingdom of God can be manifested. Let
> us not be misunderstood here. We do not say that Christians
> who are in the sects will not be eternally saved, as well as those
> gathered out, for the salvation of God reached to those who
> were outside the kingdom of Israel. The same today, but we
> do not believe that those ensnared by Satan in the many false
> systems of men *are in the kingdom of God,* or in the place
> where they can carry out the rule of God collectively on earth,
> that which Paul preached at Ephesus (Acts 20:25).

At a meeting of what were known as the elders of Great Britain,
the following six points were laid down to be accepted by all:

I. There is on earth a unique concrete thing (called in Acts
2:42 "the Fellowship") which consists of all those whom God
has brought together in a visible unity; the being in this is
conditional. It is quite distinct from the Body of Christ, the
church of Matthew 16.

II. The Fellowship finds its expression in churches of God;
and the churches are linked together in the Fellowship.

III. The existence of the present Fellowship does not admit
of a church of God coming into existence except in connection
with the already formed churches.

IV. It is the bounden duty of every man exercising oversight in the Fellowship to do his utmost to maintain the unity
of the Fellowship.

V. Does the responsibility to receive into or put out from
the circle of overseers reside in the circle of overseers in a town,
or in that of a county or district?

VI. When overseers in a given circle have a difficulty in
becoming of one mind in the Lord, the next larger circle of
overseers should come in to assist in producing the desired
oneness of mind.

Because the leaders from Scotland refused to accept points five and six, they were all cut off, thus making two rival confederacies of "churches of God." The Needed Truth division never got any real foothold on the American continent but similar teaching has been widely propagated, and there are, both in Canada and the United States many so-called Open Meetings that are in reality Needed Truth Meetings without the name. The following utterances from a Colonel W. Beers some years ago show what these meetings stand for:

> According to I Cor. 5:12, 13 God has a within and a without. Those within it is the prerogative of the assembly to judge, and bye and bye they will "judge the world" (I Cor. 6:2). Those "without" God judges: "therefore," says the apostle, "put away from among yourselves the wicked person," and since the Epistle is addressed to the church of God at Corinth, it is to that divine organization this command is given. Nowhere in the Word of God do we read of God, in the present age, judging unbelievers; they are condemned already; their judgment is future, and coming swiftly; but God is now judging His people only. See I Cor. 11:30-32; I Peter 1:17. Therefore when we read in the passage before us "them without God judgeth" (I Cor. 5:13) it is His people that we are referred to, and not unbelievers.

This teaching has made its way in many places and often with very sad results. People have been cast out of assemblies, not for any wickedness in life or evil in doctrine, but because they could not conscientiously endorse such extravagances. Instances have been known where believers were actually excluded from fellowship on the ground of *adultery* or *fornication,* and when they indignantly protested against such abominable accusations, they were calmly told that the sin consisted in having attended some meeting held for Christian testimony apart from the "Assemblies of God" and that to go to such a meeting was to be guilty of spiritual adultery, which was in God's sight worse than the carnal sin. I know of a specific instance where a godly brother was excommunicated as guilty of fornication because he preached, by invitation in a city mission. This, of course, is based upon the idea that all of Christendom has now gone into Babylon and these meetings of "gathered saints," alone are the house of God being rebuilt at the place of the Name!

It is surely a far cry from the beautiful simplicity of the early Brethrens' meetings to such pretentiousness as this.

In beautiful contrast, as it seems to the present writer, are the Catholic views set forth by the late J. R. Caldwell in "The Gathering and Receiving of Children of God," some extracts from which will help to clarify the questions under examination:

> It has been fully proved in the past that God does not own "high church" claims. In the providence of God, that which assumes to be, or even to represent, "the church of God on earth," has always been quickly proved to be wanting, and a very few years have sufficed to reduce it to fragments. So must it ever be, for God will never attach His power to that which assumes to be what it is not . . .
>
> It has also been contended that the very mention of a "within" and a "without" (I Cor. 5:12) involves a corporate and formal receiving into the church; but when we turn to the last glimpse historically of the church found in Scripture, namely, in III John, and find there the apostle John and the more spiritual of the saints "without" and Diotrephes and his followers "within," it is vain to assert now, when confusion has developed a thousandfold, that any circle of confederate assemblies forms a full and divinely recognized "within." As a matter of fact, the assertion is a mere assumption, and is disproved by the experience and testimony of very many who, though regarded by some as "outsiders," are really "inside," and enjoying richly the fellowship of the Father and the Son. This does not at all imply that the command to "put away from among yourselves that wicked person" is not as binding as ever, or that God will fail to give effect to such action when it is according to His Word, and carried out in faith and in the Holy Spirit. This God is able to do, and faith may count upon His faithfulness even in the midst of the existing confusion.
>
> Scriptural reception by the saints is personal and individual. It is on the ground of having been received already by God (see Rom. 14:3), and because "Christ hath received him" (Rom. 15:7). . .
>
> While Scripture lays down no rule of procedure in receiving, it is asserted that the reception of Paul at Jerusalem is typical, an example to be followed throughout the dispensation in every case. But is it not evident that the case of Paul, so far from being typical, was altogether exceptional? He very naturally,

drawn by love and desire for fellowship, assayed to join himself unto the disciples. Had it been an ordinary case of conversion, and no special circumstances known giving rise to suspicion, it seems clear that he would have had his place amongst them at once. But the saints were in fear of him: they supposed it was another ruse of the devil—they "believed not that he was a disciple." Hence the procedure adopted. Barnabas, with special knowledge of what the grace of God had wrought in Paul, knowing what all the rest were in ignorance of, set him before the apostles, assured that if they, the guides, were satisfied, no further hindrance would stand in the way of his fellowship with the saints.

But to assert that this procedure is necessary in the case of one who is well known to many as a genuine child of God, and against whose character no suspicion exists in the minds of any, is an absurdity that could only be entertained because it fits in with some theory not found in Scripture . . .

An expression in common use requires to be examined, and its use tested, namely, "the saints gathered to the name of the Lord." By this is meant a certain approved circle of assemblies to whom alone the title is applicable. Some claim it for one association of assemblies; others claim it for some other circle, but in each case it is an exclusive claim denied to all other saints or gatherings . . .

This use of the term "gathered to the name of the Lord" we have searched for in vain in Scripture. The expression betrays the thought that the object in view is a reconstruction of the church of God upon a new and narrow basis unknown to Scripture.

I may add that it should be remembered that many Exclusive Brethren have through the years become discouraged and even disgusted with the bewildering divisions among themselves and have sought a way out by going in among the Open Meetings. These have carried with them much that they had learned in their former associations and the result is that many Open Meetings are now much more like Exclusive Meetings than in past years. It will not, therefore, be cause for surprise that thousands of godly Brethren in all the various fellowships are looking longingly toward one another and crying to God to make plain some means whereby fellowship might be re-established between the different factions and that all together may present a united testimony in defense of the great fundamental truths for which all Brethren have stood from the beginning. With the various parties of Exclusives, this is comparatively an easy problem as, being more used to acting together, it is simply a matter of convincing leaders among them that there is no cause for further separation; but much more difficulty is experienced when it comes to negotiating with Open Brethren on account of their lack of organic union, and even if, in a given locality Open and Exclusive Brethren are able to come together and bury their differences, that does not necessarily affect Open Meetings in nearby places nor perhaps others in the same city.

CHAPTER TWELVE

AN ABORTIVE ATTEMPT AT RECONCILIATION

IN SPITE OF ALL the divisions and differences of judgment among the people of God there is a most blessed sense in which our Lord's prayer for His own "that they all may be one" has ever been answered. One in life and in family relationship they are. And because of this precious fact the renewed soul ever longs for the practical display of that unity with fellow-believers.

And, divided though the Brethren became, it has generally been leaders who have kept the sheep in the various separate corrals. Left to themselves they would soon flock together around the one Shepherd. So it becomes a real pleasure to be able to tell of an honest effort on the part of godly leaders toward mutual understanding, though it failed at the time to accomplish what was desired.

The Montreal division took place as we have seen in 1884. A few years later there developed among the so-called Grant Exclusives an uneasy feeling that their attitude toward Open Brethren was not entirely consistent with the position they themselves had been forced into through the operation of tyrannous ecclesiastical principles unwarranted by Scripture. Evangelists and teachers moving about among assemblies frequently came in contact with Christians from the Open meetings whose piety and general soundness in the faith they could not but recognize as being of a very high order. Was it right to go on treating such as wicked persons because they were supposed to be identified by association with something that had occurred in a distant land over forty years ago? A new generation, and even a second, had come on the scene since the unhappy Bethesda division. Was it to be for ever made a test of fellowship?

Both the Grants, Robert and Frederick, were keenly exercised about this, as were many other recognized leaders—both of those wholly given to the ministry of the Word and those having local oversight. Could Scripture—clear-cut definite passages from the Word of God. not hazy deductions labeled "divine principles"—be found to warrant continued exclusion of godly believers because blessing had come to them through the Word ministered by preachers in the Open, instead of the Exclusive, meetings? The Egyptian could enter into the congregation of the Lord in the third generation. What of fellow-members of Christ's body, holding similar teaching and walking largely in a similar path? Must they be excluded for ever?

Lord Chesterfield wisely said in one of his "Letters": "Individuals forgive sometimes, but bodies and societies never do." Even among Christians this often seems to be true. However, so real were the exercises referred to above that on Oct. 15, 1891, a letter was sent out by the "Grant" leaders to their own assemblies at home and abroad, and to Open Brethren also, inviting all who were interested to come to a general conference to be held in the following year at Plainfield, New Jersey, to consider the questions that separated them.

Even before this there had been much coming and going but without really cementing fellowship. Instead, suspicion was raised as to the integrity of those who, as some put it, "tried to play fast and loose with divine principles." And often Exclusives found themselves as unwelcome in Open meetings as the Opens were among Exclusives.

However, the letter referred to above was sent out and saints were asked to spend much time in prayer before the proposed conference, which was scheduled to convene in July, 1892. It was felt that there would be great opposition in some quarters and there was a danger of hasty action in others, so in the letter they inserted the following paragraphs:

> And now, beloved brethren, the object of this letter is to inform you of this, and at the same time earnestly and affectionately to entreat you to a patient waiting upon God during this interval. . . . We feel constrained, dear brethren, in all love, earnestly to entreat you not to take any hasty or independent action whatever in this connection. Our earnest desire is that we may all look at it together.

The desire was for a happy unanimity of judgment.

The letter brought joy to many, but numbers were distrustful. Among Open Brethren, leaders like Donald Ross, Donald Munro, John Smith and others, refused to attend, but drew up a letter declaring their adherence to Scriptural principles and sent it on to the meetings. Mr. J. H. Burridge from Great Britain came to speak for the Open Meetings and many local Brethren from these gatherings attended. Upwards of a thousand brethren, Open and Closed, came together at the appointed time and after ten days of frank brotherly conference the following letter was sent out as giving the judgment of the meeting.

PLAINFIELD, July 12, 1892.

TO THE BRETHREN IN THE LORD WHOM IT CONCERNS: GREETING.

In response to the call sent forth to brethren to assemble here to consider the questions in connection with our relation to (so-called) "open" brethren, a large number came together. We would thankfully recognize the Lord's grace in enabling us to feel our dependence upon as well as our responsibility to Him, with love also to those that are His people. Several days were devoted to the consideration of the matter from all sides, and free expression of judgment was given. The following conclusions were accepted with great unanimity, for which we give thanks to God.

As to their condition, proofs were given that there is no present association with evil doctrine, and this both from those amongst them and others outside. An authoritative circular from leaders amongst them in this country, agrees with the testimony of some well acquainted with them at Bethesda, Bristol, England, as well as elsewhere, that this is the case.

The *"Letter of the Ten"* has been, from the time when it was put forth to the present, a main hindrance to communion. In this it was stated that, supposing a teacher "were fundamentally heretical, this would not warrant us in rejecting those who came under his teaching, until we were satisfied that they had understood and *imbibed* views essentially subversive of foundation-truth." It is, however, stated by the leaders in Bethesda, "We do not mean that any would be allowed to return to a heretical teacher. He would become subject to discipline by doing so. Our practice proves this. We had no thought of intercommunion with persons coming from a heretical teacher when that sentence was written."

In the same way Mr. Wright's letter, at a much more recent date, affirming upon the face of it the same principle with the *"Letter of the Ten,"* has been explained not to mean inter-communion.

We dare not say that we accept these statements as really satisfactory; and there are still others, as in E. K. Groves' more recent book *("Bethesda Family Matters,"* p. 133), which show, to our sorrow, that all among them are not yet clear. Yet the late statement from leaders in this country, accepted by those in Bethesda itself, together with the testimony from all sides as to their actual present condition and practice necessitate our acceptance of the conclusion, in the "love that thinketh no evil," that looseness in this respect does not now exist. There are doubtless gatherings still "open" in this unhappy way, but from these we have every reason to believe that the brethren to whom we refer are really separate. In this belief, which it is a joy to be permitted to entertain, we shall be able to welcome them among us, as we do other Christians.

We only regret to have to express our inability to go further; the insistence upon certain views of baptism hindering the liberty of the Spirit in ministry, and which becomes thus in our judgment, a grave evil; questions also as to the past still remaining, with other matters of real importance, compel us, at present, to stop here. But we are thankful to be able to go thus far, and to show our sincere desire to take all hindrances to genuine Christian fellowship out of the way, as far as we can justly do it.

In conclusion, we feel for ourselves the necessity of much prayer and patience, and great respect for one another's consciences, that these desires for unity may not be used by the enemy to foster further division. "Whereto we have already attained, let us walk by the same rule, let us mind the same thing" (Phil. 3:16). "Let us therefore follow after the things which make for peace, and things wherewith one may edify another" (Rom. 14:19).

> B. C. GREENMAN,
> SAMUEL RIDOUT,
> F. W. GRANT,
>   *and others.*

Some among the Grant Brethren viewed this letter with alarm and felt it was the beginning of what would eventually be a complete surrender to independent principles. Others hailed it with delight as indicating that the divisions would soon come to an end and happy fellowship be enjoyed together. Open Brethren generally felt it did not go far enough and were disappointed. But others among them were grateful to God that it went as far as it did, and hoped it would lead to a better understanding and fuller fellowship in the future.

Some Exclusives felt the decision had been hastily arrived at, forgetting apparently the months of prayer that had preceded it.

In several cities efforts were made to go beyond the circular by combining the Open and Exclusive meetings, but with few exceptions the results were unsatisfactory and the attempt even led to greater distrust of each other. The two classes of Brethren had been apart so long and had been trained in such different schools that they found it hard to lay aside preconceived notions and walk together in the love of the Spirit.

In Great Britain, the Bahamas and New Zealand pronounced opposition developed. Mr. William Rickard, a much respected English brother, editor of *Words in Season,* a monthly publication of considerable merit, wrote expostulating with American Brethren for their haste in committing themselves to a position which Old Country assemblies could not endorse. I have been unable to find a copy of his letter but its contents can be gathered in great measure from the following lengthy answer which I give in full because of the vast amount of information it contains:

To our brother, Mr. Rickard, and those Brethren who signed the late Circular with him:

Beloved Brethren: In owning receipt of your letter of Oct. 1st, 1892, and before referring to the main subject therein considered, we would explain that it was through no oversight or carelessness on our part that you were not at once fully and directly informed as to the result of our meeting here on July 12th. Twenty-five copies of our circular were forwarded at once to our brother Blatchley, and must have unaccountably miscarried. We regret that this should have happened; but we trust, dear brethren, that this explanation will show that we had no thought of keeping you "in the dark," as you speak.

With reference to your next complaint that no "representative brethren of the United Kingdom were present," we certainly felt quite sure of the fellowship and sympathy of at least one brother, and even up to the last moment expected his presence, which we should sincerely have welcomed; but if we have failed in not making our invitations more general, we can only ask you to forgive us.

Recognizing your right to receive full information and satisfaction as to our action in the recent gathering at Plainfield with regard to our relation with so-called "open" brethren, we desire to give you this to the utmost of our ability, as sincerely desirous of the maintenance of fellowship in truth and holiness.

We do not believe that our principles have changed in any wise. They resolve themselves, as far as we are now concerned with them, into the responsibility to "endeavor to keep the unity of the Spirit in the bond of peace"—the *living* unity of the church of God; therefore in separation from evil, as what destroys this. This separation we hold, as we did before, to be from all fundamental error, as well as moral wickedness, and from those knowingly in association with these. Upon this ground, we had refused those in fellowship with open brethren, as "open" to receive from gatherings infected with false doctrine. And this was, as to those so-called in America, most certainly true that they were so in the past.

But a change has come with the advent of certain evangelists and leaders, principally from Scotland, who disclaim having ever been upon this loose ground. The old gatherings were either repudiated or purged from the evil, and others sprang up, and are springing up in various places, with which the old and Scriptural test failed to show evil. The question was raised, and more and more pressed upon us, how could we maintain the old attitude toward those who, while still called "open brethren," were in fact another people from those formerly known as such.

But there was still a link that remained, as we believed, with evil, not here, but in England,—the link with Bethesda,—a name of distress and reproach among us for many years, and as to which we believed we had recent testimony of unsoundness, above all in Mr. Wright's letter. This for a time held us back from any general clearing, even of these newly formed gatherings, from the charge of complicity with evil.

We are now, however, in a different position. First of all, we have a statement, concurred in by a number of their leaders in America, expressly repudiating fellowship with those in as-

sociation with evil. Then, a letter from D. D. Chrystal, formerly
in our own fellowship, as to Bethesda's present position being
in accordance with this. Of another from Col. Molesworth to
the same effect we have no copy. Another statement from
forty-eight leaders of the open brethren in England, extracted
from *"What are the Facts?"* published by Hawkins of London,
is not perhaps so explicit, but still repudiates "all identification
with unsound doctrine" such as they name. Another testimony
was given by a brother, J. H. Burridge, from among them,
present at the meeting, who assured us that he had personally
inquired into the looseness charged against them in W. K.'s
tract, and found that the meeting in question was not in fellowship. A letter from our brother, W. Scott, also read at the
conference, acquits them of any present fellowship with evil.
All that we know as to America agrees with this.

The explanation of the *"Letter of the Ten"* was unsatisfactory,
and many of us were unable to believe that it could be rightfully interpreted as not meaning inter-communion; but the
"pastors and elders" who gave the interpretation to "Philadel-
phos" (Mr. Bewley) were not perhaps any of those who had
written the letter. Mr. Wright's, of later date than either,
showed clearly to us remains of the old spirit, and yet was
taken by them with the same reserve, that there could be no
inter-communion with heretical meetings. As to their practice,
they invite personal visitation and examination on the part of
some accredited persons; and in all this, however evident it may
be that the old failure has not been judged as one desires, yet
it is clear that the mercy of God has come in, and the evil is
not there in present activity. In individuals, it may not be re-
pented of; but as a body, even in Bethesda itself, the open
brethren are committed against fellowship with evil; and it
surely should be a "joy" to believe that this is so.

Can we accept this testimony! How is it possible to refuse
it? It is not merely their own, but that of others as to them.
They give it openly, challenging examination. You, beloved
brethren, do not show that it is false. And, indeed, who ever
heard of a large body of Christians, numbers of them allowed
to be most earnest and devoted, putting forth as their principles
and practice what all amongst them must know to be false and
deceptive? We might well lose faith in the power of the gospel
over men's hearts and lives if this could be. Does the Lord
require us to go behind this? Is not sufficient witness to be

received? And this is the witness of thousands practically, who by their silence at least agree with it. Are we not bound in the "love that thinketh no evil," to receive it?

The blot upon the past can scarcely now be removed. It may be turned even to profit, if it rebuked the Pharisaism so tending to rise up, and which has, we must fear, sadly marred our own later history. May not God even thus make the last first? And are we to refuse, on account of a blot like this, Christians personally as godly as any, who were not themselves implicated in the Bethesda trouble, and *whose principles and practice,* as regards this attitude toward evil, *are as pure as our own?* Is it not to be sectarian to do so?

Does this reception of individuals mean that of the whole? It is said they are on the ground of the one body, and so we have no option! Some of themselves most earnestly deny that they are on the ground of the one body, and this principle has been stamped by a leader among them as the first "heresy" into which those who leave them for the "exclusives" fall, the second being household baptism. Would that they could show us, or that they *cared* to show us, that they are not rather a Baptist body with at least independent principles, though more or less "open" as to communion! But they are brethren—children of God, as we, to whom our hearts should quicken as such, and who are making a firm stand now against the false doctrines and unbelief at present so fearfully spreading; and if compared with other Christians round about, we shall find them nearer to us than any outside of the other bodies of so-called "brethren," which, to the loss and shame of all, are broken asunder from one another. Should it not be "joy" to us to be *able,* by recognizing the change referred to in our brethren, to get back to the simple ground on which we once were, and to find a path which will not turn even the feet of the lame out of the way? Should it not be "joy" to be able *rightfully* to throw down any existing barriers to fellowship among those who once were united, and to say, "Brethren, the sin shall not be ours of dividing the body of Christ: let us walk the rest of the way together"?

In all this, we do not believe that we are giving up principles. Perhaps the Lord is teaching us more that, after all, we are in days of ruin, and that, as those self-judged before him, we must carry those out in tenderness and grace more than we have done. Of some amid dead Sardis the Lord Himself says, "They have not defiled their garments." How is it that, with us, just those spiritually nearest akin to us are those who, in the breaches that have taken place, are to be most religiously refused and turned away from? May He turn our hearts to one another, and Judah vex Ephraim no more! What a promise of blessing yet for us would be in this!

Show us, however, that the open brethren are not what they profess to be—that they do, in principle as well as in practice, let in evil,—then, with whatever pain, we shall be compelled to retrace our steps. Show us gatherings acknowledged as in fellowship with Bethesda, Bristol, which are in this way guilty, not of mistake and failure, but of willful wickedness of this kind, and from which they will not purge themselves, and you will have done us essential service, for which we shall be most thankful. If these cannot be found, how can we be leavened by contact with that which, according to the best judgment we can make of it *is not itself leavened?*

And this brings us, beloved brethren, to your closing sentences, in which you pronounce "judgment" and "condemnation" upon us for what you term "a new departure," and which you tell us is a "dishonor to Christ," a "denial of the truth of the one body," "another secession from the true ground of the church of God." Solemn words! and although of late years, we fear, far too frequently and lightly spoken, still such as can never be heard by any to whom "the light of his countenance is better than life," and who know, too, something of their own feebleness, without serious consideration and heart-searching. But if they are not lightly to be *heard,* even far less are they to be lightly *spoken*; and awful indeed must be the error, grave indeed the sin, that could justify your charging us with dishonoring our blessed Lord Jesus Christ, with denying the truth of the one body, with seceding from the ground of the church of God! Surely nothing less than our hands joined with corrupt doctrine or evil practice,—some willful association with wickedness by which we have become wicked and corrupt. Is there a word in your letter to show this? No, you do not; and, in the fear of God, we say you *cannot* find grounds for such charges against your brethren. Instead of this, you reason in this way:—

(*a*) "Here is a sentence, written nearly fifty years ago, involving a wicked principle of association with evil."

(b) "This has never been repudiated, withdrawn, or even modified."

(c) "You, in opening the door of fellowship to any who are in any way connected with the gathering where this sentence was written, partake of the evil it embodies, and—we cannot follow you."

This reasoning, dear brethren, is not only weak, but false. Your conclusion depends upon your premises, and if the latter be incorrect, the former must necessarily be so too. The principle of evil association involved in the sentence quoted from the *"Letter of the Ten"* has been repudiated again and again, as we have shown you above. Even your own quotation—"We do not mean that any would be allowed to return to a heretical teacher. He would become subject to discipline by doing so," etc.—is sufficient to show how wrong is your statement that it has not been "even modified." Surely, but a very little measure of the love that "thinketh no evil," that "believeth all things, that hopeth all things," would see a very important *modification*, at least, in these words, and we would venture, as brethren, to press this a little upon you. But in our judgment, it speaks even more than simple modification; and, when we remember that it is now forty-five years since the original letter was penned, and that leaven must from its nature, have spread through and through Bethesda, and far and wide in those connected with her, in that time, surely you can have no difficulty in showing us clear proof of this;—if not, (and we can speak with some authority for this side, that you cannot,) is it not again proof that your statement that "it has never been repudiated or even modified" is incorrect?

Upon better consideration, therefore, we may trust that you will find the judgment you pronounce as to this matter to have been at least premature, and will be happy in withdrawing it. Give us only the proof of present evil sanctioned by those whom our circular simply restores to the common rights of Christians, and we will be with you heartily in the judgment of it. Apart from this, to cut off the members of Christ's body, would not this be really to secede from the ground of the church of God, and grieve and dishonor Him whose prayer for His own is, "that they all may be one"?

With true love in Him, believe us, dear brethren, ever yours in bonds that cannot be broken—

Signed,—	In behalf of the gathering at
JAMES BROWN, G. H. GRAHAM,	New York.
JAMES CARR, EDWARD G. MAUGER,	South Brooklyn.
H. E. LAMPE, PAUL S. COHN, S. NORSWORTHY,	Rutherford, New Jersey.
C. MARTY, C. NELSEN,	Passaic, New Jersey.
F W. GRANT, T. O. LOIZEAUX,	Plainfield, New Jersey.
J. T. McFALL, JOHN F. GRAY, JOHN F. GILMORE,	East Brooklyn.

Writing about the same time to some in the Bahamas who were troubled, Mr. F. W. Grant pertinently said:

> What could we do but withdraw charges we believed no longer truthful? Surely there was no alternative if we would retain uprightness ourselves. Our brethren who reject the circular cannot (we believe) put their finger upon one gathering today in admitted fellowship with Bethesda, Bristol, and which is "open" to receive fundamental evil. Certainly they do not attempt it. If the thing were true, it could hardly help being (at the present time) notorious. *A door is not long left open for evil without evil being found to enter in at the door.*
>
> But our brethren urge that as to the past, Bethesda has not cleared herself. We wish much we *could* say that in our belief she had, but we have not been able to say this. We fear there are those connected with her at this day that are not clear; and that the original false step never has been openly judged we know. But that was taken a generation since; and the principles involved being refused by them today, the mass cannot be charged with that with which they had nothing to do, and which in any evil sense of it they do not uphold. All agree that there are among open brethren thousands of godly souls.

> Is it of God to cut off wholesale these godly ones? Surely, surely, Scripture cannot be produced for this.

This is all plain and distinct, and seems to be the utterance of one who had thoroughly investigated the whole matter and was clear before God as to his course.

Some will be amazed to learn that inside of a year afterwards, not only Mr. Grant, but many of the others, who signed the letter to Mr. Rickard, had completely reversed themselves. What led to this will be taken up in the next chapter.

CHAPTER THIRTEEN

THE ATTEMPT AT UNION THWARTED

IT HAS BEEN pointed out already that from the first, there were leaders among the "Grant" Brethren who did not look with favor upon the effort to reconcile Open and Exclusive Brethren. Mr. Paul J. Loizeaux, the able evangelist whose fiery eloquence had made him the outstanding preacher in this particular section of the movement, dreaded any apparent lowering of the standard and shrank from re-opening a question which it was felt the fathers had settled. Yet his sense of fairness, was such that once an attempt was determined upon he entered into it heartily, placed his beautiful grounds at the disposal of the Brethren as a meeting place and personally bore a large share of the expense, far more than one in his position might seem well able to afford. When the Plainfield decision was arrived at he accepted it, though with misgivings, and sought to act upon it until he felt convinced of its impracticability. Others shared his exercises and pursued a "policy of watchful waiting."

A protest couched in no uncertain terms was soon forthcoming from the Stuart or Reading Meetings as we have seen, who wrote a solemn letter charging American Brethren with ignoring many facts of importance, acting hastily and on faulty information. This letter insisted on the unchanged character of Bethesda and declared that the fact that the *Letter of the Ten* had not been withdrawn or its principles repudiated, made fellowship impossible.

Mr. J. H. Burridge who had appeared at Plainfield to speak on behalf of Open Brethren gave out the following statement in regard to Bethesda which re-assured some troubled ones but did not go far enough for others:

> 1st. Bethesda gathering has had no fellowship with Mr. Newton from the time of the seven church meetings in which his heresy was considered very fundamental.

2d. No intercommunion of those meetings with Mr. Newton has ever been allowed.

3d. Hundreds of the Lord's people have been kept by grace in happy harmony and fellowship together without division for nearly fifty years.

4th. Though during this time she has been the object of attack from all parts; brethren have tried again and again, but in vain, to fix the charge of unscriptural looseness and heresy upon her; but it has never been proven. May she not forget that she is still dependent upon the same grace that has kept her.

5th. Though to our shame be it said, the company known as exclusives have been shattered into half a dozen pieces. May our gracious Lord gather us more undividedly around Himself!

6th. At the present time Bethesda has about thirteen hundred in fellowship who meet in four different meeting rooms, and over twenty brothers laboring in foreign mission work, and for the last ten years has proved to be a place of refuge for many an exclusive brother distracted and perplexed by division and strife.

7th. Any brother or brothers may visit Bethesda to see for themselves if the above is not true.

Mr. Walter Scott of Hamilton, Scotland, widely known as a teacher of repute, came over to America in 1893 to verbally back up the protest of English and Scotch Brethren against any recognition of the Open assemblies. He was armed with a multitude of documents which seemed to show that these meetings were honeycombed with moral and doctrinal evil, and he practically threatened a complete disruption between the Grant and Stuart Brethren unless the action of the Plainfield conference was rescinded.

This opposition was at first firmly met and with seeming decision by F. W. Grant and others of prominence. They insisted that ample time had been allowed to produce any such evidence in the months' interval between the printed call to Plainfield and the conference itself, and that it was neither fair nor honorable to bring it forward at so late a date, unless indeed new facts had come to light that were not available earlier. On the other hand they felt a statement was due their Brethren to allay suspicion and distrust, and to make clear just what their attitude was, so the following letter was drafted and sent far and wide:

New York, JUNE 1st, 1893.

TO OUR BRETHREN IN CHRIST, IN ENGLAND AND ELSEWHERE, GATHERED WITH US TO THE NAME OF THE LORD JESUS.

BELOVED BRETHREN:

In view of the evident misapprehension on the part of many brethren in this country and elsewhere, as to the meaning and intent of the Plainfield Circular of last July (which we are free to admit was imperfectly expressed), it was deemed advisable to have a conference of brethren in these parts, to consider the subject and express a judgment as to the result of the Plainfield meeting, and the true meaning and object of the circular.

Accordingly such a conference was held on the afternoon of Tuesday the 30th ult.

It was agreed that intercommunion with those in fellowship with Bethesda—or Open Brethren, so called—was *not* contemplated so long as *The Letter of the Ten* with its evil principles was unjudged and allowed to stand. At the same time, godly persons, unintelligent as to their associations, ought not to be denied fellowship amongst us should they desire it.

This action is found especially necessary from the fact that certain laboring brethren from amongst us have construed the matter differently, by fellowshiping with "Open" gatherings, practically denying that there has been occasion for division in the past, and assuming that the evil principles of Bethesda have been really judged, which we should be only too happy to learn, but of which we are sorry to say there exists no evidence.

We also generally feel that we have allowed ourselves to go too far in fellowshiping certain persons from among them, giving thereby cause for the alarm which some have taken.

Humbled through the events which have transpired among us of late years, we sincerely desire to increase in love toward *all* our brethren in Christ, whatever ecclesiastical position they may occupy. At the same time we realize that these are no times to grow slack, but contrariwise, increase in vigilance, remembering the promise and the warning, "Behold, I come quickly: hold that fast which thou hast, that no man take thy crown" (Rev. 3:11).

> E. G. MAUGER, South Brooklyn.
> JAMES BROWN, New York.
> F. W. GRANT, Plainfield, New Jersey.
> W. S. HERON, South Brooklyn.

GEORGE BEZER, South Brooklyn.
JOHN F. GILMORE, Brooklyn, E. D.
H. E. LAMPE, Rutherford, New Jersey.
C. JOUARD, New York.
JULIUS OVERBURY, Orange, New Jersey.
A. McGILCHRIST, New York.
JAMES MANAHAN, Jersey City, New Jersey.
G. H. McCANDLESS, Elizabeth, New Jersey.
JAMES WELSH, Elizabeth, New Jersey.
W. S. ROLSTON, Elizabeth, New Jersey.
T. O. LOIZEAUX, Plainfield, New Jersey.
PAUL J. LOIZEAUX, Plainfield, New Jersey.

Shortly afterwards a statement was sent to America, signed by representative Open Brethren in Great Britain endeavoring to make clear their position in regard to the much-discussed *Letter of the Ten,* which many trusted would have settled the entire controversy. I give it in full:

STATEMENT

It has been suggested that brief statement on the subject of fellowship of saints might, with God's blessing, prove helpful towards "keeping the unity of the Spirit in the bond of peace," and therefore we gladly mention a few points with a view of removing misapprehensions from the minds of any believers, especially in America, and we trust that this statement will be received with the same sincerity with which we make it.

1. Those commonly known as "open" brethren only seek to maintain liberty to carry out all the will of God, as unfolded in the Scriptures, and to receive all believers who are not plainly disqualified by the Word of God, because of evil doctrine or immoral practice.

2. Intercommunion is not permitted with assemblies where the false doctrine of annihilation or other fundamental error is tolerated.

3. Although cases of reception of persons holding such false doctrines have been alleged, they have not been substantiated when proof was requested.

4. On the contrary, cases have now and again occurred (though we are thankful to say not frequently) in which persons holding such doctrines have been put away from fellowship.

5. When Christians who are sound and careful as to fundamental truths, but without sufficient light to renounce a sectarian position, desire to break bread, as being of the one body, and are permitted to do so, we believe that it is on the ground that each one is responsible to Christ as Lord of the conscience and in the hope that by remembering with them the love wherewith all His members are loved they may be helped to learn the way of God more perfectly.

6. Though ourselves conscious of much shortcoming it is our desire to carry out our Lord's Word, "He that doeth truth cometh to the light." We do not strive to make a party, but we endeavor to hold the Head, and we trust that where there is a similar aim, misconception regarding us, though of long standing, will be removed. The name of our Lord Jesus will thereby be glorified, we shall receive mutual comfort and help and the father of lies be defeated.

7. With regard to difference of judgment on points not involving vital doctrines, we seek to give ourselves to humiliation and prayer, knowing that God would have us to be of one mind, while exercising forbearance with one another and carrying out our convictions as to the truth.

8. We must add that we do not attach our signatures as representing the assemblies with which we are connected, but, rather as those who have had more or less lengthened experience, we give according to our personal knowledge the information that is desired.

Finally. We would love and serve all who unfeignedly love our Lord Jesus Christ, and would cultivate fellowship with all who aim at walking in the truth, and, though declining controversy on this subject, some of us will gladly reply to any brotherly enquiry, so far as time allows.

    C. UNDERWOOD — For over 40 years in fellowship at Orchard Street and Welbeck Street, London.

    JOHN C. McVICKER—Now of Clapton Hall, London. For over 30 years among those known as "open" brethren.

    GEORGE MUELLER—Ashley Down, Bristol.

    G. FRED BERGIN — For over 30 years in fellowship at Cork, Cardiff and Bristol.

    JAMES WRIGHT—For 50 years in fellowship in "Bethesda," Bristol.

HENRY DYER—For 50 years meeting with fellow saints to the name of the Lord, namely: from 1843 to 1848 at Rawstorne Street, London, and elsewhere, and from 1848 till now, to the same name of the Lord, with those known as "open" brethren, Bournemouth, Hants.

J. L. MACLEAN—Bath.

THOMAS COCHRAN—Patrick, Glasgow.

JOHN R. CALDWELL—Glasgow.

F. C. BLAND—5 Upper Fitzwilliam Street, Dublin.

MARTIN SHAW—Belfast, in fellowship from 1860 (part of the time, 1863, in Dublin).

ROBERT E. SPARKS—Belfast, in fellowship for 26 years.

W. H. BENNET—Yeovil.

To this was added a personal explanation by the godly and esteemed W. H. Bennet of Yeovil, the last of the signatories:

If there is anything I can say to help our brethren whose consciences are troubled by false statements, and who are not sufficiently acquainted with us to know that they are false, I would be glad to do so.

But may I again draw your attention to the statement dated February 9th, 1894, and signed by several brethren?

No. 1 and No. 3 clearly state that we only receive "believers who are not plainly disqualified by the Word of God because of evil doctrine or immoral practice," and that any who make allegations to the contrary have not been able to substantiate such allegations "when proof was requested."

But is not No. 2 as clear on the question of *association?* It says, "Intercommunion is not permitted with assemblies where the false doctrine of annihilation or *other* fundamental error is tolerated."

If this assertion had been received with the candor with which we made it, ought it not to have settled the question? What is understood by "intercommunion"? Does it not denote *receiving from* and *going to* or *commending to* any meeting? Then if we *specified* "annihilation" only, it is because that is the doctrine which has been more often referred to of late; but we were careful to say *"other* fundamental error" in order to make it inclusive. That this clause refers definitely to assemblies that profess to be gathered to the Lord's name, on what is called church ground, should such be found tolerating "fundamental error," ought, I think to be evident, because it is in No. 5 that we refer to the mode of dealing with "Christians who are sound and careful as to fundamental truths; but without sufficient light to renounce a sectarian position."

We have no desire, dear brother, to seek "self-justification." That we have been indifferent in the matter of association with evil, we *cannot* allow; but whenever any beloved brethren who had charged us with this, have, by patient and honest investigation, discovered that they had been mistaken and have met us before the Lord, they have found us as ready to bow in confession and self-judgment as they themselves were, and far indeed from seeking to "fasten sin or failure" upon them. And if some will not thus meet us, but persist in refusing to give us credit for common truthfulness in our statements, we seek rather to humble ourselves before God than cherish hard thoughts of them.

With love in our Lord,
Yours affectionately in Him,
W. H. BENNET.

Before these letters were actually in the hands of the American Brethren another grave barrier was raised up in the publication of a paper by a Mr. H. G. Holborow, of Selsley, Gloucestershire, England, designed to allay the fears of those who were not sure but that evil teaching as to Christ had been definitely held by Mr. Henry Craik, so long associated with Mr. George Muller at Bethesda. It had been reported at the time of the Newton difficulty that Mr. Craik had said that our Lord's humanity was of such a character that he would have died of old age, or if he had drunk a cup of poison —thoughts abhorrent to the Scripture-taught mind—as He Himself so distinctly affirmed His death to be voluntary in the solemn words, "No man taketh my life from me, but I lay it down of myself."

As the calumny in regard to Mr. Craik had been repeated by many who had never taken the trouble to investigate it, Mr. Holborow evidently considered it due to the memory of this departed brother to clear him of such imputation. But he was unfortunate in his effort, owing probably to his unfamiliarity with the theological terms, for he left the distinct impression upon the minds of his readers that he personally considered the body of the Lord on earth as mortal, or subject to death. I cannot find a copy of his pamphlet at this time, but the answer to it sent out by Mr. R. T. Grant entitled *Some Remarks on Mr. Holborow's Doctrine* indicates by direct quotations the error into which he had inadvertently fallen:

SOME REMARKS ON MR. HOLBOROW'S DOCTRINE

It is a little strange that a pamphlet sent out to prove the justice of Bethesda's cause should need, in the very part which refers to doctrine, to be patched with the pen so extensively, after being printed. I refer, of course, to one entitled *Correspondence about Bethesda in 1892,* and being circulated in the hope of justifying the position taken by O. B. (That is, Open Brethren, Ed.).

To one or two points in it I desire to call attention, and to the sad fact that Mr. Holborow's statements are extremely bad, and defective, to use the mildest term possible, where they ought to enunciate the truth emphatically. I fancy that many of the Lord's dear people who are in fellowship with Bethesda, will hardly feel very comfortable, as they read what Mr. H. says in defense of his party. The accusation brought by Mr. Rickard reads thus:

"But what do we find was taught by the man whose name appears first to the *Letter of the Ten,* Mr. H. Craik? 'If the Lord Jesus had taken poison, would he not have died?' Another says of him, 'We have heard, and we do believe, a shameful, irreverential, and vile expression attributed to Mr. Craik.' Mr. Trotter says of him, 'What he says there of the Lord's humanity, leaves no room for doubt that he does, to a great extent, sympathize with Mr. N.'s unsound views.' Mr. Wigram, in *An Appeal,* page 8, thus writes:

"He (Mr. Craik) said with great warmth the other day, that J. N. D. and his followers made too much of the humanity of the Lord Jesus, and that he believed if the Lord had not been crucified, He would have lived to be a shrivelled old man, and have died a *natural death;* and more to a similar effect."

On page 10, and paragraph 35, Mr. Holborow says, after some words of extenuation, speaking of Mr. Craik: "He never admitted that he had been correctly reported, but explained he *uttered the phrases in question* in opposition to assertions which appeared to him to involve a denial that Jesus Christ came in flesh, and was perfectly human as well as Son of God." The italics are mine, and making all due allowance for what is said in the first part of the sentence, the words italicized, involve an acknowledgment that in substance he said what was imputed to him. (But see note * below, Ed.)

In paragraph 36 Mr. H. begins his defense of the statements, and I would call attention to the Scriptures he refers to: first as to Heb. 2:17, evidently the Spirit of God would teach by these words, "being made like unto his brethren," that in his life of suffering, and on the cross, He who by title was exempt from it all, underwent what gave Him His acquired perfectness, or fitness for the place which He fills for us with God. Always perfect, He yet had to be perfected, and the latter through suffering; yet nothing of this involves the idea of what Mr. H. asserts of the Lord's humanity being "identical with ours." These last are Mr. H.'s words, but the need of some correction has been felt, and with a pen is added, "as God made ours." He is not satisfied with "veritable flesh and blood" (page 180), which Mr. R. uses to state his view of the Lord's person; but insists it was "veritably identical with ours," the danger of which statement was felt evidently when with the pen some corrector has added, "as God made ours."

With Mr. Holborow *"being made like* unto his brethren" is taken for identity in nature, whilst it evidently refers to something entirely different. The "brethren" are fallen, sinful men, and to be made like them in the sense in which he would have the passage taken, would *involve* what no one who loves the Lord Jesus truly could accept. I do not say Mr. H. would allow such a thing or tolerate the thought, but his view of the passage is dangerous in the extreme, and involves it.

A lot of unhappy reasoning follows (page 180) as to what *could have happened,* but unfortunately all these things only help to hinder clear seeing for simple souls, and one fatal defect is that they leave out and ignore the character and ways of God. It is *not true* that God *could* have sent these marks of age and infirmity upon the Lord Jesus, nor the things of which Mr. Craik spoke, and one has to ask what makes these brethren write so, as to the Holy One of God, if there is not something radically unsound in their views? Why speak of things as possible to Him, which were only possible to a sinner? The Scripture pictures the Lord Jesus growing up from infancy to perfect maturity, manifesting at each step and in every circumstance,

* It was afterwards proven that what Mr. Craik really said was that if it had been the will of God the Lord might thus have died. But it is a pity such a subject was ever broached.

His own inherent perfection, and there it stops; and to say that anything else could have happened is to involve the Lord in the consequences of the fall, and one wonders how one who owes his salvation to the humiliation of the Son of God, can do other than reject with indignation such unholy trifling. Referring to the Lord's body after death Mr. H. asks: "Why does he say, 'Neither wilt thou suffer thine Holy One to see corruption,' concerning the Lord's body, if before there could have been natural decay its very nature must be changed?" "Is not the interposition of God here clearly indicated?" he adds. The answer is simple and evident, that is, that the Lord had given himself up to the judgment of sin as the Substitute for others and had been brought by the holy hand of God down to the dust of death, the consequence and penalty of sin. When all had been done that was needed to satisfy the claims of divine righteousness and glory, the answer came in the power of God raising Him from the dead. Thus was fulfilled the Scripture, and thus was secured God's glory, and no indignity was permitted, nor could be, that was not absolutely necessary for the work accomplished; to this the character of God was pledged, even to the providing the new tomb of the rich man wherein never man had been laid; according to Isaiah 53:9, and to use the words of the Holy Spirit as to the dead body of Christ, "Thou wilt not suffer thine Holy One to see corruption," to justify Mr. Craik's assertions, is a sad proof of what has to be defended.

Does Mr. H. not know that the things named as possible to the Lord, could not even have happened to an obedient Israelite, if such could have been found? Decay is the way to death and dissolution, and can only be the consequence of sin. Yet Mr. H. says (page 18): "Mr. Craik's statements involve no imputation of sin to Christ, nothing impossible to the humanity of our Lord. (! !): but he was wrong in predicting such things *would* without his authority." Then Mr. Craik did predict they would happen, and Mr. Holborow undertakes to defend and extenuate such expressions! Is there no leaven at work in Bethesda? Saying such things *would* come on the Holy One of God then is no serious outrage upon the person of the Lord for "he (Mr. R.) has to prove Mr. C. a heretic before he can talk about 'Craik's heresies' (page 18). But if this is not counted heresy by Mr. H. he asserts at the end of the same paragraph that those who hold the doctrine maintained by Mr. R. as to the Lord's person would not be suffered in fellowship at Bethesda! ! A reference to page 17 will show what it is Mr. H. thus stigmatizes as Gnosticism and which would therefore be refused.*

But I turn back to consider a moment the second of Mr. H.'s quotations from Hebrews 11 (page 10, paragraph 36): "Forasmuch then as the children are partakers of flesh and blood, he also himself likewise took part of the same," etc. To this Mr. H. adds, "and you cannot deny that the statements Mr. Craik made are true of his brethren; it is just as wrong to deny them as to assert them"; "for with God all things are possible," is added here in ink in the copy I have before me. What does this mean? These things are true of his brethren, and the passage is quoted from Hebrews to preface the sentence, and it is "as *wrong to deny* the assertions attributed to Mr. Craik; and Mr. C. was just as wrong in asserting them." I am perplexed to know what to understand here, but I leave it with the reader to unravel the knot, and content myself with the thought that if it was true it would not be wrong to assert it, nor if false to deny it; and it is either true or a *very grave* departure from the truth.

It is unhappy for Mr. H.'s doctrine, but an unspeakable comfort for those who do not tolerate what, if followed to its legitimate results, would put a blemish on the Holy One of God, that neither of the passages he relies on afford the least foundation for what they are cited in support of, but the opposite. If the reader will turn to Hebrews 11:14 and look it up in the Greek Testament, there will be seen something of the care of the Spirit of God in guarding against such irreverent notions. The children were *partakers* of flesh and blood "and he also himself *took part* of same." Now two different words are used in this passage. The children are *partakers* of flesh and blood: the word used is *koinoneo,* or a sharing in common, connected with the word communion. Had this word been used as the Lord's participation in humanity there might have been some ground for Mr. H.'s views, but the word *took part* is *meteko,* and by referring to Luke 5 the difference is clearly seen. There are two words translated "partners" in verses 7 and 10. In verse 7, "they beckoned to their *partners* which were in the

---

* Note:—Mr. Rickard says: "That Holy Thing which was born of Mary was essentially free from every element of decay. Before there could have been natural decay its very nature must be changed."—"It was real humanity, but it was *His,* in our human circumstances never subject to decay or dissolution." This is branded by Mr. Holborow, as "a most dangerous error, and it must be exposed at once."

other ship, that they should come and help them." *Partners*
here is *metokos,* and might better be translated *fellows*; that is,
they were fishermen also, but did not share equally in the pro-
ceeds of the fishing. It is the verb of this noun that is used of
the Lord in Hebrews 11, *"took part* of the same," and the same
word in Hebrews 1:9: "Above thy *fellows."* In verse 10, of
Luke 5, we have, "which were *partners* with Simon." These
were truly sharers in the full sense with Simon, and the same
word is used as in Hebrews 2, "The children were *partakers* of
flesh and blood"; they shared it in common, were alike iden-
tically. This has been often noticed, and it is a wonder Mr. H.
could have overlooked the importance of it. (See a note on
Heb. 11:14 in the new translation by J. N. D.)

Let me add in conclusion that in writing what I have, it is as
deeply deploring the controversy, and the need of it; but the
attack has come from themselves, and from the persistent effort
to force upon us unrestricted fellowship, whether we wish it
or not. A forced fellowship would be a poor substitute for
that which the Spirit of God produces. I know no way amidst
the sad discord and humbling divisions of today, but to cultivate,
as far as can be, within the prescribed limits of the Word of
truth, brotherly love towards those manifestly the children of
God according to Ephesians 4, and no fleshly zeal can accomplish this.

Mr. Burridge sought to get a retraction of his erroneous views
from Mr. Holborow, but the latter at first did not seem to sense the
gravity of the situation. Later he sent out the following letter of
withdrawal and explanation:

LETTER FROM MR. HOLBOROW,
SELSLEY, NEAR STROUD, GLOUCESTERSHIRE,
April 18th, 1895.

MR. J. H. BURRIDGE.
DEAR BROTHER IN CHRIST:

Your letter of 8th instant just to hand. In reply, after reading
its contents, I pen you an *unqualified withdrawal* of the sections
of my paper, *Correspondence About Bethesda, 1892,* in question;
those I have already particularlized in my letter to Mr. Buss.
I withdraw them because the language is faulty, and capable of
being understood in a different sense from what I intended—
and therefore in that light they are wrong; also because they
have a savor that is not godly about them; they have a spirit

of strife about them that cannot be right, and they dwell upon subjects that it is impossible for a finite mind to adequately express in language that is not the very words of the *Holy Spirit*. And I am sorry I ever wrote them.

But, in writing the above, I do not justify the perversions and false witness concerning them that have been circulated by some. In confessing wrong on my own part, I should not be right in justifying what is wrong in others.

It will be asked, *"Why did you not say this before?"* I explain—because the perversions I refer to draw my mind away from a calm consideration of the nature of my words in the light of the Word; but I told a brother in England last summer, that I did not like my own expressions on recurring to them again. May the brethren forget all about them—that they ever existed—and forgive me for ever sending them out. My only plea is this: that I did not like to see Mr. Craik so spoken of, and that I simply endeavored to explain that the expressions attributed to him did not necessarily convey the evil teaching some have sought to attach to them.

H. G. HOLBOROW.

Open Brethren generally repudiated the doctrine, but did not consider there was any further step necessary after this letter had been published, as Mr. Craik had long since definitely refused any such thoughts as had been attributed to him, and was with his Lord long ere the question was again raised by Mr. Rickard.

Nothing however could now allay the feeling among many of the Exclusives that there was something radically evil, still unjudged, in the Open fellowship and the most amazing charges were made by utterly misinformed men and circulated as truth. It was even declared that Mr. Muller maintained frequent intercourse with Mr. Newton and had "all his books in the Bethesda lending library." To this slander Mr. Muller replied as follows:

NEW ORPHAN HOUSE, ASHLEY DOWN,
BRISTOL, AUGUST 23, 1895.

MY DEAR BROTHER:

1. Neither Mr. Newton nor any of his friends have been in fellowship with us since 1848. If the contrary is stated, I ask who and where?

2. I have only seen Mr. Newton once since 1848, to know

of his present state; this was about 10 years since; yet you say I attend his Bible readings. See how false! !

3. You state that Bethesda library contains *all* his books. False. We have no Bethesda lending library. There is a library at the Orphan Houses, for the teachers, a *private* library, in which there are three books of Mr. Newton's on prophecy. They are quite sound.

Yours in our Lord,
GEORGE MULLER.

But it seemed that nothing could be done to stem the tide of distrust that had set in against any further effort to bring about communion with Open Brethren. Already in July, 1894, at a conference in Pittsburgh, Pennsylvania, a letter had been sent out signed by twenty-three laborers repudiating the Plainfield circular. A similar letter had also gone out from New York City. Later another went forth from a conference at Dunkirk, New York.

The direct result was most unhappy. Division and dissension spread throughout many of the Canadian and American assemblies. When the clouds had somewhat cleared there was a new party to be reckoned with, known as the "Independents," who steadfastly refused to repudiate the Plainfield letter and have ever since sought to keep their doors open to Exclusives or Opens alike, who desired to commune with them. On the other hand many of the Grant meetings have gone steadily on, receiving godly, properly-commended saints coming from Open or Independent meetings, as they have never recognized the authority of the Pittsburgh and Dunkirk circulars. This was the attitude of Mr. R. T. Grant himself and has been consistently followed by many others through the years, in spite of the opposition of some of a more legal tendency. But the definite declaration of Mr. F. W. Grant that "the refusal of simple godly souls has never been contemplated," makes any other course plainly inconsistent, even though full inter-communion cannot yet be enjoyed.

CHAPTER FOURTEEN

LATER DEVELOPMENTS AND CRITICAL COMMENTS

IT WAS IN THE YEAR 1896 that I became identified with the movement of which I have been writing; at first going into fellowship with the so-called Open Brethren and a little later, after some distressing experiences, casting in my lot with the Grant Exclusives. I have never thus far had occasion to regret the step I took at that time and I have, generally speaking, been greatly blessed, and I hope been permitted to be a blessing to others, notwithstanding the fact that "I have seen an end of all perfection" and have long ago been obliged to take the place of lowly confession and say "I and my people have sinned."

For a few years I regret to say I was under the soul-withering influence of very legal and narrow views regarding both service and fellowship, but as time went on God graciously gave deliverance and led me to see, at least in some measure, how far I, and others, had departed, not only from New Testament teaching but from the original principles of the Brethren themselves. With this came an ever-widening sphere of service as I recognized my responsibility to seek to help all believers, and to reach the lost wherever the Spirit of the Lord opened a door of opportunity. When called to succeed the devoted Dr. P. W. Philpott as minister at the Moody Memorial Church it was only after much prayer and exercise that I became assured such was for me the undoubted will of God. As the years have passed I do not find my love for the Brethren, nor my appreciation of the precious things of Christ for which they stand, growing less, but rather do I value them more. The preparation of these chapters has been a labor of love buoyed up by the hope that they may be used of God to call many back to the joy of simplicity and spiritual freshness of early days.

Heretofore I have been writing of events all of which can either be verified by reliable documentary evidence, or were communicated to me by men who could speak with authority. If I attempt to trace the further history of the movement to any extent I must of necessity rely largely on my own fallible judgment and, I would doubtless often find my estimates of men and their actions decidedly at variance with others far more gifted and godly than I. Therefore I think it wise to close this very imperfect record with a general review of present-day conditions, touching only on principles or referring to documents which are easily accessible.

After the Dunkirk and Pittsburgh circulars and the consequent rejection of many godly brethren like Mr. F. C. Jennings, Messrs. Edward and Nicholas Mauger and other brethren who had ever been esteemed as "guides" among the Grant Brethren since the early days of the movement, there was as we have seen considerable agitation and unrest in the American assemblies.

Brethren beloved and longed-for, against whom there was no charge of wickedness or evil teaching, found themselves in opposite camps and as the years have gone on there has been very little change on the part of the older generation. It is noticeable, however, that the younger believers of all the different fellowships are becoming more and more restive about being whipped into party lines and all are yearning for a broader and more Scriptural fellowship— a return to the first principles of the Brethren which we have seen have been so largely given up.

Shortly after the death of Mr. F. W. Grant in 1898,* Mr. Alfred Mace wrote a very full confession of failure in the matter of the Montreal division and henceforth repudiated the very exclusive position he had previously held. A little later Mr. Walter Scott (who had so successfully blocked the *entente cordiale* of the Exclusive and Open Brethren in 1893) found himself excommunicated by the Stuart party in Great Britain for the very grave offense of breaking bread with a simple company of believers not recognized as in any particular circle of fellowship! Awakened at last to see what Brethren had drifted into he wrote an arousing appeal entitled, *Shall the Sword Devour For Ever?* This was circulated all over the world and produced a tremendous reaction. The present writer, however, ventured to reply to it in *Help and Food,* pointing out that he

* An obituary in *Help and Food* (September 1902) records F. W. Grant's death on Friday, July 25, 1902, and his burial "on Lord's day, his sixty-eighth birthday."

who first asked that question—Abner—was himself a fomenter of division, and until his own confession of wrong done to the scattered people of God was forthcoming, his appeal could be of little weight. It was probably presumption on my part so to write. It showed the training I had been under. Walter Scott was ever after counted among the "Independent Brethren," until his death at a very advanced age.

Since those days effort after effort has been made to bring about a better understanding, and certainly party spirit is rapidly declining among the mass, but a few in all parties, generally known as "diehards," still insist on the old rigid geographical and disciplinary tests of fellowship. It is noticeable that where Christian liberty prevails the meetings flourish, souls are saved, and a warm spiritual atmosphere is found. But where the opposite is true there is very little in the way of active evangelizing or of edification of believers.

With the new yearning for a more Scriptural basis of communion has come increased exercise as to gospel testimony both at home and abroad. Many have been getting their eyes opened to see the folly of exalting century-old methods as though of equal force with divine revelation and so there has come a better understanding and appreciation of the apostle's words, "I am made all things to all men if by any means I may win some." Hence it is not uncommon now to find assemblies putting on earnest evangelistic campaigns with hearty gospel singing and common-sense advertising. In many places it had become an iron-clad tradition that any singing accompanied with instrumental music was opposed to the spirit of the New Testament, through failure to distinguish between singing as an act of worship and singing to attract the needy and careless to hear the gospel. Hence there were in nearly all of the Brethren's assemblies many unused gifts—people who had divinely-given talents which they did not dare use lest they come under the censure of the more conservative.

To many also has come an awakening as to the way they have neglected the apostolic injunction: "Let all things be done respectably and by arrangement" (I Cor. 14:40, literal rendering). The result has been a recognition of the importance of more systematic service for the Lord, which is already bearing blessed fruit. Needless to say, they who prefer human tradition to the present energy of the Holy

Spirit look with disfavor on any change from methods and practices that have become hoary with age, but have no more actual Scriptural authority than methods more in accord with the times.

What the future holds in store for this movement if our blessed Lord tarry but a few years longer no man can predict. But one thing is absolutely certain: Brethren must either break from traditionalism and go on with God, as the Spirit leads through the opened Word and the sanctified judgment of men who have understanding of the times, or they will themselves be literally broken to pieces; in which case the unity they originally aimed at keeping may be nearer than we think. The late Captain R. Carey-Brenton, one of the most devoted missionaries ever in fellowship with the assemblies, who died in Mexico a few years ago, said to me once: "I have been so burdened about our divisions, and have been praying that God would bring our divided gatherings together. Lately I was watching a man break stones and I observed that it was only when the boulders were all broken to gravel that they became one. It may be that God will have to deal in the same way with us!" His words are impressive and well worthy of our consideration.

Perhaps the gravest failure we have made as a people has been in dissociating ourselves in thought from the great mass of our fellow-Christians. It is a common thing to make a distinction between "Christians in systems and believers gathered to or in the name of the Lord Jesus Christ." To consider this a special privilege is but spiritual pride of the most elusive kind. And each fellowship of Brethren is as truly a system as any other body of believers. If any one doubts it let him venture to act on his own initiative, or as he believes the Spirit leads, contrary to custom, and he will soon find out how sectarian an unsectarian company of Christians can be!

Nevertheless it seems to me any unprejudiced student of the movement who really knows his Bible must see that the primary object of the Brethren has been to get back as nearly to New Testament order and teaching as is possible in days of apostasy such as we live in. But the mistake has been in claiming the presence and authority of the Lord in a way other Christians cannot claim them. Some years ago Dr. James Black* of Edinburgh, Scotland, pub-

---

* Knowing Dr. Black personally I am sure this gracious and kindly minister did not intend to misrepresent the "Brethren."

lished a lecture in which he attempted to appraise the Brethren movement, which was reasonably fair though containing some inaccuracies, undoubtedly the result of faulty information. The following answer appeared in *The Witness,* an organ of the Open Brethren and may be of interest in giving the view-point of one of the people thus criticized by the learned Doctor:

DR. JAMES BLACK ON THE "PLYMOUTH BRETHREN"

On a recent journey to Edinburgh, the writer enjoyed a pleasant conversation with a Presbyterian fellow-traveller, in the course of which Dr. Alexander Whyte was referred to, and afterwards his successor, Dr. James Black, of St. George's, Edinburgh.

Dr. Black, I was informed, had been giving recently a series of lectures on "Freak Religions," in the course of which he had ably exposed Mormonism, Russellism, and other American patents, a particularly useful thing to do.

A day or two later I saw the July number of the United Free Church magazine, *The Record,* and found there an article by Dr. Black on *"The Plymouth Brethren: How They Arose and What They Believe,"* and was led to wonder whether this was the substance of a later lecture which classified the people so nicknamed among the freaks! I hope the Doctor doesn't place these much-abused folks in the same category as the Mormons!

Be it said, that the article is kindly in tone, and written without bitterness. It is somewhat in the style in which a venerable Cardinal of Rome would write of United Presbyterians. The only approach to warmth is when the writer deals with the views of "Plymouth Brethren" on the subject of the Christian ministry, and any man may be pardoned if he wax warm defending his hearth and home.

Some of the writer's strictures are fully deserved. Sorry divisions in the history of these protesters against sectarianism give ample room for many a jibe; but the Doctor is merciful, remembering, no doubt, how hard unity is to preserve; so hard, indeed, that even Scottish Presbyterianism hasn't succeeded in it.

In one or two matters Dr. Black is evidently either misinformed or uninformed. For instance, it is less than fair to speak of "present ineffectiveness at home and abroad of 'Plymouth Brethren.'" With all humility, their record in the foreign field is grievously wronged by such a statement. The Doctor cannot have read *Echoes of Service,* or have perused their *Missionary Prayer-list,* or he would not have made this statement. As regards work at home, we take leave to inform Dr. Black that in spite of the allurements of the times, the social auxiliaries from the pulpits of our land, there is a great and growing volume of young life in and about the churches of those whom he terms "Plymouth Brethren." Things are not important in proportion to the noise they make.

His suggestion of the origin of "Plymouth Brethren" will not do. The naughty-boy-who-ran-away-from-home theory does not fit the facts. The separate and spontaneous movements in British Guiana, Ireland, England, Italy, Russia, and Germany cannot be so accounted for. The "movement" at the first was a return to the Scriptures as affording all requisite instruction and guidance for corporate as well as individual Christian life; an endeavour to carry out what is written without qualifying or nullifying it by giving equal authority to sub-apostolic traditions, medieval Church councils, or "modern thought." The need to maintain such a position is more urgent today than ever, and Dr. Black simply misses the whole point when, with fatherly benevolence, he bids "Plymouth Brethren" recognize that their day is past, and come back like naughty children now repentant to the bosom of mother-church.

As to their "not seeking to save the world, but to save a people out of it," their *"rejecting* the ancient practice of all the true 'Catholic' churches (being educated, we had all along imagined there was but *one* Catholic Church) of baptizing the children of believers," and their "celebrating the Lord's Supper every Sunday," they plead guilty; but are prepared to discuss these things over an open Bible with Dr. Black or anyone else who can show therefrom the error of them.

That they have no separate, ordained, educated, and maintained ministry or clergy is a statement that is only partly true; for they recognize a separated, educated, and maintained ministry, though the manner of its separation, education, and maintenance differs from that considered essential in Presbyterianism.

The humorous account given to the Doctor by the two young people who were leaving "Plymouth Brethren" for Presbyterianism, of how in the church they were leaving, "the Spirit always 'led' the same boring old elder," could be matched by the accounts of some who prior to coming out from Presbyterianism have been bored fifty-two Sundays per annum for half a lifetime by a dry-as-dust "educated" minister, without hope that the boring process would be interrupted until the Lord took him to Heaven.

The views on "ordination" most shock the Doctor, however. "It shocks me," he says, "to think that any stray man, without preparation, is presumed to be able to lead and guide the worship and thought of the people." It shocks "Brethren" also to think such a thing. They are yet more sure than Dr. Black that "many so-called 'lay' members can do this more usefully than many ministers"; so sure that they believe every member of a church to be under direct obligation to the Lord to fulfil whatever measure of ministry has been committed to him, and accordingly seek to give him opportunity so to do; being convinced that not even to Dr. Black has the Lord given *all* the gifts whereby He would minister to the needs of the congregation year in and year out, for "the Spirit divideth to every man severally as He will" (I Cor. 12:11).

On this subject Dr. Black appeals to history—if to the history of the church they are deaf to such an appeal—but if to the inspired history of the New Testament, they ask for one instance of a man being chosen by a church to be its teacher or pastor, or to evangelize; for one instance of a salaried minister under agreement to be responsible for the ministry of a particular church.

That an educated ministry is essential, they agree with Dr. Black; but as to the kind of education essential they differ from him. Other things being equal, a liberal education is to be preferred to a broad-school one. Yet *the* essential thing in a minister of Christ is that he shall have been educated in a way no university can guarantee—that he shall have been divinely taught, that his soul shall be rich in its experience of God and that he shall have spiritual understanding of His Word.

Since they *must* choose, "Plymouth Brethren" prefer a ministry which, though Doctors of Divinity stigmatize it as uneducated, is exercised by men whose qualification lies not in scholastic degrees merely, but in spiritual capacity, energy, insight, and devotion, rather than expose themselves to that "learned ministry," much of which is in such terrible evidence today, exercised by men whose aim appears to be to explain away on rationalistic lines every vital doctrine of our most holy faith.

Though Dr. Black may continue to regard "Plymouth Brethren" as "hard-shells" (his own expression), we assure him that some of them at least will continue to intercede that he may be kept faithful and fresh to fulfil the ministry which it is so evident he has received in the Lord.

J. B. WATSON.

A few words from one of Mr. Darby's letters, written as late as 1870, eleven years before his death, will show more clearly than any remarks of mine could do how far some of the Brethren have departed from their own first principles. If these views had been carried out the entire history of the movement might have been happier, and thousands of devoted saints helped who have rather been hindered.

DEAR ————————:

There is no difference between breaking bread as a Christian, and fellowship, though some may not be always there; because the only fellowship or membership is of the body of Christ, and if a person breaks bread and is thus recognized as a member of the body of Christ, he is subject to all the discipline of the house. *I may not enforce constant attendance with us only,* because he may come with the desire to show unity of spirit, and yet think that *his* ways are more orderly conscientiously. If his heart be pure (II Tim. 2:22) I have no reason to exclude him; but if anything in his path require he should be excluded, he is liable to it like any one else. But *I know no fellowship other than of membership of the body of Christ.* Being met, the question is has he done anything which involves disciplinary exclusion?

Only I believe Brethren alone walk in consistency with the fellowship of saints in the unity of the body; but I know no particular corporation as that body—not even Brethren—nay, these least of all. This would deny themselves. Though they have this, that they meet on principles of that unity, but for that reason must *own all its members,* on the one hand, and maintain its discipline on the other.*

Yours affectionately in the Lord,
J. N. D.

These are still the principles on which many of the assemblies act. This is particularly true in Great Britain, where Brethren are, generally speaking in the very fore-front of real evangelical testimony. It is to be hoped that in days to come there will be an even more widespread return to early practices.

* Italics mine. H. A. I.

APPENDICES

Miscellaneous Papers Pertaining to Brethren's
History, Methods and Doctrines

J. N. DARBY'S OWN ACCOUNT OF THE ORIGIN
OF THE MOVEMENT

The following letter, written in French, to Prof. Tholuck about 1857-9, is printed, as giving an interesting account of the remarkable work of God which took place in the early part of the last century, and of the spiritual exercises passed through by the one much used of God in bringing to light truths long lost to the Church. When we reflect upon the spirit of devotedness and separation from the world, as well as the definite recognition of the claims of Christ over the Christian—body, soul and spirit—which breathes through this letter, we might well ask ourselves, as we search our own hearts: Do these things mark the saints of God today as they did then?

DEAR BROTHER IN CHRIST, — Since I saw you, I have been continually on the move, so that it has been difficult for me to prepare the account which you desire to receive. It seems to me that the best way will be for me simply to mention the various circumstances as they transpired, in as far as I was personally concerned, at the time when this work of God first commenced. You will easily understand that numbers of others have laboured in that field, and many with much more devotedness than I, and with a far more marked result as regards the blessing of souls. But my concern now is with the work of God, and not our labours; so that you may gather from the account what will suit your purpose.

I was a lawyer; but feeling that, if the Son of God gave Himself for me I owed myself entirely to Him, and that the so-called Christian world was characterized by deep ingratitude towards Him, I longed for complete devotedness to the work of the Lord; my chief thought was to get round amongst the poor Catholics of Ireland. I was induced to be ordained. I did not feel drawn to take up a regular post, but, being young in the faith and not yet knowing deliverance, I was governed by the feeling of duty towards Christ, rather than by the consicousness that *He* had done *all* and that I was redeemed and saved; consequently it was easy to follow the advice of those who were more advanced than myself in the Christian life.

ORDAINED

As soon as I was ordained, I went amongst the poor Irish mountaineers, in a wild and uncultivated district, where I remained two years and three months, working as best I could. I felt, however, that the style of work was not in agreement with what I read in the Bible concerning the Church and Christianity; nor did it correspond with the effects of the action of the Spirit of God. These considerations pressed upon me from a Scriptural and practical point of view, while seeking assiduously to fulfil the duties of the ministry confided to me, working day and night amongst the people, who were almost as wild as the mountains they inhabited. Much exercise of soul had the effect of causing the Scriptures to gain complete ascendancy over me. I had always owned them to be the Word of God.

When I came to understand that I was united to Christ in Heaven, and that, consequently, my place before God was represented by His own, I was forced to the conclusion that it was no longer a question with God of this wretched "I" which had wearied me during six or seven years, in presence of the requirements of the law. It then became clear to me that the Church of God, as He considers it, was composed only of those who were so *united to Christ,* whereas Christendom, as seen externally, was really the world, and could not be considered as "the Church," save as regards the responsibility attaching to the position which it professed to occupy—a very important thing in its place. At the same time, I saw that the Christian, having his place in Christ in Heaven, has nothing to wait for save the Coming of the Saviour, in order to be set, in fact, in the glory which is already his portion "in Christ."

The careful reading of the Acts afforded me a practical picture of the early Church, which made me feel deeply the contrast with its actual present state, though still, as ever, beloved by God.

What was to be done? I saw in that Word the Coming of Christ to take the Church to Himself in glory. I saw there the Cross the divine basis of salvation, which should impress its own character on the Christian and on the Church in view of the Lord's Coming; and also that meanwhile the Holy Spirit was given to be the source of the unity of the Church, as well as the spring of its activity, and indeed of all Christian energy.

As Preacher

As regards the Gospel, I had no difficulty as to its received dogmas. Three persons in one God, the Divinity of Jesus, His work of atonement on the Cross, His resurrection, His session at the right hand of God, were truths which, understood as orthodox doctrines, had long been a living reality to my soul. They were the known and felt conditions, the actualities, of my relationship with God. Not only were they truths, but I knew God personally in that way; I had no other God but Him who had thus revealed Himself, and Him I had. He was the God of my life and of my worship, the God of my peace, the only true God.

The practical difference in my preaching, when once I began to preach again, was as follows: When a parson, I had preached that sin had created a great gulf between us and God, and that Christ alone was able to bridge it over; now, I preached that He *had* already finished His work. The necessity of regeneration, which was always a part of my teaching, became connected more with Christ, the last Adam, and I understood better that it was a real life, entirely new, communicated by the power of the Holy Spirit; but, as I have said, more in connection with the person of Christ and the power of His resurrection, combining the power of a life victorious over death, with a new position for man before God. This is what I understand by "deliverance." The Blood of Jesus has removed every spot from the believer; every trace of sin, according to God's own purity. In virtue of His blood-shedding, the only possible propitiation, we may now invite all men to come to God, a God of love, who, for this object, has given His own Son. The presence of the Holy Ghost, sent from Heaven to abide in the believer as the "unction," the "seal," and the "earnest of our inheritance," as well as being in the Church, the power which unites it in one Body and distributes gifts to the members according to His will; these truths developed largely and assumed great importance in my eyes. With this last truth was connected the question of ministry. From whence came this ministry? According to the Bible, it clearly came from God by the free and powerful action of the Holy Ghost.

MINISTRY

At the time I was occupied with these things, the person with whom I was in Christian relation locally, as a minister, was an excellent Christian, worthy of all respect, and one for whom I have always had great affection. It was, however, the principles, and not the persons, which acted on my conscience; for I had already given up, out of love to the Saviour, all that the world could offer. I said to myself: "If the Apostle Paul were to come here now, he would not, according to the established system, be even allowed to preach, not being legally ordained; but if a worker of Satan, who, by his doctrine, denied the Saviour, came here, he could freely preach, and my Christian friend would be obliged to consider him as a fellow-laborer; whereas he would be unable to recognize the most powerful instrument of the Spirit of God, however much blessed in his work of leading multitudes of souls to the Lord, if he had not been ordained according to the system." All this, said I to myself, is false. This is not mere abuse, such as may be found everywhere; it is the *principle* of the system that is at fault. Ministry is of the Spirit. There are some amongst the clergy who are ministers by the Spirit, but the system is founded on an opposite principle; consequently it seemed impossible to remain in it any longer.

I saw in Scripture that there were certain *gifts* which formed true ministry, in contrast to a clergy established upon another principle. Salvation, the Church, and ministry, all were bound together; and all were connected with Christ, the Head of the Church in Heaven, with Christ who had accomplished a perfect salvation, as well as with the presence of the Spirit on earth, uniting the members to the Head, and to each other, so as to form "one body," and He acting in them according to His will.

In effect, the Cross of Christ and His return should characterize the Church and each one of the members. What was to be done? Where was this unity, this "Body?" Where was the power of the Spirit recognized? Where was the Lord really waited for? Nationalism was associated with the world; in its bosom some believers were merged in the very world from which the Lord Jesus had separated them; they were, besides, separated from one another, whilst the Lord Jesus had united them. The Lord's Supper, symbol of the unity of the Body, had become a symbol of the union of this latter with the world; that is to say, exactly the contrary of what Christ had established. Dissent had, no doubt, had the effect of making the true children of God more manifest, but here they were united on principles quite different from the unity of the Body of Christ. If I joined myself to these, I separated myself from others everywhere. The disunion of the Body of Christ was everywhere apparent rather than its unity. What was I to do? Such was the question which presented itself to me, without any other idea than that of satisfying my conscience, according to the light of the Word of God. A word in Matthew 18:20 furnished the solution of my trouble: "Where two or three are gathered together in My Name, there am I in the midst of them." This was just what I wanted: the presence of the Lord was assured at such worship; it is there He has recorded His name, as He had done of old in the temple at Jerusalem for those who were called to resort there.

SEPARATION

Four persons who were pretty much in the same state of soul as myself came together to my lodging; we spoke together about these things, and I proposed to them to break bread the following Sunday, which we did. Others then joined us. I left Dublin soon after, but the work immediately began at Limerick, a town in Ireland, and then in other places.

Two years later (1830) I went to Cambridge and Oxford. In this latter place some shared my convictions, and felt that the relation of the Church to Christ ought to be that of a faithful spouse.

By invitation I went to Plymouth to preach. My habit was to preach wherever people wished, whether in buildings or in private houses. More than once, even with ministers of the national Church, we have broken bread on Monday evening after meetings for Christian edification, where each was free to read, to speak, to pray, or to give out a hymn. Some months afterwards we began to do so on Sunday morning, making use of the same liberty, only adding the Lord's Supper, which we had, and still have, the practice of taking every Sunday. About that time also some began to do the same in London.

The unity of the Church, as the Body of Christ, the Coming of the Lord, the presence of the Holy Ghost here below, in the individual and in the Church; an assiduous proclamation of the truth, as well as the preaching of the Gospel on the ground of pure grace and that of an accomplished work, giving in consequence the assurance of salvation when received into the heart by the Spirit; practical separation from the world; devotedness to Christ, as to Him who has redeemed the Church; a walk having Him only as the motive and rule; and other subjects in connection with these— all these truths have been largely spread abroad.

A good many ministers of the National Church left nationalism in order to walk according to these principles, and England became gradually covered with meetings, more or less numerous. Plymouth being the place where most of the publications originated, the name "Plymouth Brethren" became the usual appellation given to such meetings.

On the Continent

In 1837 I visited Switzerland, and these truths began to be known there. I returned there more than once.

At the same time, quite independently of what was going on in Switzerland, a brother who was laboring in France had awakened an interest in a considerable district where the people were, in general, plunged in infidelity and darkness.

Almost about the same time, in the eastern part of France, a like work had begun, independently of this one. It has also been visited, so that at the present time the work extends from Bale to the Pyrenees, with a fairly large gap in the districts of which Toulouse forms the center. The country is more or less covered with meetings, and the work, by God's grace, is still going on.

I ought to say that I have never meddled in any way with the calling nor with the work of the brethren who studied the Bible with me. I only helped them in the study of the Bible, in communicating to them the light which God had given me, but leaving entirely to themselves the responsibility of their calling for the work of evangelization or teaching.

Conferences

We had the custom of gathering together occasionally for some time, when God opened the way for it, to study Scriptural subjects together, or books of the Bible, and to communicate to one another what God had given to each. During several years, in Ireland and England, this took place annually in conferences which lasted a week. Two years later, helped, I believe, by the knowledge of these truths, but entirely independent of this work, a movement of the Spirit of God began at Elberfeld. There was in that town a "Brotherhood" which employed twelve laborers whom the clergy sought to forbid from preaching or teaching. Enlightened as to the ministry of the Spirit, and moved by love for souls, they would not submit to this interdict. Seven of these laborers, I believe, and a few members of the "Brotherhood" detached themselves from it, and certain of them, with others whom God raised up, continued their Gospel work, which spread from Holland to Hesse. Conversions have been very numerous, and many hundreds assemble at the present time to break bread.

Gospel preaching in Switzerland and England has led to the formation of some meetings amongst emigrants to the United States and Canada; the evangelization of negroes led to others in Jamaica and Demerara, as also amongst the natives of Brazil. The English colonies of Australia have also meetings.

DOCTRINES

Brethren do not recognize any other body but the Body of Christ, that is to say, the whole Church of the first-born. Also they recognize every Christian who walks in truth and holiness, as a proved member of Christ. Their hope of final salvation is founded on the Saviour's expiatory work, for whose return they look, according to His Word. They believe the saints to be united to Him already, as the Body of which He is the Head, and they await the accomplishment of His promise, expecting His Coming to take them to Himself in the Father's House, so that where He is, there they may be also. Meanwhile, they have to bear His cross and to suffer with Him, separated from the world which has rejected Him. His person is the object of their faith, His life the example which they have to follow in the conduct. His Word—namely, the Scriptures inspired of God; that is to say, the Bible—is the authority which forms their faith; it is also its foundation, and they recognize it as that which should govern their conduct. The Holy Ghost alone can make it effectual both for life and practice.

JOHN NELSON DARBY.

THE DOCTRINES OF EARLY BRETHREN

A Letter Written to a French Catholic Newspaper by J. N. DARBY in 1878.*

I BELIEVE THAT the Christian calling is a Heavenly one, that the Christian is not of the world as his Master is not of it, and that he is placed down here as an epistle of Christ to manifest the life of the Lord Jesus amongst men, whilst waiting for the Lord to come to take him to be with Himself in the glory.

As editor you will quite understand that articles written in order to inculcate such principles as these would little suit a political newspaper. Now I live only for these things—a life feebly realized I am ready to confess—but I live only for them. However, I will communicate to you what appears to interest you, namely, what has led me, and others with me, to take up the position in which we find ourselves as Christians.

It is well perhaps, in view of the infidelity which is spreading everywhere, to begin by saying that I hold, and I can add that we firmly hold, all the

FOUNDATIONS OF THE CHRISTIAN FAITH—

the Divinity of the Father, of the Son, and of the Holy Ghost, one God, eternally blessed—the Divinity and humanity of the Lord Jesus, two natures in one Person—His resurrection and His glorification at the right hand of God—the presence of the Holy Ghost here below, having descended on the Day of Pentecost—the Return of the Lord Jesus according to His promise.

We believe also that the Father in His love has sent the Son to accomplish the work of redemption and grace towards men—that

* In answer to an inquiry from the Editor of a Catholic paper, *The Francais*, as to "The Brethren, their Doctrines, etc." A useful statement for all Fundamentalists.

the Son came, in that same love, to accomplish it, and that He has finished the work which the Father gave Him to do on earth.

We believe that He has made propitiation for our sins, and that after having accomplished it, He ascended to Heaven—the High Priest seated at the right hand of the Majesty on High.

Other truths are connected with these, such as the miraculous birth of the Saviour, who was absolutely without sin—and yet others; but, you will readily understand, that my object is not to give a course of lectures or a theological summary, but to make it quite clear that it is in nowise on the giving up of the great foundations of the Christian faith that our position is based. Anyone who would deny one or other of these fundamental truths would not be received amongst us, and anyone who, being amongst us, adopted some doctrine which would undermine one or other of these same truths would be excluded, but only after all proper means to bring him back to the truth had been exhausted. For although these are dogmas, we hold them as essential to living faith and to salvation, to the spiritual and Christian life which we live as born of God.

But you wish to know not only the great truths which we hold in common with others, but also

WHAT DISTINGUISHES US FROM OTHERS.

Now, without in the least professing to give a course of Christian doctrine in connection with the truths I have just pointed out, I am anxious, indeed I would heartily desire, to set them forth as the foundation, recognizing as true Christians and members of the Body of Christ all those, who by the grace of God, and by the operation of the Holy Ghost who has been given to them, truly believe these things in their souls.

Converted by the grace of God, I spent six or seven years under the rod of the law, feeling that Christ was the only Saviour, but not being able to say that I possessed Him, or that I was saved by Him—fasting, praying, giving alms—always good things when done spiritually—but not possessing peace, whilst at the same time feeling that if the Son of God had Himself forgiven me, I owed myself to Him — my body, soul, and means. At length God gave me to understand that I was in Christ united to Him by the Holy Ghost—"At that Day ye shall know that I am in My Father, and ye in Me, and I in you" (John 14:20), which means that when the Holy Ghost, the Comforter, should have come, the disciples would *know* these things.

The promise of the Spirit is given to all those who have part in the remission of their sins, for "he that is joined unto the Lord is one spirit" (I Cor. 6:17). Hence, Christians are temples of the Holy Ghost. "Your body is the temple of the Holy Ghost, who is in you" (I Cor. 6:19).

At this time the Word of God became for me an

ABSOLUTE AUTHORITY AS TO FAITH AND PRACTICE,

not that I doubted it previously, but it had now become such from conviction, implanted by God Himself in my heart. In this way the assurance of salvation through the work of Christ, the presence of the Holy Ghost dwelling in us, by whom "having believed, ye have been sealed for the day of redemption" (Eph. 1:13, 14), salvation known and possessed, and this indwelling of the Holy Ghost giving us the assurance of it, constitute the normal state of the Christian. He is no longer of this world, save to pass through it peacefully, doing the will of God. Bought with a great price, he is to glorify God in his conduct.

This brings in the thought of the Church and of its unity. For me the Body of Christ was now composed of those who were united by the Holy Ghost to the Head—Christ in Heaven. If we were seated in the Heavenly places in Christ, what were we still waiting for? For Christ to come to place us up there in fact. "I will come again," said the Lord, "and receive you unto Myself, that where I am, there ye may be also" (John 14:3). We have been converted "To wait for His Son from Heaven" (I Thess. 1:9, 10).

Hence the presence of the Holy Ghost dwelling in him, and attitude of waiting for the Lord constitute the normal state of the Christian. But all those who possess this Spirit are, by that very fact, one Body. "For by one Spirit are we all baptized into one Body" (I Cor. 12:13). This baptism took place on the Day of Pentecost.

All those around me had not reached that point, at any rate they did not profess to have, and it was easy, reading Acts 2 and 4, to see how far we had got from what God had set up on the earth.

Where Was I to Look for the Church

I gave up Anglicanism as not being it. Rome, at the beginning of my conversion, had not failed to attract me. But the tenth chapter of the Epistle to the Hebrews had made that impossible for me: "For by one offering He hath perfected for ever them that are sanctified" (Heb. 10:14).

Then again it rendered impossible the idea of a sacrificing priesthood down here between me and God; seeing that our position, as the result of the work of Christ, is that we have direct access to God in all confidence. "Having therefore, brethren, boldness to enter into the holiest by the Blood of Jesus" (Heb. 10:19).

I am stating facts; I am not entering into controversy; but faith in an accomplished salvation, and later on the consciousness that I possessed it, hindered me from turning in that direction; whilst having grasped the fact of the unity of the Body of Christ, the various dissenting sects no longer attracted me. As to the unity to which, as we all know Rome pretends, I found everything in ruins. The most ancient Churches did not want to have anything to say to her, nor did Protestants either, so that the great majority of those who profess Christianity are outside her pale. On the other hand, it was not a question of seeking this unity amongst the Protestant sects. Besides, whatever their ecclesiastical position might be, most of those who call themselves Christians are of the world, just as much as a pagan might be.

Now the 12th chapter of the 1st Epistle to the Corinthians shows clearly that *there is a Church formed on the earth by the descent of the Holy Ghost.* "For by one Spirit are we all baptized into one Body;" and it is evident that this is on the earth, for "Ye are the Body of Christ, and members in particular" (I Cor. 12:27).

The Assembly of God, then, has been formed on the earth, and ought always to have been manifested. Alas! it has not been so. In the first place, with regard to individuals, the Lord had pointed this out beforehand. "The wolf catcheth them and scattereth the sheep," but, thank God, "No one shall catch them out of My hand," said the same faithful Shepherd (John 10:12, 28).

But this is not all: the Apostle Paul, bidding farewell to the faithful of Asia, said: "I know this, that after my departing shall grievous wolves enter in among you, not sparing the flock, and of your own selves shall men arise speaking perverse things, to draw away disciples after them" (Acts 20:29, 30). Jude declares that already in his time, deceitful men had crept in among the Christians, and which is of all importance, they are marked out as being the object of the judgment of the Lord when He comes again (Jude 4).

He warns us that "All that will live godly in Christ Jesus shall suffer persecution. But evil men and seducers shall wax worse and worse" (II Tim. 3:12, 13) ; but he gives us as a safeguard the knowledge of the person from whom we have learned those things which we believe; it is the apostle himself, with the Scriptures, which can make us wise to salvation by the faith which is in Christ Jesus. He assures us that "All Scripture is given by the inspiration of God, and is profitable for doctrine, for correction," etc. (II Tim. 3:16).

Thus we have proof that evil, having entered into the Church, would continue.

"The Mystery of Iniquity,"

says the apostle, "doth already work; only he who now hinders will hinder until he be taken out of the way. And then shall that Wicked be revealed, whom the Lord Jesus shall consume with the breath of His mouth, and shall destroy by the brightness of His Coming" (II Thess. 2:7, 8). The evil which was already working in the time of the apostle was, then, to continue until the Wicked One himself should be revealed. The Lord will destroy him then by His Coming; and although it be not spoken of the Church properly so-called, the same thing is revealed to us in regard to Christendom, for we learn that tares have been sown in the place where the Lord had sown good grain. When the servants desire to pull up the tares, the Lord forbids them, saying, "Let both grow together until the harvest" (Matt. 13:24-30). The evil done to the Kingdom of God was to remain in the field of this world until the judgment. Christ will doubtless gather the good grain into His garner, but the crop is spoiled down here. You will tell me, "But the gates of Hell are not to prevail against that which Christ has built." Granted, and I bless God for it with all my heart, but we must distinguish here as the Word of God does. There is on the one hand the work of Christ, and on the other what is done by men and under their responsibility. The enemy will never destroy what Christ built (we speak of the Church of God), nor will he prevail against the work of the Lord.

Whatever be the evil that has come in — for that there are heresies and schisms we do not deny — that which Christ works has endured and will endure for ever.

This is what the Word of God presents to us historically and prophetically in the New Testament: this Word, addressed by the teachers to the faithful, is our resource when these perilous times should come; and, if that were necessary, the facts have borne out all that it says.

What is to be done? The Word declares to us that where two or three are gathered to the Name of Jesus, He will be in their midst (Matt. 18:20).

This is What We Have Done

There were only four of us to do it at the first; not, I hope, in a spirit of pride or presumption, but deeply grieved at seeing the state of that which surrounded us, praying for all Christians, and recognizing all those who possessed the Spirit of God—*every true Christian wherever he might be found ecclesiastically*—as members of the Body of Christ. We were not thinking of anything else than of satisfying the need of our souls according to the Word of God. The same needs caused others to follow the same road, and thus the work has extended in a way of which we had not the remotest idea. It commenced in Dublin, to spread in the British Isles, in France, where a great number of persons, open unbelievers, were converted; in Switzerland, where the work on the Continent had commenced; in Germany, in Holland, in Denmark, where it is commencing, in Sweden, where a great religious movement is going on at this moment. The path we follow has spread to a considerable extent in the British Colonies, and in the United States, in Asia, in Africa, and elsewhere. The Spirit of God acts and produces needs of soul to which the religious systems offer no answer.

In a word, this is definitely the position of those brethren who rest on the authority of the Word of God. Christ is seen in this Word as the Savior in three different positions: first, as accomplishing redemption on the Cross; then as seated at the Father's right hand, the Holy Ghost being thereupon sent down here; finally as coming back to take His own to be with Himself. These Christians believe these things, have the assurance of their salvation, having faith in the efficacy of this redemption; and finally, being sealed with the Holy Spirit, who dwells in every true Christian, they wait for the Son of God from Heaven without knowing the moment of His Coming. We believe in the promise, "I will come again, and receive you unto Myself; that where I am, and there ye may be also" (John 14:3).

Absolute faith in the efficacy of redemption; the seal of the Spirit which gives the assurance of salvation and the consciousness of being children of God; the attitude of waiting for the Lord—this is what characterizes these Christians. Bought with a great price, they are bound to regard themselves as no longer belonging to themselves, but to the Lord Jesus, to please Him in everything and to live only for Him.

I do not mean to say that we all walk at the full height of the Heavenly calling, but we acknowledge

THE OBLIGATION TO DO SO.

If anyone fails openly in what becomes a Christian—in point of morality or in what concerns the faith—he is excluded. We abstain from the pleasures and amusements of the world. If we have evening parties, it is for the purpose of studying the Word and of edifying ourselves together. We do not mix in politics; we are not of the world; we do not vote. We submit to the established authorities, whatever they may be, in so far as they command nothing expressly contrary to the will of Christ. We take the Lord's Supper every Sunday, and those who have gift for it preach the Gospel of salvation to sinners or teach believers. Every one is bound to seek the salvation or good of his neighbor according to the capacity which God has given him. Feeling that Christendom is corrupt, we are outside the Church-world, by whatever name it is called. As to the number of those who follow this course I cannot tell you what it is; we do not number ourselves, wishing to remain in the littleness which becomes Christians. Besides, *we reckon as a brother in Christ every person who has the Spirit of Christ.*

You ask me what is the advantage of this course. Obedience to the Word of God suffices to decide us. To obey Christ is the first requirement of the soul which knows itself saved by Him, and even of every soul acknowledging Him as the Son of God, who has loved us so much and has given Himself for us. But in fact, in obeying Him, in spite of weakness, faults, and failures, which, on my part I own, His presence manifests itself to the soul as an ineffable source of joy, as the earnest of a bliss where failures, blessed be His Name for it, will no longer be found, and where He will be fully glorified in all believers.

Appendix C

CRITICISMS

Perhaps one of the best cures for any tendency to spiritual pride is to see ourselves as others see us. So I venture to incorporate here some kindly criticisms written by a well-known man of God who walked apart from the Brethren while rejoicing in much of the truth for which they stood.

The following two editorials are from the pen of that doughty champion of our common faith the late Dr. James H. Brookes and appeared years ago in *The Truth*. They may seem somewhat caustic in places, but it is well to remember that the author had himself been criticized very sharply by many among the Brethren for not fully identifying himself with them. Brethren are generally keenly sensitive about criticism directed against themselves, but I regret to say are much more indifferent to criticism of others not counted as of their number.

Dr. Brookes knew and loved many of them. His pulpit had often been opened to them. J. N. Darby, Malachi Taylor, Paul J. Loizeaux and others had preached in his church at various times.

He wrote as follows:

Two pamphlets have been received from those known as "Brethren," who are writing against "Brethren." More than sixty years ago a movement was started, which promised to be of incalculable service to multitudes. The leading spirits were J. N. Darby and B. W. Newton, both men of decided ability, extensive learning, profound acquaintance with the Word of God, and ample means to publish and disseminate their views. They began by emphasizing certain half-forgotten truths, the absolute inerrancy of the sacred Scriptures, the deity of the Lord Jesus Christ, His vicarious atonement, redemption by His blood alone received by faith alone, a present and certain salvation, and the second coming of the Lord.

Their books and tracts were largely circulated, bringing comfort and peace and joy to thousands of souls, quickening interest in the study of the Bible, and spreading like a wave of blessing through the church of England and other religious bodies. Dr. Anthony Groves, one of the original number who met in Plymouth to pray and search the Scriptures, declares that it was not the purpose of the leaders at first to form a separate organization, but to permeate existing denominations with the truth of God. But alas! the flesh was in the best of them as they themselves affirm, and they soon determined to cast off fellowship with other Christians, while envy, jealousy and rivalry took possession of the principal teachers, each of whom desired to be chief.

The result has been from that day to this a most painful and humiliating scene of strife, bitterness and factional disputation, until there are now twenty-four parties or sects in London alone, none of whom will have anything to do with the others.* In this country there are the Darbyites, the Newtonites, the Kellyites, the Stuartites, Cecilites, the Grantites, the Ravenites, the Bex Hillites, the Exclusives, the Open, the Needed Truth, the Neutrals, and many independent congregations, all belonging to the "Brethren," and each claiming to be the one and only assembly. It is enough to bow one's head in shame before God. In their protest against sectarianism they have become the narrowest and most bigoted sect on earth, and they are truly described in Scriptures as "living in malice and envy, hateful, and hating one another" (Tit. 3:3).

One of the pamphlets received was written by a good and faithful and true man, who has belonged to the "Brethren" for twenty-five years, and who is now one of their most godly and instructive teachers. He speaks of them as follows:

> "What is manifest now is, all are separated, avoiding one another, and *filled* with malice, and the three leading characteristics *are selfishness weakness, legality,* and the result is that great *multitudes* of infidels are being made and added to Mr. Ingersoll, and multitudes of godly saints are cut off. What a contrast, both as to principle and practice,

* Those who have followed these chapters carefully will realize that Dr. Brookes erred as to the number of divisions (H. A. I.).

from what it was at the beginning . . . It is no longer
'admonish,' 'convert' or 'restore.' It is *excommunicate* on
the slightest pretext . . . It is truly all *chaos,* and needs
the Holy Ghost to brood over it, and God to let the light
into it, to reveal its *terrible* condition, and allow the Word
of God to purge it, before there can be fruit which will
be acceptable to God."

The italics are his own, and there is much more of the same
sort which there is not space to quote. Near the close of
his pamphlet he describes them as fairly represented in II
Samuel 2:

> "Both parties were Israelites (types of believers); both
> companies had parted company with David (lost sight of
> Jesus) and were away from Hebron (out of communion)
> verse 11, and were in Gibeon (iniquity), and they came
> there to *fight* to please the leaders (verse 14). They did
> not take each other by the hand, but by the *head;* they did
> not seek to comfort each other's *hearts,* but stuck a dagger
> into their brother's side, and *both* fell together; there was
> a "very sore battle," but not with David's enemies, it was
> between themselves, and to their shame (verses 16, 17).
> The loss to David is seen in verses 30, 31."

Such is the testimony of one of their most useful teachers,
who clearly sees their wretched failure. He still insists that they
occupy the only "true church ground"; but who can tell which
one of the forty or more wrangling parties occupies the true
church ground, and of what use is it to talk of true church
ground, when the Spirit has departed, and I-cha-bod is written
on the walls? Well does the Holy Ghost say to them. "Ye
are yet carnal: for whereas there is among you envying, and
strife, and division (margin, factions), are ye not carnal, and
walk as men?" (I Cor. 3:3)

The cause of their downfall it is easy to trace. "Knowledge
puffeth up, but love buildeth up" (I Cor. 8:1). They were
more diligent students of the Bible, and came nearer to the
heart of God's revealed will, than other people, and their earlier
literature was exceedingly precious for its testimony to the truth.
Then they grew conceited, and looked with contempt upon other
Christians who did not join them, and said of ministers in
"systems" who proclaimed the gospel, "Oh, they preach 'Brethren' truth," and would not listen to them, however faithful,

and labored far more zealously to lead believers out of "systems" than to lead a lost soul to our Lord Jesus Christ, and in their fight with "systems" became the closest system ever devised, and then fell to fighting with themselves.

No wonder God forsook them, and made them a shame and reproach, as they are this day, among all Christians. It is the saddest wreck in the history of the church. When they started upon their career, it seemed that they were to do a work for the cold and formal and legal religious denominations, as important in extent and usefulness as the work of Luther, Zwingli, Calvin and Knox at the time of the first Reformation. But pride, vain-glory, self-seeking, took possession of them, and they plunged to a depth proportioned to the height of the elevation to which God had exalted them. Well might they remember the text written of one newly come to the faith, "Not a novice, lest being lifted up with pride he fall into the condemnation of the devil" (I Tim. 3:6).

The late C. H. Spurgeon and Dr. A. J. Gordon gladly acknowledged in their respective periodicals, that there are thousands of ministers in various "systems" throughout Europe and America who, without the least sympathy with the peculiar "church views" of the "Brethren," gratefully recognize their indebtedness to them for a better understanding and a fuller preaching of the Word of God. To these it is a real grief to see the present deplorable condition of "Brethrenism," and although many of them have suffered from the base slanders and cruel insinuations and causeless hatred of those in this little "system," yet with tearful eyes and loving hands would they bury the remains of what was once a true witness of our Lord Jesus Christ.

Letters have often been received, charging rival factions of the same sect, not only with unsoundness in doctrine, but with laxity of morals. Of course these have not been published, but it is sad enough to see that such charges can be brought against their own "Brethren." They have surely forgotten the exhortation, "Brethren, ye have been called unto liberty; only use not liberty for an occasion to the flesh, but by love be in bondage to one another" (Gal. 5:13). It is humiliating to notice that while many of them, at least, still hold to the letter of the Word, they have gone all to pieces in other respects, showing that truth, unattended by the Holy Spirit, is of no avail.

There is but one hope for a revival of the testimony that

formerly was a blessing and power. Let the "Brethren" of every name get together, not for discussion, but for deep humiliation, and heart-felt confession. Let them cease from their miserable hair-splitting distinctions, worthy only of the schoolmen in the dark ages. Let them turn from hatred of one another and of believers in "systems," and exhibit a spirit of real, practical Christian love. Let them not raise some little point, which no one can see, to a place of prime importance, but rally in these last and perilous times around the great essential truths of God's holy Word. But this suggestion will be received with a sneer of derision. "Cease ye from man, whose breath is in his nostrils; for wherein is he to be accounted of?"

Thousands of Brethren will say Amen! to this last paragraph and are earnestly seeking to carry out this most salutary advice. Nor would they be angry because the good Doctor unintentionally exaggerated the real conditions and the number of divisions. They are deeply grieved to think that they did not present a better testimony and so adorn the doctrines in which they delight.

Dr. Brookes' second article follows:

In the May issue of *The Truth* there appeared an editorial on "Plymouth Brethren." It has called forth numerous letters, some in hearty commendation, most in fierce denunciation, of the article. The latter have been too numerous and too lengthy, even to read carefully, and they have been thrown into the waste basket. It is simply impossible to answer them personally.

Those who read *The Truth* must have seen that the men and ministers of any denomination, system, or sect, who depart from the Word of God are not spared, whether they are Baptists, Congregationalists, Episcopalians, Methodists, Presbyterians, or by whatever name they are called. Who are the "Brethren," that they should be exempt from merited criticism, when they go astray from the sacred Scriptures?

The very claim they make, that those who mention their faults and failures are guilty of a sort of profanation and sacrilege, shows their arrogant assumption of constituting the only true and infallible church. It is a claim, equal in effect of that of the Roman Catholic or the highest church Episcopalian, which says, "You may assail others, but you must not touch the 'Brethren.'" They remind one of a little meeting place in London, in which some branch of the "Brethren" assembled, that had

over the door a strip of cloth bearing the inscription, "JESUS
ONLY." By the wind, or in some other way, the first three
letters of His name were torn off, so that the sign read, "US
ONLY."

If the "Brethren" imagine that they are sacredly guarded
against admonition and rebuke, they will find themselves decidedly mistaken. Nay, they are far more blameworthy, because
they know more truth than most of the denominations, and
have more shamefully departed from it in practice towards each
other, and towards other Christians. They recall the substance
of a remark made somewhere by J. G. Bellett, one of their best
writers, who says that truth, received through the ear, and finding lodgment in the mind, but going no further, is of little
value. It must touch the heart and life, if it is a real blessing.

Most of the letters received charge that the divisions, into
which the "Brethren" are now found in fighting factions, are
grossly exaggerated in the editorial of two months ago. This
may be, but the statement was made on the evidence of the
"Brethren" themselves. One of them, a faithful teacher, or as
people in "systems" would say, a preacher or evangelist, was
asked, "How many sects exist among the 'Brethren' in this
country?" He promptly replied, "At least half a dozen." One
of them is authority for the assertion that there are twenty-
four in London. Perhaps he included every little gathering of
two or three disgruntled "Brethren."

The worst of it is, that they not only refuse to "break bread"
with each other, but decline to have anything to do with one
another socially, sometimes expressing disgust at the necessity
that compels them to sit in the same room, as at a funeral,
and rejecting the proffered hand of mutual acquaintanceship.
To them it is absolutely nothing that the New Testament is
full of such injunctions as the following: "Let all bitterness,
and wrath, and anger, and clamor, and evil speaking, be put
away from you, with all malice" (Eph. 4:31).

Since the article was written to which violent exception is
taken, two pamphlets have been received, written by "Brethren"
against "Brethren," with the request that they shall not be
made public. The request is granted, so far as to withhold
names, but it is essential to truth and righteousness to give a
few extracts from one of the pamphlets, prepared and published
by perhaps the leading teacher among the "Brethren" in the
world:

"What is the use of professing to maintain the truth, while manifesting a spirit contrary to the whole of the New Testament? What we need is to maintain the truth in our lives and conduct, as the truth in itself cannot be touched. My dear brethren, are we not at this time giving the lie by our practice to a most blessed truth, which we hold and preach with the lip, namely, that the people of God are one—the unity of the church? If our practice in relation to our brethren is quite the opposite of what is inculcated everywhere in the New Testament, and thoroughly inconsistent with the relationships into which we are brought, are we not giving the lie in our practice to the truth, while with our words we profess to be maintaining it? . . . Depend upon it that there has been something radically wrong in the practice of the Lord's people, who have been professedly gathered to His name. Is it not manifest by our present condition? Shall we still go on blaming every party but our own? Or shall we not rather, my beloved brethren, humble ourselves as a whole in real confession before our God? . . .

"And oh! the bitterness of spirit, the terrible fightings, the barbarous treatment meted out to each other. The truth of the text, 'With what measure ye mete it shall be measured to you again,' has been verified upon almost every party in its turn . . . I do not like to use such words as dishonesty and shuffling, but they certainly seem the most appropriate here . . . This is despicable. Why do not these two brothers meet the question straightforwardly? But their line of conduct in this again is worthy of their cause . . . I repeat, this is positively false; and may the gracious Lord forgive our brother for such calumny; he stands by this convicted of a *direct* falsehood . . . Though to our shame be it said, the company known as Exclusives have been shattered into half a dozen pieces . . . Do not, by any means, show the bad spirit, bitterness and want of grace that, alas! has been so characteristic of 'Brethren' in times of trouble . . . What is to be more deplored than even the divisions of the 'Brethren' is the bitterness, party prejudice, graceless spirit, and un-Christianlike, if not barbarous, conduct toward each other; which ignores amongst ourselves, and belies before the world the most blessed and intimate relationships and divine unity into which we are brought. It is no use to

deny the existence of this shameful state of things, and it
is adding sin to sin to excuse it by any pretext whatever."

Nothing half so severe as this is found in the article which
has evoked such a stream and storm of indignant protest, and
the terrible arraignment of "Brethren" is drawn up by one of
the most prominent "Brethren." Curiously enough, it is addressed to one who was himself kicked out of communion by
the Exclusives a few years ago, because he did not recognize
the difference between the Old Testament saints having life
from Christ, and New Testament saints having life *in* Christ.
Many years ago Colonel McClung, a noted duelist of Mississippi
and celebrated for his rash courage, kicked a noisy gambler out
of a hotel in Vicksburg, and along the streets. A week later
he was in Natchez, and saw a man kicking another man. Going up to the kicker he said, "Are you not the fellow I kicked
in Vicksburg the other day?" The gambler replied, "Yes,
Colonel, I am, but you and I both know whom it is safe to
kick."

The "Brethren" have been largely engaged in kicking each
other, in trying to get earnest Christians out of "systems," in
forbidding their people to listen to preachers who preach the
truth in different denominations, in rejecting fellowship with
other believers, in lofty and ridiculous claims to be *the* church
without the ability to tell the inquirer which one of the twenty
or more fighting factions among themselves occupies the true
church ground. Mr. Darby, to whom thousands are so greatly
indebted, once said, "I would not be surprised if they exclude
me after a while"; and then the noble old man added, "The
comfort I have is that no man can call me a Darbyite."

He greatly missed it in failing to recognize the permanent
offices of pastor and elder or deacon, because, as he said, "there
is no apostle to ordain them." This, for so strong a man, was
extremely foolish. He might as well have said there can be
no church, because there is no apostle to organize it. If the
"Brethren" had the New Testament officers to regulate their
unruly members, if they had grace to give up their hairsplitting
and nonsensical divisions, and to come together for honest humiliation and confession, what a power they might be for good!
But it is too late. They are wrecked, like the other denominations, and will hasten the time when a sad negative must be

given to the question of our Lord, "When the Son of man cometh, shall he find faith on the earth?" (Luke 18:8).

Dr. Brookes' criticisms were greatly resented at the time by many of the Brethren, but one would have to be a very strict party-man who would resent them today. They rather cause conscientious Brethren to hang their heads in shame and to seek grace from God to so behave toward his dear saints in other communions that they will be attracted to the truth instead of being repelled. It is interesting to know that Dr. Brookes broke bread after all with an assembly of Brethren one Lord's day just shortly before he was called up higher.

APPENDIX D

THE TEACHING OF THE SO-CALLED PLYMOUTH
BRETHREN; IS IT SCRIPTURAL?

REPLY TO AN ATTACK IN DR. STRONG'S
"SYSTEMATIC THEOLOGY"

The following paper appeared some years ago in the periodical "Help
and Food." It is here reproduced as giving the present writer's matured
views as to the general teaching of the Brethren.

A CORRESPONDENT lately called the writer's attention to some statements made against so-called "Plymouth Brethren" and their views,
by Dr. A. H. Strong, the well-known Baptist theologian, in his
"Systematic Theology," 7th edition, pp. 498, 9. Though averse
to controversy, and seeing little to be gained by what might look
like self-vindication, it seems there is enough in question to demand an examination of the Doctor's remarks with positive denial
and refutation of some of them.

First, let me say that I rejoice in the orthodoxy, as it is commonly
understood, of the learned author and preacher whose work is referred to. It is a pleasure to note his faith in the Lord Jesus Christ,
his apparent loyalty to Holy Scripture, and evident zeal for the
gospel. As to the teachings he attempts to expose as unscriptural
and heretical, it is charitable to believe he has not familiarized himself with them enough to know what these "brethren" really hold.
I take it for granted he has been too ready to credit the statements
of heated controversialists like the late Dr. Reid, from whom he
quotes, in place of seriously examining the writings of the brethren
criticized — an unwise course for any one to take in determining
the exact views of any people, and especially unwise in one whose
ipse dixit many lesser lights readily accept as authority.

Let us take up the quotations from Dr. Reid first, though these
come in last in Dr. Strong's summing-up of the case against

"Plymouth Brethrenism." He writes: "Dr. Wm. Reid, in *Plymouth Brethrenism Unveiled,** 79-143, attributes to the sect the following church principles:

"(1) The Church did not exist before Pentecost; (2) the visible and invisible Church identical; (3) the one assembly of God; (4) the presidency of the Holy Spirit; (5) rejection of a one-man and man-made ministry; (6) the Church is without government.

"Also the following heresies:

"(1) Christ's heavenly humanity; (2) denial of Christ's righteousness as being obedience to law; (3) denial that Christ's righteousness is imputed; (4) justification in the risen Christ; (5) Christ's non-atoning sufferings; (6) denial of moral law as the rule of life; (7) the Lord's day is not the Sabbath; (8) perfectionism; (9) secret rapture of the saints—caught up to be with Christ. To these we may add: (10) pre-millennial advent of Christ."

Taking these up categorically as given, we beg the reader to lay aside prejudice and examine each statement in the light of Holy Scripture. "To the law and to the testimony; if they speak not according to this word, it is because there is no light in them" (Isa. 8:20).

The "Brethren" are said to hold and teach: (1) *that the Church did not exist before Pentecost.* Can Dr. Strong, or anyone else, prove that it did? Is the congregation of Israel to be confounded with "the Church of the first-born written in heaven?" Was "the Church in the wilderness," mentioned by Stephen (Acts 7:38), the same as that which the Lord Jesus spoke of as a future thing, when He said, "Upon this Rock I *will build* my Church, and the gates of hell shall not prevail against it?" Mark it well—not "I have built," nor, "I am building," but, "I will build"—future tense. Does Dr. Strong see nothing of the great truth of the formation of believing Jews and Gentiles into "one body" (Eph. 2:14-16)— the Church of the new dispensation? One can hardly believe that any well-instructed teacher of our day could be in ignorance as to this. Not only "brethren," but so many well-known teachers in evangelical denominations have taught, both orally and in writing, along these lines for so many years that it seems unbelievable that

---

* Dr. Wm. Reid was fully answered at the time by another Wm. Reid, in "Accusers of the Brethren," now out of print, though occasionally to be found in Tract Depots.

Dr. Strong could be ignorant of the distinct calling of the Church, the body of Christ, as distinguished from both the congregation of Israel and the saved of the nations in past dispensations. "Brethren" make no apology for the teaching here ascribed to them. They do *not* believe the Church existed before Pentecost. They emphatically believe the Church was formed on that day by the Spirit's baptism, uniting saints on earth into one body (I Cor. 12:13), and to their glorified Head in heaven. Without this there could be no Church in the full New Testament sense.

(2) *The visible and invisible Church identical.* At this "Brethren" demur. Where, in all their writings, is such teaching found? Every well-instructed man among them distinguishes carefully between the Church, according to the mind of God, and the Church in its present outward aspect; or, between the Church as the "Body of Christ," including every saved soul in the present dispensation, and excluding all false professors, and the Church as the "House of God," largely committed to man, in which saved and unsaved are sadly mixed together. "Brethren" do not find the terms "visible church" or "invisible church" in the Bible, and consequently seldom use them. They know well what Christians mean when they do use them; only "Brethren" believe the invisible Church *would be everywhere visible* but for human failure. They do not believe that this failure excuses them from responsibility to "depart from iniquity," and to "follow righteousness, faith, love, peace, with them that call on the Lord out of a pure heart" (II Tim. 2:19, 22), for they have learned from Scripture that separation from evil is ever the path of faithfulness to God.

(3) *The one assembly of God.*—What fault can anyone find with so eminently Scriptural an expression? It is well-known that "church" and "assembly" are but different translations of the Greek word *ecclesia*, "a called out company." Would the Doctor object to the doctrine of "the one *Church of God?*" If not, why object to the other expression which means the same thing? "There is one body and one Spirit, even as ye are called in one hope of your calling" (Eph. 4:4); does not that passage teach that there is but one assembly of God? "For His body's sake, which is the Church," or "the assembly," says Scripture (Col. 1:24)—how many bodies has Christ? "One," Scripture answers. And what is that body? It

replies, "The assembly." What is its full name? Paul tells us, when
he says, "I persecuted the Church (assembly) of God"; and again,
"Give none offence, neither to the Jews, nor to the Gentiles, nor to
the Church of God" (I Cor. 10:32). And, be it observed, as
"Brethren" believe in the one assembly of God, when thinking
of the body of Christ as a whole, so they believe in assemblies of
God when speaking of local companies of believers gathered by
the Spirit to the name of Christ. Such assemblies should consist
of saved persons only, though evil men may slip in unawares.

(4) *The presidency of the Holy Spirit.*—Can it be possible that
any spiritually-minded Christian objects to this? Do Christians in
the systems not believe in the presidency of the Holy Spirit? Again
and again we have heard ministers pray that the Holy Spirit might
take charge of the meeting. Did they not mean this? Were these
only deceptive words—not meant as spoken? Granted, that if they
are bound to carry out their own programs, people can get on better
without the Holy Spirit than with Him; still, we have supposed it
was at least an article of faith that He was on earth to preside
in the assemblies of saints. Does Dr. Strong know anyone better
fitted to preside than He, the third Person of the eternal Trinity?
Yes, "Brethren" *do* believe in and insist on "the presidency of the
Holy Spirit," much as they may sometimes fail in recognizing Him
practically. To fail, while seeking to walk in the truth, is surely
less serious than to substitute human expediency for the revealed
will of God.

(5) *Rejection of a one-man and man-made ministry.*—If we
mistake not, it was once the boast of Baptists that they too rejected
these. Do they now endorse what they once repudiated? The term
"a Baptist clergyman," is, we believe, of very late origin. The older
was "a Baptist minister," a far better one, to our mind. And
"Brethren" believe in the ministry given by the Spirit, and desire to
reject all other. They have no clergymen, but in God's grace, many
ministers, who labor in word and doctrine. They reject a one-man
ministry as well as any-man ministry; while they thankfully accept
ministry, from one or several, if it manifestly accords with the
revealed Word of God. A man-made ministry they positively refuse.
Nor would intelligent men among them designate gifted and godly
Baptist ministers as man-made, simply because humanly ordained.

With "Brethren" ordination adds nothing to the God-given ministry. A man may be a God-made, and God-given minister, though he has received ordination and wears a surplice, but "Brethren" believe his ministry would be just as profitable, and more becoming, if he dressed like other Christians, and had not gone through the form of ordination. Real ministers are men called of God, gifted by Christ, and sent forth by the Holy Spirit. "Brethren" rejoice in all such.

(6) *The Church is without government.*—What an astonishing declaration! Some have charged "Brethren" with being all government! The fact is, "Brethren" believe all needed directions for the government of the Church are embodied in the Word of God. And in the Church there are "helps, governments," "elders who rule well," etc., who are responsible to seek to guide the saints in ways according to Christ. Because they reject the artificial organizations of the day is no reason to argue that "Brethren" are an unorganized mob. Where the Word is bowed to there will be godly order and Scriptural discipline, and these they seek to practice.

Now that we have disposed of the "Church principles," let us have a look at the "Heresies." It is an unbrotherly thing to charge people with being heretics who are "of like precious faith"; and it would seem that here, as above, the Doctor has been exceedingly rash and has passed on second-hand information without investigation.

(1) "Brethren" are said to teach the heresy of *Christ's heavenly humanity.* Like some Baptists, "Brethren" have not always been as careful as they might in using terms liable to misconception. The expression, "heavenly humanity," has been used by some, though not endorsed by "Brethren." But what was meant thereby? Simply that Christ's humanity was sinless and holy; heavenly in origin, because brought into existence, not by natural generation, but by the direct operation of the Holy Spirit who prepared that body in the womb of the virgin. Is not this orthodox and Scriptural? "The Second Man is the Lord from heaven," in contrast to the first man, who was "of the earth, earthy." (See I Cor. 15:47-49.) Christ partook of true humanity, apart from sin, but it was not humanity after an earthly order, for He had no human father—whatever modern theology may say—but was virgin-born. Is there any heresy in this?

(2) *Denial of Christ's righteousness as being obedience to law.—* The question is too large a one to go into at any length here, but one need only say that Christ certainly became in all things obedient to the law of God as a man on earth; yea, He "magnified the law, and made it honorable." But we suspect that this is not at all what Wm. Reid meant in the past, nor what Dr. Strong means now. When they write of "Christ's righteousness," they probably mean "God's righteousness," and we must frankly state "Brethren" do not believe that God's righteousness, or "the righteousness of God" (Rom. 3:21-22), means obedience to the law. It is God's consistency with Himself, His ways with men in accordance with the holiness of His nature. When divine righteousness demanded the punishment of sin, Christ the righteous One, became the propitiation for our sins, and thus righteousness is now on the believing sinner's side; it demands the justification and not the condemnation of all who trust in Christ. God is just and the Justifier of all who believe in Jesus. This is divine righteousness.

(3) *Denial that Christ's righteousness is imputed.* This links up with what has been touched on. Nowhere does Scripture say *Christ's* righteousness is imputed. Scripture is clear—"God imputeth righteousness." To whom? To all who believe. Such are "made the righteousness of God in Christ"; as saved and justified from all things, they display, they are the proof of, God's righteousness in dealing thus with them; since Christ has taken their place, they are righteously given His place. God is righteous in reckoning them righteous, because full atonement has been made for their transgressions; and freely imputes righteousness instead of guilt to all who believe in His Son. It is not that Christ wrought out a righteousness to cover us as a cloak, but that His death has met every claim that was against us, and God imputes righteousness apart from any works on our part; even as it is written of Abraham: "Abraham *believed God, and it was counted unto him for* [*as*] *righteousness*" (Rom. 4:3).

(4) *Justification in the risen Christ.*—This expression is objected to even by some "Brethren," but to our mind it well sets forth the truth of Scripture. When Christ died, He took my place, and died in my stead. I have therefore died with Him. But He is

risen; and I am in Christ, having received life through His name. In Him, I am beyond the reach of condemnation. Therefore I am justified. So I am "justified in the risen Christ." If Christ be not raised, my faith is vain and I am yet in my sins. But Christ has been "delivered for our offences and raised again for our justification"; and "there is therefore now no condemnation to them which are in Christ Jesus." Christ is risen for our justification. All that are "in Christ" are uncondemned. They are in Him as risen; therefore they are justified in the risen Christ. Is there anything illogical or unscriptural about that? Why then call it heresy? Theological hair-splitters may quibble over it as they will, but simple Christians will believe it and rejoice.

(5) *Christ's non-atoning sufferings.* — It is very questionable whether Dr. Strong has any conception of the theme he dismisses so curtly. Are there any Christians who do not believe Christ endured sufferings that were not in themselves atoning? Do we not rejoice in a Great High Priest who suffered, being tempted? Is that atoning? Do we not adore Him for His tender, human sympathies, which could not but cause Him to suffer greatly in a world like this? Did such sufferings make atonement? He suffered in the Garden, in view of the Cross. Was that atonement? If so, why go to the cross at all?

The subject is too sacred and holy for controversy. Dr. Strong had better study his Bible on the great theme of Christ's sufferings, until he can distinguish clearly between Christ's sorrows as the Servant of God and man *on the way to the cross,* and His atoning sufferings when our sins were laid upon Him, and He was made sin *upon* the cross. It will open up a wonderful vein of truth that will stir the heart to worship and move the lips to praise.

(6) *Denial of the moral law as the rule of life.*—Well, if "Brethren" are heretics because they teach that *Christ,* not the law of Moses, is the rule of life, they are in excellent company—with many devoted and enlightened Baptist ministers who teach the same. Literature on this subject is abundant.* No one need be in the dark as to what is taught on the important subject of "law and grace." "Brethren" teach that "the righteous requirements of the

---

* C. H. M.'s little booklet, "The Law and the Gospel," is clear and convincing. Any of the "Brethren's" expositions on Romans or Galatians are helpful.

law are fulfilled in us who walk not after the flesh but after the Spirit." We are not under law (Rom. 6:14). We are neither saved by the law, nor under it, as a rule of life; we are not lawless, but "under law (enlawed) to Christ." We stand firmly by the apostle Paul when he declares, "I through the law died unto the law that I might live unto God" (Gal. 2:19). Is Christ Himself a lower standard than the law given from Sinai? Or is the latter needed to complete the former? Surely no intelligent believer would so speak. This is not antinomianism, but its very opposite. It is subjection to Christ as Lord of the New Dispensation and Mediator of the New Covenant.

(7) *The Lord's day is not the Sabbath.*—If it is, let Dr. Strong produce the scripture that says so. The sabbath was the seventh day, the Lord's day is the first day of the week. The Sabbath was given to an earthly people, and its observance prescribed under severest penalties for disobedience. The Lord's day is kept by a heavenly people, with no legal requirement or penalties attached. The Sabbath was for Israel; the Lord's day for the Church. They that love the Lord gather together on that resurrection day to remember the Lord's death till He come.

(8) *Perfectionism.*—One is here wholly at a loss to know what is meant. When and where have "Brethren" ever taught the doctrine of perfectionism, save that perfection which all believers have in Christ? But *that* Dr. Strong himself evidently believes; so he must mean "perfection in the flesh." This is a doctrine that "Brethren" have ever *refused,* and constantly confuted. Believing that the sinful nature remains in the believer so long as he is in the body, and is ever ready to act if there be a moment of unwatchfulness, how can they be truthfully charged with holding to perfectionism? Any who so accuse them, are either wilfully ignorant of their real teaching, or utterly fail to understand its import.*

(9) *Secret rapture of the saints—caught up to be with Christ.*— Yes, if this be heresy, "Brethren" are heretics; for they do indeed teach that at the coming of the Lord to the air all His saints will be caught up to meet Him, and the world left to pass through the great tribulation. But he is a bold man who would dub this

---

* Having, myself, written a book on this theme, "Holiness, the False and the True," I beg leave to commend it to the inquirer who is anxious for a fuller statement of the subject.

"blessed hope" heresy in the face of I Cor. 15:51-56; I Thess 4: 13-18, and kindred passages. And again, be it remarked, "Brethren" are in good company, for Dr. Strong need not go outside his own denomination to find a host of honored servants of Christ who believe as thoroughly as "Brethren" do in the "secret rapture of the saints." But it passes our comprehension how any man, or set of men, with an atom of genuine love for the Lord and His people, can deliberately brand as heretics fellow-believers whose lives are generally fragrant with Christian graces, who stand unflinchingly for the inspiration of the entire Bible, simply because they hold different views on prophecy. Dr. Strong evidently does *not* believe in the secret rapture of the saints, but in the coming of the Lord in judgment at the end of the world. "Brethren" would not brand him as a heretic for this, though they feel he has lost much by his defective views. The same general remarks apply to the last charge of heresy—gratuitously hurled at "Brethren" by the Doctor himself.

(10) *Pre-millennial advent of Christ.* It is true that "Brethren," without any written creed, have learned from Scripture itself that the descent of the Lord from heaven will precede His millennial reign. Together with a goodly fellowship of saints in all the centuries since Christ's first advent, they are waiting for His second coming. Seeing no warrant in Scripture to expect a Millennium before He appears, their expectation is for Himself, according to John 14:3, and they find this glad hope has purifying power, and is a marvelous incentive to Christian life and service. They deeply regret that the Doctor, with many another, unconsciously says, "My Lord delayeth His coming." Is it because of this that such begin to belabor their fellow-servants and to call them heretics and schismatics? But whether or no, "the coming of the Lord draweth nigh," and "Blessed are all they that wait for Him."

Having briefly noticed the charges of heresy brought against those whom Dr. Strong calls "Plymouth Brethren," let us now consider some further remarks he has made concerning them and their teaching.

Dr. Strong believes there is evidence in the Bible "of a developed organization in the New Testament Church, of which," he says, "only the germ existed before Christ's death." He first attempts to trace this out by citing the different names used to denote the children of God or Christ's followers, as "disciples" in the Gospels (and in the Acts, though he overlooks this) ; then in the Epistles, as "saints," "brethren," "churches." This, he thinks, proves clearly that the Church is not "an exclusively spiritual body, destitute of all formal organization, and bound together only by the mutual relation of each believer to his indwelling Lord."

While his argument is not clear, one can readily admit that his conclusion is correct in measure; for surely the Church is *not* what he describes, either looked at as the Body of Christ, or as expressed by local churches or assemblies.

The "one assembly of God" consists of all believers baptized by the Holy Spirit into one body. Of this Dr. Strong seems to know nothing. It is not here a question of being "bound together only by the mutual relation of each believer to his indwelling Lord"; this is not Paul's doctrine of the Church at all, nor is it what "Brethren" maintain. They believe that before Pentecost believers were individually all children of God, were all possessors of eternal life, were all bound for heaven, and waiting for "the promise of the Father"; and on the fulfilment of this promise, something altogether new was formed. The Holy Spirit having come upon them, He baptized the believing Jews and Gentiles into *one body.* This is the Spirit's unity, and to this body every Christian belongs. There are no unsaved persons in it.

But when believers are gathered locally together, it is evident that some among them may be unreal, and when manifested it calls for discipline. This, as we have seen, is connected with another aspect of the Church—as the "house of God," not as the "body of Christ."

When Dr. Strong attempts to show what "Brethren" hold as to this, his biased mind throws all into confusion. He goes on to say: "The Church upon this view, as quoted above, so far as outward bonds are concerned, is only an aggregation of isolated units. Those believers who chance to gather at a particular time constitute the church of that place or time. This view is held by the Friends and by the Plymouth Brethren. It ignores the tendencies to organization inherent in human nature, confounds the visible with the invisible Church, and is directly opposed to the Scripture's representations of

the visible Church as comprehending some who are not believers.
Acts 5:1-11—Ananias and Sapphira—shows that the visible Church
comprehended some who were not true believers. I Cor. 14:23—
'If therefore the whole Church be assembled together, and all speak
with tongues, and there come in men unlearned or unbelieving, will
they not say that ye are mad?' Here, if the Church had been an
unorganized assembly, the unlearned visitors who came in would
have formed a part of it. Phil. 3:18—'For many walk of whom I
have told you often, and now tell you even weeping, that they are the
enemies of the cross of Christ' . . . The Plymouth Brethren dislike
church organizations, for fear they will become machines; they
dislike ordained ministers, for fear they will become Bishops; they
object to praying to the Holy Ghost, because He was given on
Pentecost, ignoring the fact that the Church after Pentecost so
prayed." Then Dr. Strong cites Acts 4:31 as a proof-text! I have
quoted at length, that his argument may be connected, but one is
pained by the irrelevant use he makes of Scripture to prove the un-
provable, and to bolster up what had best be torn down.

The Friends can speak for themselves; but so far as those whom
Dr. Strong calls "Plymouth Brethren" are concerned, I say unhesi-
tatingly, that he (either through ignorance or malice—the former,
I feel sure) completely misrepresents their teaching.

The Church can never be "an aggregation of isolated units," for
all believers are united into one body by the Spirit, as we have seen.
Has Dr. Strong never learned this? Does he know nothing of the
great "mystery" which formed the burden of the apostle Paul's
ministry? Has he never read I Cor. 12, or Eph. 3 and 4, or Col. 1
and 2? It would be well for him to consider these scriptures if
he honestly desires to know what "Brethren" hold as to the Church.
Believers everywhere constitute the Church as the body of Christ.
All believers in a given place—whether met together or not—constitute the Church of God in that place. Wherever two or three
such are gathered together unto His name, our Lord vouchsafes His
presence (Matt. 18:20). What more could be desired? Will formal
organization give us anything better than this? *Christ in the midst
is enough for every emergency.* It is true that "Brethren" care very
little about "the tendencies to organization inherent in human nature." There are a great many other things inherent in human

nature we seek grace to judge and mortify. But has God not already organized His assembly? The Church is a *divine organism*; every member is set in its place there by God Himself. Can man improve on that?

As we have said, when believers come together locally, unreal ones may be among them. Such may "creep in" and "feast themselves without fear," but they are only in the assembly in its outward aspect—they are not actually in the body of Christ.

As to Ananias and Sapphira, has the learned Doctor inside information not given to others? Is he absolutely certain they were not true believers? It is true they sinned grievously, and were judged therefor; but how many saints before and since may have to confess sin as grave as theirs?

I Cor. 14:23 has no bearing on the case. "The whole Church" is assembled together, and an unbeliever comes in afterwards. How can he be said to be a member of the Church?

"Brethren" are not engaged in building organizations, not because they "dislike" them, or "fear" what they might become, but because they find no Scripture for this—only the "inherent tendency in human nature," which they dare not substitute for "Thus saith the Lord." They have no humanly-ordained ministers because, though they have read their Bibles well, they have never been able to find a case of a man being ordained to preach or teach. If the passage is in the Book, let it be produced. Men were ordained to serve tables and ordained as elders, but where were they ordained as ministers of the gospel?

As to Phil. 3:18, would Dr. Strong include "enemies of the cross of Christ" in his church? "Brethren" believe such have "neither part nor lot in this matter."

His readers are further told that the "Brethren" would "unite Christendom by its dismemberment, and do away with all sects, and are themselves more narrow and bitter in their hostility to existing sects than any other." Again we find complete misunderstanding as to the aims, methods, and spirit of those whom he criticizes. "Brethren" are not attempting to either unite or dismember Christendom. They know too well that outward unity will never be again displayed until "the coming of our Lord Jesus Christ and our gathering together unto Him." Meantime they simply seek to walk together as brethren, acknowledging the Lordship of Christ and the presence of the Holy Spirit in the Church to guide them through the written Word. In believing this, they desire not to judge others who do not see eye to eye with them, but rather to pray for all men, and seek to manifest the compassion of Christ to all His sheep, wherever found.

It must be owned that some may have shown an uncharitable spirit toward fellow-saints remaining in the sects but this has ever been condemned by the spiritually-minded among them. One whose writings have had a larger place than those of any other in moulding and influencing his weaker and less instructed brethren, wrote once, "I do not believe attacks on anything to be our path, but to be superior, and for the truth in grace." Such was the spirit of J. N. Darby, and such will ever be the spirit of those who endeavor to follow him as he followed Christ.

With only one more quotation and a few brief comments, this already too lengthy paper must be brought to a close.

Dr. Strong tells his readers that "the tendency to organize is so strong in human nature, that even Plymouth Brethren, when they meet regularly together, fall into an informal, if not a formal, organization: certain teachers and leaders are tacitly recognized as officers of the body; committees and rules are unconsciously used for facilitating business. Even one of their own writers, C. H. M., speaks of 'the natural tendency to associate without God—as in the Shinar association or Babel-confederacy of Gen. 11, which aimed at building up a name upon the earth. The Christian Church is God's appointed association to take the place of all these; hence God confounds the tongues in Gen. 11 (judgment); gives tongues in Acts 2 (grace); but one tongue is spoken of in Rev. 7 (glory).'"

To C. H. M.'s apt remarks we add a hearty "Amen!" and are astonished that the Doctor should quote such words and not see how well they answer his own objection to "Brethren's" position. It *is* indeed ever the tendency of human nature—even in saved and enlightened people—to confederate, and seek by human organization to accomplish what would be better done in simple obedience to the Word. Undoubtedly "Brethren" also have failed in this very thing. But does failure to act on a right principle invalidate or vitiate the principle itself? Surely not. To the C. H. M. referred to, a man once said: "Do you know that Dr. ——, the —— minister, is lecturing against the Brethren?" To which C. H. M. replied, "Give him my compliments, and tell him I am doing the same in the Brethren's hall. Only he is lecturing against their principles, and I against their practices."

As gathered to the name of Christ, "Brethren" thankfully accept all spiritual ministry, and seek to recognize the gifts the ascended Christ has given for the upbuilding of His Church. As they bow to the instruction of Holy Scripture they find no need for human organization nor man-made rules, inasmuch as no eventuality can arise that is not provided for in the Book. They do not claim perfection, however, but mourn over their low estate, desiring grace daily to enter more fully into the mind of Christ, and be sanctified by the truth.

That their fellow-believers and fellow-members of Christ's body may find the same blessing, is their earnest prayer.

Appendix E

As illustrating the more enlightened views of liberal-minded yet deeply spiritual leaders among brethren today regarding some things which have disturbed many assemblies of Brethren in past years, I am glad to submit the following from the pen of Mr. Harold St. John one of the outstanding men of God among the British meetings:

Liberty as to Methods

In many parts of the world I have come across Christians deep in controversy on details such as the time and character of meetings, the use of an organ or a solo, or an after-meeting; it is often quite seriously advanced that these matters can be settled by an appeal to the text of the New Testament, which only shows *how easy it is to become silly when we most want to be solemn.*

The state of society in the first century, when Christians were largely of the slave class, allowed of one meeting a week, usually at midnight or at an hour when they could be spared from their work, and our modern multiplication of meetings is the fruit of the more favorable conditions produced by the Providence of God; such things as hymn books, Sunday Schools and Bible readings in the modern sense are as likely to be met with in the New Testament as motor cars!

The question may be asked, "Then by what rule shall our use of methods be governed?" To this the reply is simple, viz., by precisely the same law as our general conduct; all things are lawful for us, but at every crossroad of life three points must be considered: (1) Will the proposed step "free my feet" for the race to God? (2) Will it tend to bring me into bondage? (3) Will it edify and help my neighbor? (I Cor. 6:12; 10:23). Any method that will pass the threefold test, Godward, self-ward and manward may safely be used as long as it serves its purpose.

HAROLD ST. JOHN